FROM STRANGERS TO NEIGHE

FROM STRANGERS TO NEIGHBORS

Post-disaster Resettlement and

Community Building in Honduras

RYAN ALANIZ

UNIVERSITY OF TEXAS PRESS *Austin*

Requests for permission to reproduce material from this work should be sent to:
    Permissions
    University of Texas Press
    P.O. Box 7819
    Austin, TX 78713-7819
    utpress.utexas.edu/rp-form

♾ The paper used in this book meets the minimum requirements of
ANSI/NISO Z39.48-1992 (R1997) (Permanence of Paper).

LIBRARY OF CONGRESS CATALOGING-IN-PUBLICATION DATA

Names: Alaniz, Ryan, author.
Title: From strangers to neighbors : post-disaster resettlement and community
building in Honduras / Ryan Alaniz.
Description: First edition. | Austin : University of Texas Press, 2017. |
Includes bibliographical references and index.
Identifiers: LCCN 2016058635
ISBN 978-1-4773-1383-1 (cloth : alk. paper)
ISBN 978-1-4773-1409-8 (pbk. : alk. paper)
ISBN 978-1-4773-1410-4 (library e-book)
ISBN 978-1-4773-1411-1 (non-library e-book)
Subjects: LCSH: Community development—Honduras. | Disaster relief—Honduras—
Citizen participation. | Disaster relief—Social aspects—Honduras. | Hurricane Mitch,
1998—Social aspects—Honduras. | Honduras—Social conditions.
Classification: LCC HN160.C6 A53 2017 | DDC 363.34/92283097283—dc23
LC record available at https://lccn.loc.gov/2016058635
doi:10.7560/313831

THIS BOOK IS DEDICATED TO ALL THOSE WHO HAVE BEEN DISPLACED AND CONTINUE TO STRUGGLE TO REBUILD THEIR LIVES. IT IS ALSO DEDICATED TO MY SONS, SANTIAGO AND KAVIEN. MAY YOU GROW UP WITH A DESIRE TO SERVE THE MOST VULNERABLE.

CONTENTS

Campo Cielo (a pseudonym) was initially imagined by an international non-governmental organization as a resettlement to serve the most vulnerable Honduran survivors of Hurricane Mitch (in 1998)—impoverished single mothers with children. This organization, whose aim is the development of infrastructure for those in need, was the first to build houses and move families out of temporary shelters and into new homes. For many women, the resettlement was a dream come true, offering a safe place to raise their children and create a life far from Tegucigalpa, which continually ranks as the second-most-violent city in one of the most violent nations in the world (World Bank 2016a; SJP 2014). Soon after construction was finished, the organization moved on to construct more houses in another part of the country.

It was not long until the resettlement, beautiful on the outside, began to encounter serious internal social problems. With rampant crime and an ineffective Honduran police force, Campo Cielo soon found itself under the control of a gang, targeting the impoverished mothers to pay an *impuesto de guerra* (war tax) in order to stay in their homes, or face dreadful consequences. Only with the help of a United Nations special military operation years later was the resettlement finally freed of gang influence. The still-struggling Campo Cielo reveals that resettlement efforts must include more than empty houses for survivors. In addition to infrastructure, what mechanisms and characteristics are necessary to support the development of a resettlement into a healthy community?

Resettlement is an increasingly important component of what scholars are calling the *new normal*. The new normal (in which climate change produces a greater number of increasingly more extreme natural disasters) will compound vulnerability to rising poverty and inequality and the increasing growth of marginal periurban areas (slums), and exacerbate the consequences of ineffective government disaster responses. As I write these words, changing conditions—sea-level rise impacting Pacific Island nations, permafrost melt in Alaska, salinity intrusion in Bangladesh, and refugees fleeing from the Middle East to Europe—are forcing families and nation-states to discuss resettlement options. Yet little is known about successful resettlement and, as the World Bank (2015b) has admitted, it is a continual struggle to do it well.

While volunteering at an orphanage in Honduras (2001–2002), I had the opportunity to visit different resettlements built for survivors of Hurricane Mitch near the capital city, Tegucigalpa. Most of the new residents arrived from the same affected areas of the city and had similar demographics. The social environments within each of the resettlements, however, were markedly different. In some, people greeted each other by name, worked together on projects, and took care of each other when in need. In others, residents did not trust each other, homicide and theft were ongoing problems, and there was no functioning leadership. If the social aspects of community can be portrayed as a spectrum of strangers to neighbors, the resettlements presented both extremes and everything in between. This experience left a lasting impression. Eight years later, as I was investigating dissertation research topics, the contrasting resettlement development trajectories came to mind. If residents were similar initially, what were the mechanisms that promoted positive long-term social outcomes in certain resettlements and not in others? In other words, what are the conditions that support strangers working together collectively to create a sense of community?

This book is written for a general audience interested in relocation, resettlement, and community development. Besides rich description of the cases, the book offers four insights that may be useful to scholars, policymakers, and nongovernmental organizations involved in long-term resettlement.

DISASTER SURVIVORS ARE OFTEN OVERWHELMED BY THE CHALLENGES OF RESETTLEMENT AND NEED LONG-TERM EXTERNAL GUIDANCE AND SUPPORT

Before undertaking this project, I did not realize the level of survivor and resettlement-community vulnerability, which hampered survivors' agency to develop functioning institutions and a common community culture in their new home. Many residents are traumatized, impoverished, and isolated from their social networks in the new environment. In the weak state of Honduras, there are threatening external forces—gangs, corrupt government officials, dysfunctional organizations, power-hungry and greedy residents—that may quickly derail the development process. Under ideal conditions, community development is difficult. Nevertheless, survivors are often immediately tasked with, and expected to succeed in, running the resettlement—governing, creating economic opportunities, addressing crime, building and fixing infrastructure, negotiating conflict among individuals and groups, forming a community identity, establishing a community culture, and so forth. This responsibility is often overwhelming, impeding the social development of resettlement toward community.

From the perspective of governments and nongovernmental organizations (NGOs), successful resettlement is often based on infrastructure or economic measures. What continues to be underexamined is the long-term failure of resettlements from the perspective of residents. Despite billions of dollars poured into resettlement projects globally, they can be worse places to live than temporary shelters due to the social environment. Many policymakers and development workers also believe that if the project is built and paid for, residents will have the agency to create the social environment on their own or with little assistance. This is often not the case, however, and vulnerable survivors likely need significant external support to build a sustainable health community.

IN HETEROGENEOUS RESETTLEMENTS, A HYBRID TECHNICAL ASSISTANCE AND SELF-HELP COMMUNITY DEVELOPMENT APPROACH IS MOST EFFECTIVE

This is not the conclusion I expected to find. My knowledge of the community development literature combined with twenty years of working in international development arenas led me to believe that promoting a deliberate and self-directed process that empowered residents would lead to the most successful outcomes. Yet, due to survivor vulnerability and initially weak community political, economic, and social institutions, expecting survivors to build community on their own was unrealistic. My research suggests that external actors, such as sponsoring NGOs, play a critical role in providing technical assistance to survivors in the beginning stages of resettlements. Of the seven resettlements studied, the most successful were those in which organizations intervened heavily in resettlement affairs and supported neophyte institutions early on, decreasing their influence over the course of a decade. The least successful were those in which sponsoring organizations provided little more than infrastructure.

It is not just the amount of support, but the type of approach implemented. Of the many strategy variations I found in Honduras, two stand out in opposition. The first, a hybrid of technical assistance and self-help, what I call *sustain, accompany, guide, and empower* (SAGE) resettlement development, enabled the organization to intervene when social problems arose while also empowering residents and community institutions to work toward a common self-defined vision over an extended period. More concretely, this meant that the organization could utilize its resources to keep gang members or corrupt residents from obtaining a foothold in the resettlement while also providing technical assistance for the creation of a new culture and strong institutions. Once a new culture had gained traction and institutions had a secure foundation, a self-help empowerment model was implemented to decouple the resettlement from the sponsoring organization. The second strategy is a partnership approach, which is a type of self-help strategy wherein organizations encourage residents to drive the development process and intercede only when requested. The partnership strategy did not offer enough supportive structures to protect residents and neophyte community institutions. On their own, groups of residents had little power to deal with large structural issues (economic development, political disintegration, crime, etc.) and external negative forces, such as gangs and drug dealers. In addition, social problems overwhelmed the weak governing institution, inhibiting leadership efforts to maintain social norms and a common vision, leading to poorer social health outcomes.

SOCIAL HEALTH IS AN IMPORTANT SUPPLEMENTAL MEASURE IN DETERMINING THE LONG-TERM DEVELOPMENT OF A RESETTLEMENT

Historical recovery and resettlement strategies have often measured success by infrastructure built or economic growth. Recent scholarship and major NGOs have recognized the need for a more robust metric that takes into account the social aspects of relocating disaster survivors and refugees, especially over the long term.

Bridging the disaster and community development literatures to resettlement resident needs, I define resettlement social health as a combination of crime, social capital, collective efficacy, a common vision, and civic participation. Each characteristic provides a different component of community life that is recognized as important to creating a cohesive group with a common identity whose members are willing to work together toward communal goals. These characteristics have also been found to support community resilience when confronted by future natural hazards or social problems. By examining each as a single feature and in combination as potentially self-reinforcing interactions, we can examine the social development of a resettlement in greater depth and secure a clearer picture of the success of resettlement as experienced by residents, complementing previous metrics.

THE INITIAL CULTURE CRAFTED IN A RESETTLEMENT SIGNIFICANTLY SHAPES THE PROCESS AND LONG-TERM COMMUNITY DEVELOPMENT OUTCOMES

Community culture is a critically important though often overlooked component of resettlement development. Unlike established neighborhoods or communities, a new, heterogeneous resettlement initially lacks a collective culture, including an absence of agreed-upon social norms and a common vision. It becomes the responsibility of the first residents, often in dialogue with the sponsoring organization, to define, obtain buy-in, and enforce a set of values and norms among many stakeholders—or risk the resettlement fracturing into competing groups. This task is difficult to do well, as various households or small alliances compete for personal or short-term gain rather than the long-term collective good.

This research suggests that the development of a community culture can benefit from significant technical assistance from an external entity, such as a sponsoring NGO. Since it would prove challenging for an individual or small group of residents (let alone a group of vulnerable, unfamiliar disaster survivors) to ensure that a set of norms and common vision are adhered to, an external organization may have the independence, resources, and technical expertise to reconcile disputing groups and safeguard the agreed-upon culture, despite internal conflicts. Path dependence theory describes how the initial culture builds upon itself, gaining momentum and making future changes more difficult to implement. The initial resettlement culture, then, guides the resettlement development and its future social health outcomes for better or worse.

Resettlement is part of the new normal. Similarly, we must move beyond previous definitions and paradigms so that resettled survivors find their circumstances not worse, or even the same, but better. The resettlement process can be transformative, drawing people out of problematic situations and creating an opportune environment to develop into socially healthy, resilient communities. By understanding context and focusing on the quality of the resettlement development process rather than the quantity of houses built, organizations and governments can help create the atmosphere in which strangers can become neighbors.

ACKNOWLEDGMENTS

Like all manuscripts of this length, it took the encouragement and support of dozens of people and organizations to bring it to completion. Primarily, I would like to thank the residents of all seven resettlements, especially Suyapa and Pino Alto, for their openness in sharing their lives and experiences. In addition, it was the generosity of time, resources, and materials from La Iglesia and La Internacional that made this book possible.

I am indebted to the following organizations and fellowship sponsors for their financial support: the Fulbright Program, the Social Science Research Council, the Diversity of Views and Experiences Fellowship, the University of Minnesota Department of Sociology, the Bilinski Foundation, the Public Entity Risk Institute, and the California Polytechnic State University College of Liberal Arts Summer Stipend Writing Grant. Without this funding the depth and breadth of this research would not have been possible.

I wish to also thank my professors, Doug Hartmann, Pat McNamara, David Pellow, Ross MacMillan, and Bill Siembieda, for their generosity of time and wisdom, as well as three anonymous reviewers from University of Texas Press for their insightful feedback, which strengthened the book significantly. My PhD advisor, Ron Aminzade, is an inspiration personally and professionally. I cannot thank him enough for his positivity and guidance.

Finally, it was the support and patience of friends and family; the encouragement of my best friend, Julio, and his family in Tegucigalpa; feedback from my amazing partner, Jenny Holmes; the kindness of many Hondurans; and constructive critique and editing from my friend and colleague Ron Den Otter that provided the impetus to finish this book. Of course, any errors or omissions are solely my own.

FROM STRANGERS TO NEIGHBORS

CHAPTER 1

THE PERILOUS PATH:
FROM RESETTLEMENT TO COMMUNITY

In 2010, Juana—one of the leaders of a post–Hurricane Mitch resettlement, Suyapa[1]—exclaimed proudly in a political meeting, "Look at us. We have never had a violent death in our community." This was a common sentiment, espoused at nearly every gathering in Suyapa. Compared to the six other resettlements in El Valle, Suyapa was safe. The nearest resettlement, Pino Alto, had witnessed twenty-eight homicides in recent years.

Unfortunately, no one is left untouched by the violence in Honduras. Exactly sixteen years after Hurricane Mitch devastated the nation, on the evening of October 25, 2014, Suyapa was victimized again, not by another natural disaster, but by a social disaster. As four of its young men left an evangelical church meeting that Friday evening, they were gunned down, with two pronounced dead at the scene and two left in critical condition (*La Tribuna* 2014). Residents were forced to speculate about who may have been responsible for the murders. In Honduras, the underfunded and corrupt criminal justice system convicts less than two percent of murder cases (*Guardian* 2015). Neighbors concluded that one of the murdered young men had been observed flirting with the ex-girlfriend of a known gang member from the nearby Pino Alto resettlement. In retaliation, residents believe, the gang took his and his friends' lives and futures.

This tragic story, like many others shared in this book, highlights the complex social situations found within resettlements. Suyapa and Pino Alto residents possessed similar initial demographics, arriving from the same urban areas of Tegucigalpa, and both communities feature comparable infrastructure. Suyapa enjoys comparatively safe living conditions and high levels of social capital and civic participation, while in contrast Pino Alto wrestles with multiple homicides annually, low levels of trust and community engagement, and high crime rates. If residents and infrastructure of both resettlements were similar, what strategies enabled one resettlement to produce better outcomes than another?

MECHANISMS FOR SUCCESSFUL
RESETTLEMENT DEVELOPMENT

While not addressing resettlement directly, the academic literature provides numerous answers to the question above. As will be discussed in chapter 3, scholars have pointed to displacement type, resident demographics (e.g., religion, trauma, socioeconomic status), resettlement characteristics, infrastructure, community development strategies, and the role of the state and nongovernmental organizations as potential mechanisms that influence resettlement development. The question of how one defines "community" or resettlement success is also broadly debated, but researchers often evaluate one location at one moment in time. This book adds to the broader understanding of resettlement by comparing and contrasting the long-term (twelve years after the disaster) social health characteristics of seven resettlements.

This book also bridges the disaster recovery and community development literatures by discussing the difficulties faced by resettlement residents, the potential for organizations to address those challenges, and the importance of the formation and maintenance of social structures, institutions, and community culture for the development of resettlement social health. Infrastructure in and of itself does not lead to successful resettlement and, as found in Campo Cielo, may lead to worse social conditions than temporary shelters.

On the one hand, disaster scholars recognize the vulnerability of survivors and have spent ample time studying the immediate response and early recovery. Only a few researchers, however, have investigated the complex and hazardous path from resettlement to community. On the other hand, community development theories describe in detail the process of change over time, but these explanations hold numerous assumptions about the assets of residents and the openness of economic, political, and social structures to a community development project. Resettlement sits at the nexus of these literatures; drawing on the strengths of each, this book will link the two in an attempt to describe how the resettlement-to-community process happens.

Survivors face significant challenges in the post-disaster and resettlement context and may not have the resources or skills to develop their neophyte community on their own. Many are traumatized, having lost not only their homes but also family members or friends. They come from areas most impacted by the disaster, often impoverished neighborhoods. Once they arrive, the resettlement is made up of individuals from throughout the affected area, leading to low levels of initial bonding, social capital, and potential distrust. The group of strangers is relocated to a *new* resettlement, a space with no previous socially constructed meaning, symbols, or culture. Unlike established neighborhoods, new residents must create everything from scratch. This is a critical difference from the repopulation of established neighborhoods after a disaster, as meaning and purpose must be given to places and symbols, a difficult task among a heterogeneous[2] population. Even though the physical infrastructure is in place, survivors may not have the time, energy, skills, or resources to build the social aspects of community.

In the case of the seven Honduran resettlements studied, survivors were overwhelmed with many of these issues, leaving limited time, energy, and resources to devote to the development of community. This is where combining the traditional technical assistance and self-help approaches to development can be beneficial. By making available high levels of developmental technical assistance, organizations can provide the foundation for a self-help approach to be enacted. Supporting organizations, then, can play an important role in bolstering neophyte resettlements. For example, organizations can take on the role of protecting residents from exploitation (e.g., gangs), preventing the fracturing of resettlement cohesion, and building a cohesive and unifying set of norms and common vision, while empowering residents to take leadership in areas of community life. In short, they can facilitate the community development process. The two most important examples of these development strategies are described in brief below.

In post-Mitch Honduras, La Internacional is a large organization that works on numerous disaster relief fronts. Both the size and quantity of projects dilute the focus, time commitment, and long-term presence of the organization, as it is committed to helping many communities concurrently. In the Pino Alto resettlement, La Internacional took a self-help participatory or partnership approach toward community development, focusing on the empowerment of residents to induce them to take responsibility for their community without creating dependence upon the NGO. However, this independence led to low social health outcomes, in large part due to the particular challenges of the resettlement. The heterogeneous population could not create a clear vision for the community that all residents would endorse, nor was there a set of norms that were agreed upon and enforced. Essentially, handing over responsibility to the fragile and vulnerable group of 1,285 households led to fracturing, not unity.

In contrast to La Internacional's approach, La Iglesia provided more resources over a longer period toward social development, and intervened more often and more directly in the development of the Suyapa resettlement. La Iglesia's strategy, what I describe as the *sustain, accompany, guide, and empower* (SAGE) development approach, meant that the organization was involved in every facet of resettlement life, from supporting the growth of the market to holding home mortgages and having a vote in resettlement decision-making. The NGO was deeply embedded within, and continually adjusted its decisions for the perceived needs of, the resettlement. In addition, the small organization's dedication to only one project enabled La Iglesia to devote more organizational resources and make a long-term commitment (fifteen years) to the resettlement. The intervention and commitment guided the nascent community along a path of social health. When troubles arose that overwhelmed the capacity of residents (such as drug dealing, gang influence, or resident conflict), La Iglesia stepped in to find solutions. La Iglesia's support was critical in enabling the budding community to develop a unified vision and set of norms, in other words, a healthy community culture.

The divergent trajectories of each resettlement can best be investigated by looking at processes over time. Path dependence theory offers a framework for describing changes over the twelve-year period, especially in the development of culture within each resettlement. Originally developed by the economist Paul David (1985), path dependence attempts to articulate the widespread acceptance and use of the QWERTY keyboard as opposed to other, more efficient keyboards. David argues that certain technologies gain an initial advantage over others, making any future change (learning a new keyboard) costly. Political scientists and sociologists have used this perspective to further arguments describing how initial conditions can lock in a particular trajectory (see Thelen [1999] and Mahoney [2000] for an overview). Margaret Levi (1997) provides perhaps the clearest definition: "Path dependence has to mean, if it is to mean anything, that once a country or region has started down a track, the costs of reversal are very high. There will be other choice points, but the entrenchments of certain institutional arrangements obstruct an easy reversal of the initial choice." In the resettlement context, I argue that it is not just the institutional arrangements but also the social and cultural structures that shape resettlement beliefs, values, and norms that guide and bound the development process. Once these traits are locked in, the resettlement has defined its trajectory; cultural change after the fact is exceptionally challenging.

The path dependence perspective uses four time frames—initial conditions, formation of community culture, conciliation of culture, and increasing returns—to explain how an idea becomes normalized. Initial conditions are the preliminary circumstances each resettlement possessed. The commonalities of Suyapa and Pino Alto—resident demographics, resettlement infrastructure, and NGO early commitment—demonstrate that no predetermined outcome exists. The dialectical formation of community culture by the NGO and residents sets the tone for the resettlement's path to building community. More specifically, the early collective vision and social norms provided and maintained by the sponsoring organization guided the resettlement's future trajectory.

Even with collective vision and strong social norms, efforts to define community were not always smooth. *Conciliation* refers to the conflict between actors and the resulting resolution. In the case of each resettlement, tensions arose over what type of community vision and identity were to be developed as well as which social norms would be incorporated. During this time frame, residents and the sponsoring NGO reconciled their differing views and produced a unifying vision and emerging *sense of community*. Once the culture was created and conciliated, it became embedded as residents then formally and informally passed on the vision and norms to incoming residents.

The creation of culture among a vulnerable resettlement population is a slow and contentious process; once ingrained, however, it guides residents' vision and future behavior, without necessitating the influence of a sponsoring organization. At that point, the community culture is self-reinforcing and is very difficult to change.

IMPLICATIONS

Scholars have called for a multidimensional and holistic theory to address issues of disaster recovery and resettlement (Fussell 2015; Cardona 2004). Often, researchers study particular and isolated characteristics, such as vulnerability, social capital, collective efficacy, trauma, resource use and availability, economic development, and NGO development strategies, individually, without a deep investigation into the interaction or the cascading effects they can have *combined* and *over time*. By appreciating how these challenges, separately and jointly, can have a synergistic effect by creating even greater vulnerability among survivor residents with respect to their social health, supporting organizations and governments can be more effective in the process of transitioning from resettlement to community.

Discerning the mechanisms that promote or detract from the development of resettlements into cohesive communities is indispensable for both organizations and resettlements. Historically, the focus on infrastructure has provided beautiful houses that survivors may not want to live in, may not fit their needs, or may not have the social characteristics that make a place worth living in. Spending an equal amount of time and resources on social development will ensure that houses become homes and resettlements become healthy communities. Ideally, survivors should find themselves in a better situation after disasters—not only in two or five years, but also in ten or twenty years, even indefinitely.

The implications of this study may be useful to other migration and re-settlement contexts. According to the United Nations High Commission on Refugees (2015a), the number of displaced persons is the highest in history, affecting 1 in every 113 people on the planet. If refugee status were a nation, it would be the twenty-fourth most populous on the planet (UNHCR 2015b). The findings outlined in this book are particularly salient given the environmental challenges our world faces and their impacts on displacement (Black et al. 2013). Climate change is forcing millions to think about relocation. Indeed, if we continue to near the two-degree-Celsius tipping point, other natural hazards, such as flora and fauna extinction, extreme drought, and increased human conflict over scarce resources, will likely induce mass displacement and resettlement throughout the world (Esnard and Sapat 2014). The issue is so prevalent that the term *climate refugee* has become an accepted part of the contemporary lexicon (National Geographic 2016).

Of course, each migration, refugee, relocation, and resettlement context is different and must be assessed as such. It is my hope this book will, in some small way, aid governments and organizations working with small-scale resettlement development projects in creating sustainable, socially healthy communities.

DATA

With generous support from Fulbright and Social Science Research Council fellowships, I carried out ethnographic research by living in Suyapa for nine months and commuting, on average, one day a week to Pino Alto. I also visited each of the other five resettlements about twenty times in total from September 2009 to June 2010. To obtain information I needed to complete the investigation, I returned to the resettlements in 2011 and 2012 on multiweek trips.

Due to my previous experience living in Honduras, I gained entrée into both Suyapa and Pino Alto quickly. Having volunteered at the Nuestros Pequeños Hermanos orphanage in La Venta, Honduras, for thirteen months eight years earlier, I was familiar with cultural protocol and local Spanish colloquialisms. Additionally, bringing my family, especially our six-month-old child, provided a bonding opportunity, as family is a core component in much of Latin American culture (Gutmann 1996), including Honduras. Over our stay, I developed close relationships with residents and involved myself in every aspect of life—playing soccer with the kids, working on community service projects, and attending birthday parties and funerals. I even hosted an international conference, attended by residents, on resettlement and recovery for Salvadoran survivors of Tropical Storm Ida and Hurricane Mitch to share ideas about the best practices for resettlement and community development.

I administered a ninety-six-question census survey in each of the seven re-settlements, with the exception of the largest, Pino Alto, in which a random representative sample was taken (see appendix, table A.1). With the help of seven research assistants, I obtained 1,918 household surveys from the seven resettlements. The survey covered various aspects of the resettlement process and community development: demographics; quality of life over time; politics and leadership; civic participation, social capital, unity, and religion; familiarity with community and neighbors; informal social control and delin-quency; disaster trauma and NGO support; changes over time in resettlement and individual household circumstances; and open-ended questions concern-ing the positive and negative characteristics of each resettlement (see appen-dix, tables A.5 and A.6). Various statistical analytics were then used to iden-tify significant differences among resettlement outcomes.

I conducted seventy-four semistructured interviews with key NGO staff (representing various levels of responsibility), resettlement members and leaders, religious leaders, and government officials. These interviews lasted from thirty minutes to three hours and covered the same topics noted in the survey in more depth but also allowed the participant to guide discussion. Using an inductive grounded theory approach, the interviews provided the theoretical foundation for the survey. Throughout the book, pseudonyms are used for all interviewees to protect their identity.

Finally, I gathered documents from organizations, resettlements, and gov-ernment and police records. These included NGO communications, plans, and internal documents; resettlement policies and procedures; newspaper articles from 1998 to 2010; government memos; and resettlement crime records (when available). Through the triangulation of data—ethnography, surveys, inter-views, and documents—I was able to create a multidimensional image of the resettlements over time, even though many of these topics are notoriously dif-ficult to investigate.[3]

BOOK OVERVIEW

Chapter 2, "The Consequences of Hurricane Mitch," describes the disaster, its aftermath, and the social and political situation under which resettlement occurred. This context will serve as the foundation for understanding the ini-tial conditions and vulnerabilities of survivors. Additionally, each of the seven resettlements studied is described, with attention given to the case selection of Suyapa and Pino Alto.

Chapter 3, "Community Development in the Context of Disaster Resettle-ment," outlines how this book fills a gap in our understanding of the long-term consequences of particular resettlement and community development strategies. The theory of path dependence serves as a framework for analyzing how particular mechanisms lead to divergent levels of social health. This chapter also reveals how certain differences in the respective community development processes led to dramatically different outcomes in Suyapa and Pino Alto.

Chapter 4, "Measuring Successful Resettlement," elaborates on the usefulness of a multifaceted social metric (social health) to compare the long-term outcomes between Suyapa and Pino Alto. Beginning with a definition of community social health indicators, this chapter compares Suyapa and Pino Alto to one another, to Tegucigalpa, to the average of the other five post-disaster resettlements, and to national statistics. The differences are critically assessed, particularly in the areas of crime and collective efficacy, since this is one of the greatest concerns of Hondurans.[4]

Chapters 5, "Suyapa," and 6, "Pino Alto," consist of descriptions and analyses of the two resettlements and their sponsoring NGOs. Each case is analyzed in the following areas for its possible influence on the current social health of the resettlement: infrastructure; resident demographics, including livelihood and backgrounds; resettlement leadership; and NGO philosophy, practice, and relationship with residents. The final chapter, "From Strangers to Neighbors," connects the characteristics of Suyapa and Pino Alto and their respective development processes to their current social health outcomes. As these connections become apparent, I discuss the lessons of each for development practitioners engaged in current and future resettlements.

CHAPTER 2

THE CONSEQUENCES OF HURRICANE MITCH

On Wednesday, October 21, 1998, a tropical depression formed in the south-ern Caribbean Sea. The depression, named Mitch, developed into a tropical storm and slowly drifted northwest as it grew in size and intensity. After three days, the storm increased in ferocity to a Saffir-Simpson Category 5 hurri-cane. By the end of Monday, October 26, and through the following Tuesday, the winds maintained a peak of 157 knots (180 mph), just off the northeast coast of Honduras. Mitch tied for the fourth-strongest hurricane on record, stronger and much more damaging than Hurricane Katrina.[1]

A week later, the wind decreased to 105 knots but still produced mas-sive amounts of rain. On October 31, reports from the extreme southern and northern areas of Honduras recorded similar data: thirty-six inches of rain—forty-two times the expected rainfall during the same period under normal conditions. Twenty-five of those inches were deposited in less than thirty-six hours. The total rainfall over those 5 days was the equivalent of 212 days of an average year. Mitch finally drifted away from Honduras but continued north to impact Guatemala, Mexico, and Florida, finally losing its storm qualities on November 9, north of Great Britain (NOAA 1998; IADB 2000; Met Office 2011; USGS 2002).

The aftermath of the hurricane also devastated the national economy and infrastructure. A journalist following the disaster captured the economic im-pact of Mitch:

> Perhaps worst of all, he said, was the sweeping destruction of Honduras's banana and coffee plantations, which for years have been the country's main cash crops and the source of much of its foreign exchange. . . . International lending agencies estimate that Honduras and Nicaragua, the poorest coun-tries in the Western Hemisphere after Haiti, suffered about $5 billion in losses, equivalent to nearly half their gross national products. (Sengupta 1998)

According to the Honduran president, the storm put set country back fifty years in its development (Barrios et al. 2000; Jackson 2005). The former minister of health noted that nearly 70 percent of the vital national infrastructure was damaged (Castellanos 2011). Entire lengths of highway were washed away or layered with so much sediment as to be impassable, 170 bridges were badly damaged or completely destroyed, and seventy-five dams broke, flooding whole communities. The capital city Tegucigalpa's normally placid Choluteca River, which winds through downtown, reached record-level flooding and engorged to six times its normal width in some areas. It left six meters of mud on its periphery and massive destruction in its wake.

The human cost of Hurricane Mitch was almost inconceivable. Official estimates count approximately ten thousand deaths in Honduras alone, and up to twenty thousand for the isthmus, although the exact number remains unknown. More than half the population of Honduras was directly affected as Mitch displaced 2.1 million people. In Tegucigalpa alone, more than 150,000 people were left homeless and many neighborhoods, especially the city's poorest, lacked potable water. Ramon Espinol, former mayor of Morolica in southern Honduras, recalled, "I will never forget hearing people around me crying out that they had lost everything. Older people asking, 'How will I rebuild my house? Everything that I had is gone. How will I carry on living?'" (UNICEF 2010).

Throughout the city disease proliferated, especially conjunctivitis, hepatitis, typhoid, and dengue, and even a new disease was encountered—leptospirosis, a bacterial infection that can lead to kidney damage, meningitis (inflammation of the membrane around the brain and spinal cord), liver failure, respiratory distress, and even death. Food and clean water were nearly impossible to find, communication was unavailable, and people were migrating from rural areas in search of the minimal aid that was directed at cities. In addition, with the majority of the population living "without a roof, without a job, lost [dead] family members, disheartened, sick, uncertain about the future," there was considerable social instability and protest (Stefanovics 1999).

POST-MITCH RELIEF

The response to Hurricane Mitch by the Honduran government and by the global community was uneven. On the one hand, the government lacked the capacity to provide the basic resources needed to restore basic services after Hurricane Mitch. Two years before the hurricane, social scientists warned of the nation's vulnerability, noting that it did not possess the national apparatus or the capacity to deal with disaster. "In Honduras and Costa Rica, community work for disaster evacuations are not usually planned, but rather are spontaneous responses of support at the time of emergency" (Leon and Lavell 1996, 61, translated by author). In fact, the situation was much worse. While the rain was still falling, the government was already in disarray and even basic services could not be provided. Jackson (2005, chapter 10) points out that in the initial days following Mitch, the World Bank, the International Development Bank, and the United States Agency for International Development (USAID) took control of logistical issues and decided what was to be done in the relief effort and how. When asked about the Honduran emergency commission (COPECO), international financial institution staff commented that the agency "was unprepared and had no funds. It was unable to perform at all" for emergency response and relief, let alone recovery (Jackson 2005, 262; Jeffrey 1999). Due in part to the inability of the Honduran state to deal with the aftermath of Mitch, the Honduran congress had little choice but to follow the programs and actions decided upon by foreign development actors (Jackson 2005). The fragile (and minimal) social contract between government and citizenry had been broken, creating a space to be filled by international and national organizations (Alaniz 2012).

On the other hand, the outpouring of international aid was unmatched in its generosity. International organizations and governments pledged 6.3 billion US dollars to the reconstruction of Central America, the majority of which was designed to help the most impacted country, Honduras. Over fifty nation-states and multilateral organizations and hundreds of nonprofits bombarded the isthmus with support. The Inter-American Development Bank (IADB) director, Enrique V. Iglesias, summed up the hopeful outpouring: "Let us turn the tragedy of Hurricane Mitch into the springboard for a great virtue, the virtue of demonstrating international solidarity" (IADB 1999).

Shelter was among the top priorities for both the government and international nongovernmental organizations (INGOs), as Mitch had displaced 1.5 million people throughout the country (NOAA 2009). Resettlement efforts focused on the most affected areas with high population density, the urban centers of San Pedro Sula and Tegucigalpa. Most survivors in these areas were forced to find alternative places to live, having either lost their home already or having had their neighborhood defined by the government as at risk and therefore uninhabitable. According to my survey focused on resettlement around Tegucigalpa, most future resettlement residents temporarily lived in a home that was at risk but not initially condemned, had family members take them in, or had the means to rent an apartment. About one of every five displaced persons, however, either had to move into *macro-albergues* (large temporary shelters set up in partnership between the government and NGOs) or were forced to move away from the city completely.

RESETTLEMENT AS OPPORTUNITY

From this tragedy, amazingly, arose opportunity. In the aftermath of Mitch, a vision was conceived in the minds of Hondurans, foreign donors, and development workers—not only was the nation going to be rebuilt; it would be socially transformed. When donors, government officials, and Honduran civil society met in May 1999 to discuss the reconstruction effort, they signed an agreement and declared, "The Presidents of Central America made clear their view of the tragedy as a unique opportunity to rebuild—not the same—but a better Central America" (IADB 1999). As a record-setting sum of disaster donations poured into the nation, resettlements for hurricane survivors were built in geologically safer locations north and east of Tegucigalpa. Excitement spread among those who had been displaced. They had a dream, a hope of leaving the violence and poverty of Tegucigalpa behind to create new, healthy communities.

Broadly, planners envisioned how the post-Mitch resettlement effort could serve as a model for future disaster reconstruction and resettlement throughout the world. The donor-nation reconstruction agreement asserted: "Reconstruction must not be at the expense of transformation" (IADB 1999). Specifically, residents and organizational leaders in the metro area of Tegucigalpa, one of the most violent cities in the world, viewed this as an opportunity for individual families to start a new and safer life. Indeed, in comparison to the city, one resettlement resident, Don Hernán, saw his uprooting as a move to "paradise." At a media conference, an NGO president claimed, "Our goal was to create a new Honduran"—a new citizen filled with hope and the will to develop Honduras (La Iglesia 2009).

As I write, it has been eighteen years since the hurricane. Is Honduras transformed? Marisa Ensor (2010) and colleagues have found that at the national level, there were some positive societal changes, but the country as a whole remains in conditions similar to those it struggled with in 1998. The World Bank, International Federation of the Red Cross and Red Crescent, IADB, CESAL (Centro de Estudios y Solidaridad con América Latina), and the United Nations have done similar studies and found smaller-scale successes, especially in gender equity and progress toward the UN Millennium Goals. Nationally, though, the envisioned transformation did not come close to occurring. The country continues to grapple with corruption, nepotism, gang violence, one of the highest homicide rates in the world, and growing economic inequality.

THE CONSEQUENCES OF HURRICANE MITCH 13

What about the long-term development of individual resettlements? These sites, where new resettlements were to be built and new citizens created, had inspired hope that the nation could begin to develop at the grassroots level. Hundreds of millions of dollars were poured into dozens of resettlement projects throughout the country, providing opportunities for survivors to move out of the violence and poverty of Tegucigalpa and San Pedro Sula. At that time, one would have anticipated that resettlements populated by residents with comparable backgrounds would have similar outcomes.

As it turned out, the social health outcomes—such as social capital, civic participation, crime levels, a common vision, and collective efficacy—vary dramatically in El Valle, where seven resettlements were constructed and inhabited. It was not demographic or infrastructure conditions that shaped resettlement trajectory, but rather the process and type of resettlement development. Survivors of Mitch did need a new house; they also needed support in creating a vision for their community that residents could buy into, as well as the mechanisms to ensure that that vision and its accompanying culture would become a reality. In short, the resettlement needed social structure as much as infrastructure (Aldrich 2012b).

CASE SELECTION: EL VALLE

After Hurricane Mitch, tens of thousands of people in the Tegucigalpa urban area were without homes or lived in at-risk zones on the periphery of rivers and hillsides. Some neighborhoods were washed away, while others flooded, and still others were buried. Survivors flocked to find shelter in temporary structures, churches, and schools or were taken in by family members elsewhere, despite cramped living conditions. Many could not return to their homes, either due to the complete disappearance of the land or because their zones had been designated uninhabitable by the government.

To deal with the multitude of survivors who could not return home, the Honduran government and INGOs built *macro-albergues* in the major cities. From 1998 to 2004, resettlements were built to move the survivors from the wood and plastic structures of the *albergues* to permanent housing. El Valle was an ideal place to relocate survivors due to its geographic proximity to Tegucigalpa, low population density, and low risk of future natural hazards. International and national NGOs began a process of gathering donations, purchasing land, building infrastructure, selecting residents, and later moving the survivors into seven resettlements. In total, seven organizations constructed nearly four thousand new homes and resettled approximately 18,300 Mitch survivors and others in need (Reduniversitaria 2009).

I investigated six of the seven resettlements in El Valle, leaving out one because of transportation issues and safety concerns.[2] A seventh organization, Fundación Santa Fe, requested that I also investigate the social health of their new community, Santa Fe, and provide feedback on how the NGO could further support residents. Like the others, the resettlement was constructed for survivors of Mitch from Tegucigalpa (two hundred families in total). This resettlement was located in a rural area east of Tegucigalpa and approximately two and a half hours from El Valle.

SIMILARITIES AND DIFFERENCES
AMONG THE RESETTLEMENTS

Data on initial demographics of incoming residents was unattainable due to lost information and concerns about the protection of privacy. To compensate, our survey asked residents to consider their life circumstances before Mitch, right after Mitch, and a comparison between their pre-Mitch life (1998) and their current life (2009–2010). The data illustrates that there are no statistically significant differences between resettlement residents in the following areas: race and ethnicity, gender distribution, pre-Mitch socioeconomic status,[3] status as a survivor, post-Mitch trauma, remittances as percentage of income, and pre-Mitch versus current physical health.

Relocated community members also share other characteristics. Nearly all residents of each resettlement came from the same affected urban area of Tegucigalpa and its sister city, Comayaguela.[4] Less than one percent of residents in Suyapa do not come from Tegucigalpa, and two percent of residents in the other six resettlements are from outside the capital. These statistics indicate that the two groups are from the same pool of survivors in the Tegucigalpa metro area.

Likewise, in order to obtain a home in either resettlement, a person had to meet a minimum of two conditions of social vulnerability: they must have lived in a condemned area that they could not return to, and they could not own any other property elsewhere. These conditions distill the pool further to citizens who were significantly impacted and had nowhere else to live. In other words, they had the status of disaster survivor and were not wealthy, as they could not rebuild or build elsewhere.

Like resident demographics, the physical resettlements are also similar. Infrastructure and resettlement design are critical components of any recovery and resettlement process (Olshansky, Johnson, and Topping 2006; Olshansky and Chang 2009; Oliver-Smith 1992). The resettlements resemble each other in home size and location (all of which are in El Valle except Santa Fe);

all were built in an undeveloped rural area (no previous landmarks or cultural significance); and all have similar topography, flora, and fauna. All resettlements had parks, schools, community buildings, clinics, churches, roads, paths, electricity, water, sewage, and drainage (see appendix, tables A.1 and A.2 for a comparison of Suyapa and Pino Alto). House types are similar in size and functionality (Belli 2008). As will be described in chapters 5 and 6, differences in resettlement design are also key considerations for predicting long-term social health (Newman 1973).

There are also important differences between the resettlements. First, how sponsoring organizations and future residents chose one another shaped the future resettlement demographics. For example, religious organizations favored survivors of the same religion, while secular organizations were less discriminatory. Since religious groups already held similar values and beliefs, it may have been easier for religious-affiliated resettlements to create social capital and a common vision. In the same vein, the timing of relocation over a five-year period may have impacted the type of residents who applied. Did survivors move at the first possible opportunity, or did they wait for a particular resettlement? Interview data suggests a complicated push-pull process in which individual family needs and resettlement characteristics led to unique decision-making.

Second, size and design are also noticeably different among the seven resettlements. The smallest, La Colina, was built for 80 families, while Pino Alto hosts 1,250. One might conclude that resettlement size may correlate to the ease of community development processes. However, the seven resettlements illustrate that the answer is much more complex. Both a small and a large resettlement had poor outcomes, while another small and the second-largest resettlements had the best outcomes. There may be an upper limit to the size of the resettlement for successful results, but there is no clear correlation between population size and social health.

Lastly, NGO presence over time was also a factor. By 2013, most organizations had moved on to other projects. In La Tierra, the Catholic organization was forcibly removed by residents because the residents had severe disagreements with the NGO.[5] The community of Campo Cielo had not been in touch with its sponsoring NGO in years, and informally, the organization has recognized the resettlement to be a failure. In Santa Fe, the organization was only peripherally involved in economic development. They did maintain a full-time resettlement supervisor, but she mostly collected mortgage payments. In Cerro Viejo, the residents had not heard from the NGO for years, and in Valle Verde, the organization maintained only a minimal connection, mainly through mortgage payments. La Internacional and La Iglesia maintained the longest tenure in Pino Alto (nine years) and Suyapa (eleven years), respectively. They dedicated the most time and resources in community development programs; even though La Internacional officially withdrew in 2007, it maintained an office and two support staff in the resettlement until 2009. La Iglesia continued to work with residents on projects, and build homes for others in need, through 2013. The NGOs' presence, although sometimes contentious, was viewed by the majority of residents as beneficial for the resettlement.

A COMPARATIVE ANALYSIS: SUYAPA AND PINO ALTO

Perhaps the most important question in a comparative analysis is whether the objects of study are similar enough to conduct a comparison that will generate reliable results. In the social world, opportunities that provide the perfect environment to conduct such an investigation are rare. There are, however, similarities between groups, nations, institutions, phenomena, and organizations that I attempt to draw on and generalize from. In post-disaster recovery analysis, Sylves (2011) has noted that "disasters are not unique. There are commonalities and experiences that need to be understood and developed." By extension, disaster resettlement and development are sufficiently similar to make them comparable.

Since discussing all seven resettlements would be difficult, two were selected for their specific similarities and differences. Of the various models for case selection, I chose the maximum-variation cases (Flyvbjerg 2011)—resettlements that resemble each other in many important ways but also have some significant differences. Initially, I sought commonality in demographics, geographic location, long-term NGO relationships, goals and vision for the resettlement, and infrastructure, as well as differences in development trajectories.[6] Suyapa and Pino Alto are the most similar in these respects yet have very divergent social health, providing an opportunity to conduct a comparative case study in a natural environment to see what caused these different outcomes (Ragin 1987, chapter 3).

Though similar in demographics, infrastructure, and NGO length of stay, current social conditions in each community noticeably differ. Suyapa thrives economically, sustains a lower crime rate, and maintains higher collective efficacy, social capital, civic participation, and commitment to a common vision than Pino Alto. In sharp contrast, Pino Alto experiences gang problems, crime, and other social ills. Violence, including murder, has also plagued Pino Alto, and there is low trust and civic participation. This natural experiment of two resettlements starting at similar points but experiencing drastically different outcomes offers a unique opportunity for advancing our understanding of the causal mechanisms that shape developmental trajectories of resettlements.

To clarify the similarities and differences between Suyapa and Pino Alto, I have added a control group—the statistical average of respondents from five post-disaster resettlements (La Tierra, Campo Cielo, Valle Verde, Cerro Viejo, and Santa Fe). I decided to use the average survey results of all five rather than picking only one for methodological reasons. Each resettlement is unique in multiple ways. Choosing only one resettlement would create increased complexity in the comparison of Suyapa and Pino Alto. By drawing on the average of the five resettlements, outlier characteristics of any one case will be softened, thus providing a more vivid picture of what an average resettlement looks like. Combining the five resettlements into one control group also afforded a much larger N, strengthening the validity of the claims.

POST-MITCH CONTEXT AND EVENTS (ECONOMIC, POLITICAL, AND SOCIAL INFLUENCES)

The resettlement of tens of thousands of people is, of course, embedded in broader structures that shape the community development process. Since 1998, Honduras has witnessed massive upheaval, resulting in some of the highest levels of violence in the world due to increasing narco-trafficking and government instability and corruption. The following paragraphs will briefly describe the political and economic history of Honduras, then discuss the recent social turmoil and its impact on the resettlement development process.

It was from the harsh Atlantic Ocean that the name Honduras was born. From its "founding" and christening by Christopher Columbus, Honduras has been a place of extremes. The traditional story describes Columbus leading the Spanish fleet on his last trip to the New World, in 1502. Heading southwest from Jamaica, they encountered rough seas in the deep waters off the northeastern coast of the unnamed land. After arriving safely, Columbus is cited as saying, "Gracias a Dios que hemos dejado estas honduras" ("Thank God we have left these depths"). The far eastern state of Honduras received the name Gracias a Dios, and the country as a whole was called Honduras.

Since independence from Spain in 1821, Honduras has had a long history of economic challenges. Wealthy Spanish-descendent elites, along with transnational elites from the United States and the Middle East, were able to maintain control over land and property throughout the nineteenth and twentieth centuries, finding economic prosperity in land use for natural resource exploitation (bananas, minerals, fruits, coffee, fish, etc.). The two-tier society, with a small elite and large poor and subsistence citizenry, created a system of patronage and corruption, political infighting and an incompetent bureaucracy, dependency on raw materials, isolation from the broader world market, and ties with international corporations that maintained a largely poor and under-developed economy (Merrill 1995; Dudley 2016; Sieder 1995). Honduras as a nation had little opportunity to develop the strong middle class necessary for long-term sustainable growth. In 2015, 60 percent of Honduran households lived below the poverty level (CIA World Factbook 2016), and the nation, like much of Latin America, has a high GINI coefficient of 53.6 (World Bank 2016b). The inequitable distribution of income within the country is in part due to significant underemployment and low-productivity jobs. Most jobs are in agriculture (30 percent), trade (25 percent), services (16 percent), and manufacturing (15 percent) (Europa World Online 2016; for a history of the Honduran political economy, see Euraque 1996).

Impoverished conditions also laid the fertile soil for the growth of gang activity and drug trafficking throughout the nation. The late 1990s crackdown on gangs in the United States led to mass deportation of Central Americans, especially those who had a criminal record. When repatriated, deportees arrived in a politically weak state that was also going through significant rural-urban changes (Insight Crime 2015). In addition, the 1980s and 1990s drug war in Mexico and Colombia forced narco-traffickers to look for alternative locations for the production and movement of illicit drugs. Honduras, with its relatively large and unpopulated north coast, became a base of drug trans-shipment, with up to 80 percent of the cocaine that reaches the United States trafficked through the area (Sherwell 2015).

By the early 2000s, two gangs, Mara Salvatrucha (MS) 13 and Barrio 18, had become powerful social forces in Honduras. The extortion and violence created by these groups led to a severe reaction, Mano Dura (Iron Fist), by the Maduro administration (2002–2006). This approach, however, was unsuccessful at eliminating the gangs; rather, both gang organizations became more horizontal in structure (Insight Crime 2015). The resulting power struggle between MS 13, Barrio 18, and the Honduran state has created an atmosphere of fear and paralyzing violence in Honduran society (see Caldera and Jiménez 2006).

Murder is common in Honduras, especially in the cities. Ranked as the nation with the highest homicide rate per capita in the world three years running, Honduras continues to struggle with violence, especially in the cities. A 2011 *Washington Post* article entitled "Honduras: The World's Homicide Capital" graphically illustrates the problem the nation faces: 82.1 murders per hundred thousand residents nationally, with homicides tripling since 1995. Since 1996, Honduras has occupied one of the top five slots for highest homicide rate in the world. Between 2008 and 2014, Honduras had the highest murder rate

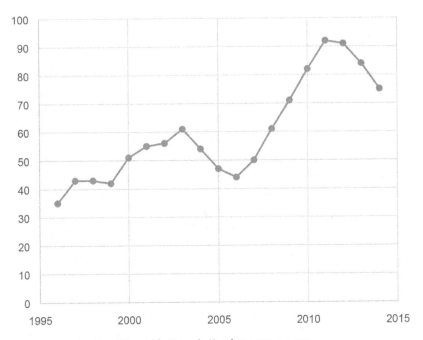

FIGURE 2.1. Intentional Homicide Rates in Honduras per 100,000
(World Bank 2016a; UNODC 2016)

in six of the seven years, ranking second behind El Salvador in 2009 (World
Bank 2016; UNODC 2016).

Although homicides are declining slightly in quantity, "atrocious crimes,"
such as decapitations and mutilations, are increasing, largely as a result of
gang violence (Palencia 2014). Due to these changes, Hondurans are losing
hope that life will be better after Mitch. Blanca Álvarez, whose child was murdered, exclaimed, "We are living in constant fear. Nothing is going to change
here. Nothing."[7]

I, too, was affected by growing violence. On December 23, 2011, my friend
Marco, whom I knew through soccer, was murdered. One afternoon, in a
supposedly safe part of Comayaguela, he was held up while driving, robbed,
and shot to death in his old pickup truck. Marco, a good man, left behind a
wife and two adolescent children. With the death of my friend, I gained new
insight into the pessimism and hopelessness felt by many Hondurans, and the
disbelief that things can ever change.

Finally, internal trust in the government is low (Ruhl 2010). A 2008 study
by Latin American Public Opinion Project (LAPOP) and Vanderbilt University, with support from USAID, found that 34.5 percent of residents in Te-

gucigalpa have been a victim of corruption (such as bribery)[8], a rate that is more than twice as high as in any other city in the country. When asked about the number of corrupt civil servants in the country, more than 70 percent of Honduras believed most public employees are corrupt, the highest level of any Latin American nation. Moreover, respondents were questioned about the ability to bribe a police officer to prevent being detained. Forty percent replied that it would be a high or very high possibility. If the answer "it depends on the situation" is added to the responses, 67 percent believe the police can be bribed (Latinobarometro 2011a). To put it in perspective, these numbers are higher than in all of the neighboring countries except Guatemala (see also *La Tribuna* 2010).

Reviewing the national statistics from 1997 until 2010, the Honduran government has had a steadily declining record of financial transparency (except for a blip immediately after Mitch due to international oversight) and is significantly less transparent than its neighbors Guatemala and El Salvador. Transparency International (2016) measures the perceived levels of public sector corruption in 163 countries around the world. In 2015, Honduras was 112th, illustrating high citizen distrust of the government and government officials. In a 2013 World Bank survey, Hondurans cited anticorruption as the second most important development priority for the country (after education). Additionally, when asked if Honduras is headed in the right direction, only 19 percent of national citizens said yes, compared to 70 percent in a similar 2004 survey.

Honduras also wrestles with weak state institutions. This is seen clearly in the June 2009 coup, in which the Honduran congress and supreme court mandated the removal of the democratically elected president Manuel Zelaya from the country. The ensuing protests led to significant violence and decreased trust in the state by citizens. Internationally, the coup was condemned by the international community, and the Organization of American States suspended Honduras as a member (Europa World Online 2016; Arnson 2009). The peaceful 2010 election of Porfirio Lobo Sosa and return of Zelaya in May 2011 marked a return to normalized international relations, but distrust continues among Hondurans.

In sum, historical and contemporary economic, social, and political structures create a national atmosphere of distrust, fear, crime, and violence. Dudley (2016) explains,

> Honduras, meanwhile, has become one of the poorest, most unequal and indebted countries in the world. Any attempts to change this system have been met with stern and often unified opposition from elites of all stripes.

And attempts to exert more regulatory control over the activities of the elites are smothered before they begin. It is little surprise then that the country offers criminals, large and small, one of the most propitious environments from which to work. On one side, an ineffective justice system and corrupt security forces, long exploited by these elites, [open] the way for large criminal groups to operate with impunity. On the other side, an impoverished populace—which sees and understands exactly how elites abuse a broken system—seeks to get its share by working directly with criminals in the illegal and legal enterprises these criminals operate. Crime, as it turns out, is one of the few forms of social mobility.

Resettlement in ideal conditions is difficult; resettlement in a nation with such wide-ranging social problems is even more so.

CHAPTER 3

COMMUNITY DEVELOPMENT IN THE
CONTEXT OF DISASTER RESETTLEMENT

In his "Meditation XVII," John Donne elucidates the interconnection we share.

> No man is an island, entire of itself; every man is a piece of the continent, a part of the main . . . any man's death diminishes me, because I am involved in mankind, and therefore never send to know for whom the bell tolls; it tolls for thee.

Yet how is the connection among individuals re-created after massive upheavals such as a natural disaster and relocation? Appreciating this interdependence in a post-disaster resettlement is all the more important as the ties that bound particular groups together are unraveled and survivors may feel, figuratively and literally, alone among strangers. This chapter attempts to synthesize the very different literatures—disaster studies, community development, and path dependence—that may answer why residents in some resettlements were able to create these connections (defined as social health) while residents in other resettlements could not.

To begin, I will review the disaster and resettlement literatures. Resettlements are unique in both infrastructure and population in comparison to established communities. This is a crucial insight, often overlooked by community development experts. The distinctiveness of post-disaster heterogeneous resettlement will be described, clarifying the unique attributes of the resettlement process and special needs of inhabitants.

With this as a foundation, the following section examines how scholars define community and explains the community development process. This area of research is vast, so I narrow it down to the two major theories of community development most relevant to the resettlement case studies, self-help and technical assistance. I also discuss the social qualities of community and the debate over whether development should be "of community" (focusing on building community characteristics, such as social cohesion and collective effi-cacy) or "in community" (focusing on individual or household-level capaci-ties, such as economic development) (Shaffer and Summers 1989). Addition-ally, in global south nations like Honduras, NGOs are often crucial actors in supporting or sponsoring resettlement and community development. The role of NGOs in post-Mitch Honduras will be described.

Finally, to draw these varied areas together, the theory of path dependence is applied within the context of resettlement. Resettlements are in a unique liminal moment in which new initiatives and community development strate-gies can be pursued. Path dependence provides a framework for investigating the long-term consequences of these interventions. Path dependence connects the disparate causal explanations of resettlement development by taking into account the initial conditions of residents within the resettlement, the NGO and resident community development philosophies and practices as a dialec-tical process, and change over time.

DISASTER RECOVERY LITERATURE IN THE CONTEXT OF RESETTLEMENT

It is well recognized that human vulnerability, natural vulnerability, and haz-ards continue to increase (Amos 2011), due in part to human-induced climate change (IPCC 2013). In response, the disaster literature is also growing. How-ever, much of the research has been preoccupied with preparedness, response, relief, and mitigation and has been limited geographically and longitudinally (Tierney 2007; Berke and Beatley 1997, chapter 1). Disaster recovery devel-oped much later (Tierney 2007) and is often understood in the context of re-construction[1] (Lizarralde, Johnson, and Davidson 2009) or resettlement, with the latter one of the least researched disaster subfields (Institute of Medicine 2015).

Within disaster recovery, long-term resettlement is understudied and im-mensely complex (Holt 1981; Jha et al. 2010; for a review see Cernea and McDowell 2000). Scudder and Colson (1982) developed one of the earliest models, focusing on how affected people and systems respond during differ-ent stages of resettlement: recruitment, transition, potential development, and handing over or incorporation. Responding to critiques of this approach, Cer-nea (1997) created the impoverishment risks and reconstruction model, which focused on the risks of resettlement in order to avoid them: landlessness, job-lessness, homelessness, marginalization, food insecurity, loss of access to com-mon property resources, increased morbidity, and community disarticulation (the breakdown of social structures and kinship bonds). Black et al. (2013) found that displacement and resettlement is only one outcome of post-disaster recovery, along with migration and immobility of survivors. Well-researched studies exist but are often very specific, investigating involuntary resettlements (Ali Badri et al. 2006), development-provoked resettlements (Oliver-Smith 2009; Hall 1994; OECD-DAC 1991), refugee resettlements (Nawyn 2006), and conflict-driven resettlements (Ellis and Barakat 1996). The strengths of these studies are recognized in the characteristics of, and policy implications for, resettlements in various contexts. The weaknesses, however, are that most investigations are done only within a few years of the initial relocation.

The bridge between recovery and long-term community development merits more scholarly attention than it has received so far. Badri and colleagues' (2006) review of resettlements in Iran eleven years after the Manjil earthquake, and Iuchi's (2010) discussion of the 2004 Chuetsu earthquake in Japan, provide the longitudinal data needed to discuss resettlements' transformation into communities, but this scholarship fails to identify the long-term consequences of resettlement for social health.[2] Ritchie's (2012) qualitative analysis of the impacts of the *Exxon Valdez* oil spill on an Alaskan community finds that there are long-term physical and mental ills associated with stress and collective trauma.

The scholarship also may lack the comparative data to describe differentiation in these consequences or may focus on individual or a small number of resettlement issues. Oliver-Smith's classic multiyear work in post-earthquake Peru (1986 [1992]) highlights four key factors for successful resettlement design: site selection, settlement design, housing, and participation. This valuable contribution, however, focuses on resettlement of residents who already have some semblance of social capital, not a heterogeneous group of survivors as in post-Mitch Honduras. Those scholars who have conducted comparative work focus narrowly on particular aspects of resettlement. Berke and Beatley (1997) provide an overview of different hurricane disasters and their devastating effects on four Caribbean islands. They propose a significant overhaul in the way governments and supporting NGOs strategize recovery efforts. Tellman, Alaniz, Rivera, and Contreras (2015) also utilize a two-nation comparison of resettled areas. In particular, the authors point out the importance of social capital in resettlements for combating fragile and violent states in El Salvador and Honduras. Furthermore, Adams, Alaniz, Bronen, and McNamara (2015) elaborate on the context of voluntary and forced resettlement as it applies to place attachment, illuminating the issue of trauma and the challenge of creating attachment to a new location, an issue faced by all who are relocated.

The anthropologist Anthony Oliver-Smith once noted, "Any discussion of a disaster and its effects on a community must consider the issues of adaptation and changes as well as drama and impact" (1992, 14). Building on this idea, discovering how resettlements adapt and change in the long-term context is distinctive and must be studied as such. Most academic post-disaster research continues to focus on themes such as physical and mental health (under the disciplines of psychology, psychiatry, and social work), mitigation (sociology and urban planning), short-term recovery of one to five years (across disciplines and by sponsoring organizations), and infrastructure (architecture and engineering). Although all of these components are important to community development, they cannot speak to the long-term social sustainability of particular resettlement development strategies.

Resettlements are also often defined by what forced survivors to relocate rather than what characteristics they share as a group. De Wet (2006) and Oliver-Smith (2009, 2010) refer to groups impacted by contemporary neoliberal projects in the global south as development-induced resettlements. Barnes (2001), in her study of the Vietnamese who fled to Australia after the fall of Saigon in 1975, identifies the population as a refugee resettlement. Du (2012) discusses ecological resettlement efforts by the Chinese government to remove populations from a sensitive ecosystem in Qinghai province. Finally, other scholars have used involuntary or forced resettlement to characterize populations that are made to leave, usually by a nation-state (Scudder and Colson 1982; Cernea 2000). While each of these concepts articulates the mode of dislocation, they say little about the characteristics of the resettlers. The context of resettlement is important; however, understanding the actors involved and their agency and constraints provides an important perspective into the resettlement long-term outcomes.

In redefining resettlements from event-focused to people-focused, scholars and practitioners can become more aware of the particular challenges and opportunities the individual group possesses. The following section discusses important characteristics of disaster survivors generally as well as those found within heterogeneous resettlements, or resettlements populated by survivors from diverse geographic locations.[3]

RESETTLEMENT CHARACTERISTICS

Governments and NGOs in disaster recovery, and, by extension, disaster resettlement, often do not take a holistic approach (Ingram et al. 2006; Cernea 2000). Frequently, institutions do not have the financial ability or time to address issues of place attachment, intentional vision, development of a community culture, and life in the "new normal" (Jackson 2003; Olshansky, Hopkins, and Johnson 2012). Moreover, without the immediate physical danger of a disaster or natural hazard, survivors may be seen as no longer need-ing help. Nonetheless, the complex social relationships within a resettlement reveal that survivors remain an extremely vulnerable population. Cernea and McDowell (2000, 363) highlight the complexity of the situation:

> It is well documented that forced displacement tears apart existing communi-ties and social structures, interpersonal ties, and the enveloping social fabric. Kinship groups often get scattered and life sustaining informal networks of mutual help, local voluntary associations, and self-organized service arrange-ments are dismantled. The unraveling of spatially and culturally based pat-terns of self-organization, social interaction, and reciprocity represents loss of valuable social capital that compounds the loss of both natural and man-made capital.

This social disarticulation shapes the social dynamic of the future resettlement.

In what follows, I will focus on six common resettlement characteristics that increase vulnerability in the creation of community. These six—trauma, poverty, heterogeneous population, low bonding social capital, intentionality, and newness—shape the initial conditions of the resettlement. They interact in complicated ways and significantly affect community development efforts and future resettlement social health. To provide concrete examples, the six characteristics will be discussed in reference to post-Mitch resettlements in Honduras.

TRAUMA AND POVERTY

Each resettlement in El Valle was inhabited by a traumatized population. Many survivors had suffered the death of family members in addition to having lost their homes and possessions. Additionally, survivors were forced to move, breaking their place attachment to previous neighborhoods. In the survey, I found that in all seven resettlements, at least 75 percent of the resi-dents had some type of trauma associated with the hurricane. Of this popu-lation, on a three-level scale of very bad, bad, and normal, an average of 44 percent of residents rated their trauma as very bad.

Trauma has been considered a significant hurdle to community recovery, resettlement, and development (Erikson 1976; Gill 2007; Ritchie 2012; Scud-der and Colson 1982; Cernea and McDowell 2000). The post-disaster trauma literature suggests that in many cases, the diagnosis of posttraumatic stress disorder (PTSD) can affect anywhere between 5 and 40 percent of survivors, depending on the type and severity of the trauma. Goenjian et al. (2000, 911) discovered that survivors of earthquakes and political violence are at a "high risk of developing severe and chronic posttraumatic stress reactions that are associated with chronic anxiety and depressive reactions." Galea et al. (2007) had a similar finding of severe trauma among survivors of Hurricane Katrina, noting that it was necessary to address those significant and long-term effects. According to Ritchie (2012), residents of Cordova, Alaska, continued to experience a collective trauma, even fourteen years after the *Exxon Valdez* oil spill. In this study, self-reported trauma was much higher, affecting between 75 and 78 percent of the resettled populations. Although scholars know trauma exists in residents, the impact on the long-term outcomes of resettlement is understudied.

Others establish that although disasters usually have a negative impact on psychological and material well-being, symptoms of trauma wane over time. Green et al. (1990) found that PTSD in Buffalo Creek disaster survivors declined from 44 percent to 28 percent from 1974 to 1986. Goenjian et al. (2000) provide a lengthy literature review on the subject, highlighting the lingering effects of trauma (PTSD, depression, and anxiety) in the case of survivors of the Mount St. Helens volcano eruption, noting that trauma abated, for many, after as few as three years, while lasting a lifetime for others (see also Nolen-Hoeksema and Morrow 1991; Neria, Nandi, and Galea 2008; North et al. 2004).

The impact of relocation and trauma continues to be debated among scholars, most of whom view it as problematic and difficult to investigate. Najarian et al. (2001) found that relocated women had higher levels of PTSD than women who remained in their original location. Boeni and Jigyasuii (2005) conclude that after the Indonesia earthquake and Indian Ocean tsunami (2004), the Bam earthquake (2003), and the Gujarat earthquake (2001), relocation was often done without the cultural and ecological considerations necessary to maintain healthy communities. Jha et al. (2010, 182), on behalf of the World Bank, highlight that "relocation disrupts lives and should be kept to a minimum."

Gill (2007) discusses relocation as a secondary trauma experience by Hurricane Katrina survivors, noting that trauma was not limited to a single event. Prolonged social disruption and uncertainty produced chronic stress within the community, diminishing social capital, which normally provides support for the individual. Kai Erikson also analyzes the severity of secondary trauma, which is then carried with survivors into the next community. Erikson (1976, 185) explains:

> Secondary trauma can be defined as a blow to the social fabric of a community caused by inadequate responses to an initial hazard event and/or

inadequate responses to secondary hazards. Events, occasions, or public perceptions that inhibit timely community recovery and prolong stress
and disruption are examples of secondary trauma . . . impacts of secondary trauma are related to diminished social capital, a corrosive community,
chronic stress and negative lifescape changes among individuals, and prolong
social disruption in communities.

One would expect that the community with higher trauma severity would
have a much more difficult time building the social essentials of community,
and that this could contribute to explaining different outcomes in similarly affected resettlements.

Trauma also negatively impacts community reconstruction and development efforts. Steinberg (2007) found that people were so preoccupied by their
trauma and personal losses that community planning was relegated to the back
burner. Unlike most community development ventures, organizations had to
address issues of trauma (Hoffman and Oliver-Smith 1999) before starting to
develop issues of social health (see also Etzioni's [1995] discussion of invert-
ing symbiosis).

However, other evidence indicates that the disruption of unhealthy neighborhoods can actually be beneficial to residents. Kirk (2015) finds that formerly incarcerated individuals who were relocated away from their previous New Orleans neighborhood after Hurricane Katrina were significantly
less likely to recidivate. To underline this point, the author cites a conversation shared by Malcolm Gladwell (2015) and an ex-convict, in which the ex-
convict explains, "Now, I hate that the storm came because a lot of people
died in the storm, but, guess what, that was probably the best thing that could
have happened to a lot of people, because it gave them the opportunity to re-
invent themselves if their life wasn't going right." Relocation can provide an
opportunity for self-improvement and new choices once certain structures are
removed.

Poverty and the education of survivors may have also posed a challenge to
recovery and resettlement (Fothergill and Peek 2004). Honduras is the third-
poorest nation in the Western Hemisphere (after Haiti and Guatemala), with
approximately 56 percent of the population living on less than four dollars a
day and 64 percent living below the national poverty line (World Bank 2015a).
It ranks second lowest on the United Nations Human Development Index
(after Nicaragua) in the Americas (UNDP 2015). Post-Mitch survivors were
not only some of the most vulnerable to natural hazards in the Western Hemisphere but also some of the most economically vulnerable in North and South
America and, as noted earlier, socially vulnerable to violence.

In order to be eligible for resettlement, prospective residents had to prove to the sponsoring NGO that they had lost their home or that their home was in an at-risk zone, and that they did not have another option for housing. These eligibility requirements restricted resettlement to survivors who were of a lower socioeconomic level and who had lived near or in dangerous areas, either along the river or on steep hillsides. Wealthy Hondurans, living in safer areas, either were not affected, were able to rebuild or reinforce their home, or were able to relocate on their own. Poverty conditions may also deemphasize community development efforts as survivors are focused on feeding their families. In sum, El Valle resettlement residents wrestled with higher levels of poverty by international and national standards and, as will be discussed in the following chapter, a weak state and minimal social welfare in the homicide capital of the world.

DIVERSITY OF RESIDENTS AND SOCIAL CAPITAL

Heterogeneous resettlements, made up of survivors with diverse backgrounds and geographies, are less likely to have bonding social capital. Other types of resettlement, such as the relocation of entire communities or slow-onset disaster relocation, maintain relationships and build on previous social capital, engaging in social reconstitution (Oliver-Smith 2005) rather than the complete invention of "community." Because heterogeneous resettlements lack the necessary embedded bonding social capital and previous common culture, they face special challenges. For example, they often do not have a common set of norms and values; may have different understandings of power, politics, and economic relationships; and may have embedded conflict based on previous areas of residence (e.g., stereotyping of neighborhoods or social identity). These issues are even more salient when it comes to creating a common vision for the future community.

As described in many resettlements studied and in the literature (Alesch, Arendt, and Holly 2009, 179–180), background diversity can undermine the formulation of a cohesive plan. As Scudder and Colson point out, "Following removal, the majority of relocatees, including refugees, can be expected to follow a conservative strategy. They cope with the stress of removal by clinging to the familiar and changing no more than is necessary" (1982, 272). In Suyapa, residents arrived from dozens of Tegucigalpa metro neighborhoods; those in Pino Alto came from more than one hundred. As will be shown, this diversity shaped much of the development process and impacted how cohesive the resettlement was to become. It also casts into relief a resettlement challenge that has yet to be fully fleshed out theoretically.

A house does not make a home, just as a resettlement does not make a community. The concept of social capital is contentious, but most scholars define it as having two parts, as originally defined by Bourdieu (1986; Coleman 1988): a social relationship that enables individuals to claim resources by their association with others, and the amount and quality of those resources. It constitutes both an instrumental and a functional explanation, emphasizing the benefits and deliberate construction of this relationship (Portes 1998, 3–4). Putnam supplements this definition by specifying the types of relationships and resources: "Whereas physical capital refers to physical objects and human capital refers to properties of individuals, social capital refers to connections among individuals—social networks and the norms of reciprocity and trustworthiness that arise from them. In that sense social capital is closely related to what some have called 'civic virtue'" (2000, 19). It is this definition, often utilized in the literature, that I will make use of. I refer to social capital, broadly, as the networks, trust, and reciprocity that shape all aspects of social life, or what has also been called bonding social capital (Putnam 2000; Aldrich 2010, 2012a, chapter 2).

Bridger (2001, 464), considering the role of social capital in sustaining communities, notes that "successful cooperation for long-term mutual benefit depends on the cultivation of social capital." Others insist that social capital can produce safer communities, more confidence in the justice system, clear communication, greater social interaction between people (Coleman 1988, S102–S103), and the development of entrepreneurial social infrastructure (Flora and Flora 2003). Putnam underscores how social capital can ease social relations, stating that "trustworthiness lubricates social life. Frequent interaction among a diverse set of people tends to produce a norm of generalized reciprocity. Civic engagement and social capital entail mutual obligation and responsibility for action" (2000, 21). Reciprocity can mean more cooperation, stronger norms, less opportunism, and better communication (Bridger 2001). Silverman (2004) asserts that the creation and maintenance of social capital constitutes a necessary component of any community-based organization in obtaining long-term goals, especially those related to democracy, grassroots empowerment, and community development. Along the same lines but in a different context, Gould (1991) discovers that informal networks such as neighborhoods are tied directly to formal membership in social movement organizations (see also Snow, Zurcher, and Ekland-Olson 1980; Meyer 2007, chapter 3). Lastly, Wuthnow (1999) and Candland (2001) explain how religion can enable social cohesion or the formation of social capital. As the case studies will show, religion did support the creation of community via bonding social capital.

Quarantelli states that social capital is "one major kind of resources that those involved in disaster-related activity might or might not have" (2005, 357) and can be useful in disaster recovery. Aldrich (2011, 2012a; Aldrich and Sawada 2015) describes how different types of social capital—bridging, bonding, and linking—were advantageous for recovery after the Kobe earthquake and recent Tohoku earthquake and tsunami. Nakagawa and Shaw (2004) note that the benefits of social capital extend beyond cultural context, as seen in community recovery after the Kobe and Guajarat earthquakes. Ritchie and Gill (2007) also found that social capital can be a useful framework for understanding the multifaceted consequences of technological disasters. Yandong (2007) corroborates this claim by finding that social capital enabled communities in eleven provinces in China to recover more quickly, particularly with higher levels of trust and networking. Chamlee-Wright (2010), in her work on returning to New Orleans neighborhoods after Hurricane Katrina, emphasizes that disaster survivors must often deal with collective action problems, including attitudes of dependency. In her view, one way to overcome these problems is to draw on previous social capital and the cultural economy in which residents and institutions create and reinforce particular norms and social capital (broadly). Lastly, Adger et al. (2005) found that social capital is useful beyond recovery and provides distinct benefits to communities in building adaptive capacity for future hazards and resilience once impacted by a disaster.

All of that said, Portes (1998) reminds scholars to approach the concept carefully, not as a political and value-laden strategy but rather as a social fact. Indeed, citing Woolcock (1998, 185), "Definitions of social capital should focus primarily on its sources rather than its consequences . . . long-term benefits, if and when they occur, are the result of a combination of different but complementary types of social relations, combinations whose relative importance will in all likelihood shift over time."[4] This is important in the case of resettlements of atomized households that already lack social capital. The development of bonding social capital before and during the resettlement process where there was very little to begin with still has not been adequately studied.

The intersection of these factors has a multiplier effect (Crenshaw 1991) on resettlement and the development of community. With higher trauma and fewer resources, and a heterogeneous resettlement with lower levels of bonding social capital, among many other factors, survivors in resettlements must overcome multiple, complicated, and often invisible obstacles in creating community. Indeed, like the development of any social condition, the necessary ingredients must be available to produce the desired outcome. In the resettlements, many of these ingredients were scarce.

NEW RESETTLEMENTS

Each resettlement is also a "new" resettlement (Beck 2001). Many barrios in Tegucigalpa were completely destroyed by either rivers or landslides during Hurricane Mitch. Rebuilding was not possible without the likelihood that the same destruction would happen again. To prevent this from recurring, resettlements were built in the geologically safe area of El Valle, where there was open, unused land and minimal population. Services for water, sewage, and electricity, along with other infrastructure—homes, roads, markets, and parks—all needed to be built. New resettlements like these must not only create material resources (including housing, clinics, markets, parks, churches, schools, etc.), but also meet many nonmaterial resource needs (such as local support networks, organized social and political structures, a new set of social norms, informal social control mechanisms, new power relations, and even a new community culture). As Barr describes in her work with resettled Zimbabwean farmers, "new villages should be thought of as highly interactive, nonlinear systems. They represent small worlds in which new and distinct cultures can evolve" (2004, 1764–1765). Because there are so few long-term, comparative investigations, how these social resources are created in the context of post-disaster resettlements is not well understood.

New resettlements are also unique in their opportunity for change. In most instances, when citizens move from one town or neighborhood to another, they are moving into a built environment that may have been occupied by others for decades or centuries. Infrastructure—including schools, parks, paths, and roads—already exists, and there is little room for flexibility or creativity to shape the physical environment. The natural environment has been contoured around the needs of the community as well. Importantly, histories, symbols, scars, personalities, and even local cultures already exist (McMillan and Chavis 1986, 10). When a family moves into such an established community, they must acclimate to the existing norms and values of the neighborhood. For residents in a *new* resettlement, the norms and values must be cooperatively created; new resettlements provide a special opportunity to define *community*, physically and socially.

When the first residents arrived in Suyapa and Pino Alto, the built and natural environments were still construction sites. The land was laid bare of its plants and curves for the efficient erection of homes. It was a blank canvas for residents to decide how they wanted to utilize the pockets of space in corners, around homes, along the road, and in the parks. This creative process was encouraged and institutionalized by La Iglesia and La Internacional. In Suyapa, the Junta de Reforestación (Committee for Reforestation) and in Pino Alto the committee of the *patronato* (governing political body) decide on the development and beautification of the natural environment. Residents, collectively though inequitably,[5] defined the new space.

The resettlements are also a place of negotiation of structures, including behaviors, beliefs, and values. Residents arrived from dozens of different barrios or *colonias* (neighborhoods) in Tegucigalpa, and all citizens brought their own understanding and expectations of community based on prior personal experiences and socialization. Like many new groups of resettlement residents, they generally lacked strong social network ties (Morrow 1999). Strangers lived next door to one another. In addition, each family brought their own particular cultural tool kit (Swidler 1986), tied to their previous neighborhood, to put to use in their new community. Resettlement culture became a process of conciliation, cooperation, and conflict on a level unseen and unnecessary in more established neighborhoods.

Culture (the values, norms, behaviors, and material goods of a group), emergent social norms (the boundaries defining appropriate behavior in a new situation), and vision (the belief about the way community should be) enabled the survivors to reimagine their lives. Most residents came from polluted neighborhoods in Tegucigalpa that were unsafe at night (and, for vulnerable residents like the elderly or adolescents, dangerous all the time). Father Carlitos, the Catholic priest who served the whole of El Valle from 2005 to 2009, told me:

> Tegucigalpa, for example, is at times a disagreeable climate to live in: the air and the natural environment are contaminated with the climate of violence. People continue to come to the capital but it is not *open* to them. [Residents] live locked inside; they do not have clean air. The children, for example, are locked inside the fence only watching the cars pass by.

Tegucigalpa is, in many ways, unhealthy. Yet when residents arrive in the valley, they have a different experience. Carlitos continued,

> Some find it hard to adapt to living in a more comfortable climate; they run, ride bikes, have space to sow plants—a green garden, not only a cement floor. There is green space; they can walk and can live in a dignified manner. But the mentality of the people is always to live locked up. This environment helps them to remove themselves from the problems [of the city], to relax more, and to not live stressed out. I think people have a change in their mindset.

Carlitos believes that moving away from the city could change people, change mentalities, and change culture. Whether this was available to each resettlement and whether residents accepted a change or drifted back into a Teguci-galpa mentality remained a choice to be made by each individual, while being shaped by each resettlement's particular cultural development.

In their newness, resettlements are also quite vulnerable due to social dis-articulation (Cernea 1997). As noted, poverty, trauma, heterogeneity, broken social networks, and restarting in a new place can be overwhelming. Previous scholarship on crime established that delinquency is more likely to happen in areas of poverty, trauma, and instability (Shaw and McKay 1942; Kawachi, Kennedy, and Wilkinson 1999; Zahran et al. 2009; Bursik and Webb 1982).

The six characteristics described above intersect in complicated ways and change and develop over time. One can see how a lack of social capital in a new resettlement can make overcoming trauma and poverty considerably more challenging. One can also imagine the opposite—the development of social capital within a new resettlement, the creation of a common vision, and people working together to build a sense of community. Academic under-standing of how community development happens, why a group would choose one path over another, continues to evolve.

DEFINING COMMUNITY

Community has been defined in many ways and in many contexts (Hillery 1955; Fromm and Maccoby 1970; Gusfield 1975; Schwartz 1981; McMillan and Chavis 1986; Goe and Noonan 2007). Two descriptions are appropriate for discussing the process of post-disaster resettlement development toward community. As described earlier, vulnerability and newness give resettlements a distinct character of intentionality. Intentional communities are most often referred to in the context of communitarian movements. According to Za-blocki in *The Joyful Community*,

> an intentional community is a group of persons associated together [volun-tarily] for the purpose of establishing a whole way of life. As such, it shall display to some degree, each of the following characteristics: common geo-graphical location; economic interdependence; social, cultural, educational, and spiritual inter-exchange of uplift and development. (1971, 19)

In El Valle, displaced residents chose to live in a bounded geographic location; to be economically interdependent; to engage in social, cultural, educational, and sometimes spiritual dialogue; and to share (to some extent) a vision for the development of the resettlements. Of course, not all members at all times did so, but survey results and interviews support the generalizability of this definition.

Furthermore, to attend to the social-psychological aspects of community (beyond the geographic, numeric, or transactional), theorists have developed the concept "sense of community." McMillan, twenty years after first articulating the concept, redefined sense of community as "a *spirit* of belonging together, a feeling that there is an authority structure that can be *trusted*, an awareness that *trade* and mutual benefit come from being together, and a spirit that comes from shared experiences that are preserved as *art*" (italics in original 1996, 315). Although robust, McMillan's characterization would be difficult to measure and discuss with residents. Therefore, within the context of post-disaster resettlement, I combined the intentionality description and the interpersonal characteristics of "sense of community" to define community as a sense of cohesion, social capital, and physical security, wherein members demonstrate a commitment to each other through collective participation, shared values, and the upholding of a common vision.

THEORIES OF COMMUNITY DEVELOPMENT

The history of community research dates back to Ferdinand Tönnies (2001 [1887]) and his analysis of changing social ties from *gemeinschaft* (community), based on traditional social rules, to *gesellschaft* (society), which was based on rational self-interest. As Gusfield (1975, chapter 1) points out, these concepts are analytical and not empirical; they help us think about change and human associations, but there are no purely traditional or self-interested groups. Building on Tönnies's work, the French sociologist Emile Durkheim (1995 [1912]) furthered this approach with his descriptions of mechanical solidarity (wherein social connections are based on kinship) and organic solidarity (in which social relationships are based on interdependence due to the division of labor). Over the twentieth century, US scholars were also theorizing the boundaries and development of community (Addams 1910; Whyte 1943; Shaw and McKay 1942; Logan 2003). Much of this research would later be cataloged under rural sociology. Since an in-depth review of the history of community development is beyond the scope of this book (see Cary 1970; Gusfield 1975; Goe and Noonan 2007; Christenson and Robinson 1989), this section will focus on the two foundational theories most relevant to post-disaster resettlement development: technical assistance and self-help.[6]

THE TECHNICAL ASSISTANCE APPROACH

The technical assistance approach (also referred to as social planning and the empirical-rational approach) is usually conducted by external organizations or institutions that provide programs, activities, or services to support the capacity of community members to achieve a defined goal. A core assumption is that people often know what the problem may be but do not have the technical expertise, experience, or resources to address the issue. However, with the support of external professionals, the collection and analysis of data, and clear planning, a community can overcome challenges. The aim of technical assistance strategies, then, is attaining a distinct end, with less emphasis on the means.

Technical assistance is often described as a directive (nondevelopment) or developmental strategy. The former can be likened to historical examples of development, in which external providers demanded that recipients change to fit the provider's vision. "Civilizing" and "Christianizing" are perhaps the most potent examples of what has been criticized as the White Man's Burden (Kipling 1998 [1899]). Although not viewed as acceptable today, there is no doubt this strategy continues to underlie broader economic development efforts (McMichael 2016). The developmental approach is one in which the recipient approaches the external provider, collaborates with the providers using an agreed-upon set of roles, and has some control over the process. As Oberle, Stowers, and Darby (1974, 61, as cited in Robinson and Fear 2011, 61) explain, development is the "process in which increasingly more members of a given area or environment make and implement socially responsible decisions." Two significant differences between the two include who controls the process of development and how provider and recipient interact within the relationship.

Three benefits of this developmental technical assistance approach are clear. First, communities often do not have the necessary resources to develop and therefore need the assistance of providers. With the support of external agents sharing best practices, new technology, or scientific knowledge, communities can jump-start their projects. Second, the development process may be more efficient, bypassing time-consuming learning processes and community decision-making and directly tackling the problem. Finally, as described above, disaster survivors who are thrown into building a community may need clarity and guidance from providers to be successful.

The strengths of the technical assistance approach have also been criticized as weaknesses. Ellerman (2007) notes that the technical assistance strategy can undercut or override (vis-à-vis Illich's "counter-productivity") recipients' identification with feelings of self-help and autonomous decision-making, and may reinforce a lack of self-confidence. Recipients may also be placed in a subservient position, creating particular power relationships that may reinforce a colonial mentality and internalized oppression, or disempower local creativity in efforts to solve their own problems (Lummis 1991; Porzecanski 1989; Escobar 1995, 44). This power imbalance between external agents and recipients may lead to providers giving resources based on what donors think residents need or what they have funding for, rather than what residents actually need. Donors or provider staff are often not obliged to any particular community. There is no lack of communities in need; therefore, providers have the power to choose who receives support and in what quantity. Providers, by the structure of the relationship, are rarely held accountable by recipient communities, only to donors. Their incentive is to ensure that donations continue despite the actual impact a development project has on the ground (Damberger 2011).

Technical assistance may also be more Band-Aid than cure (Robinson and Fear 2011, 64). It may relieve the immediate suffering but does not address the structural inequality that caused the suffering. By not questioning the social and economic structures that created the problems in the first place, it maintains the status quo in the distribution of wealth and power relations (Zizek 2010). In the case of resettlements built without state support, organizations are limited in what issues they are able to confront within their limited resources. In El Valle, what was needed was long-term, consistent support by external organizations in developing and maintaining a healthy social structure. The quick technical assistance of building houses and leaving development up to the recipients was the least successful strategy. This was the case of Campo Cielo, which received beautiful homes but no support in developing or protecting the neophyte community from gang influence.

A final problem is the notion that a "community" exists and is willing to work together toward a common cause. "Frequently in community development, we naively assume—sometimes with disastrous consequences—that sufficient levels of community exist, in the psychological and sociological senses, so that all practitioners need to do is focus attention on the substantive problems(s) at hand" (Robinson and Fear 2011, 63). In heterogeneous resettlements, as I argued earlier, a sense of community often does not exist and must be created. Deciding which project should be prioritized, let alone the implementation of the project, can be contentious and even paralyzing. Developmental technical assistance can perhaps be more useful in this context if it supports the development of social capital and cohesion to the level needed for further development approaches, such as the self-help approach described below.

THE SELF-HELP APPROACH

The self-help approach "assumes that residents possess the potential for improving the quality of life in their communities" (Green 2011, 72). This participatory, democratically based ideology claims that people know what is best for themselves, and that an agent of change must work hand in hand with potential beneficiaries to develop a successful program (Gorjestani 2001; Christenson 1989).

The self-help approach often falls into two categories: the development of social capital and the development of community assets. As discussed earlier, the creation or reinforcement of bonding social capital can facilitate the use of information and resources in the development process. Others have argued that communities often possess the assets—individuals, associations, and institutions—needed to implement self-transformation (Kretzmann and McKnight 1993; Green and Haines 2015). In both strategies, the role of development practitioners is to facilitate and promote broad representation and participatory decision-making, mobilizing the strengths of the community members to address the issue themselves.

There are many benefits to this community development approach. Unlike, technical assistance, self-help focuses on the means and the ends; building capacity in the recipient is as important as the final outcome. Self-help also engages stakeholders at all levels, giving them a voice in the process. Additionally, self-help is seen as sustainable. Whether it is creating social capital within a community or finding assets, the community will be able to draw upon these when tackling the next challenge. Finally, it promotes buy-in to the project and builds bonding social capital through an equal sharing of power by each group (Brown 1996).

Embedded in this approach are assumptions that may not fit a given post-disaster resettlement. For example, as described earlier in this chapter, a traumatized and vulnerable population may not have the necessary assets, or the quantity of resources needed. In a similar vein, associations and institutions are built over years; it will take time for these to be founded and grow within a new heterogeneous resettlement.[7] In the case of all seven resettlements studied, initially the only institutions were the supporting organizations and some churches; internal associations would later develop but were small and fragile, and many did not have the assets to support the community development process. A second assumption is that the assets could be garnered through a democratic purpose for a common good. As will be discussed, collaboration and consensus on a common goal or vision was difficult, complicated, and contentious with such a heterogeneous population. Various actors utilized their power to obtain resources for their or their families' benefit. Without clear guidance and structures, the resettlement populations were not able to control how assets were allocated, hindering the community development process (see Harvey 2013).

Finally, Dougherty and Peralta (2010) point out the US centric community development research does not take into account corruption and institutional weaknesses in the developing world. "[T]he documented successes of the asset-based development model often take place in the context of relatively effective local democracy characterized by strong institutions and minimal external influence" (69). Honduras, as described in chapter 2, is an impoverished and corrupt weak state that does not fulfill the social contract with citizens and often cannot provide even the basic resources (roads, consistent electricity, security, etc.) for economic development. A self-help approach may be less effective when community members cannot rely on basic state institutional support and must address external negative influences (drugs, gangs, crime, etc.) on their own.

"OF" VERSUS "IN" COMMUNITY DEVELOPMENT

Building broadly on the self-help and technical assistance approaches is the question as to whether community development efforts should focus on the development "of" or "in" the community (Shaffer and Summers 1989). More specifically, is "community" the causal factor in the well-being (social, political, and economic) of residents or is it denotative of the stratification system, the power structure, or the human ecology that prevails in a locality? Three major theorists take the former position. Durkheim (1984[1893]; 1979 [1897]) and later the functionalist school argue that a society creates social structures, values, and norms that play a role in maintaining a stable social whole. Alinsky (1971) emphasizes democratic citizen participation that would open channels of communication and cooperation among local groups. Finally, Summers notes (1986, 356) "The creation and maintenance of social structures . . . which mediate between individuals and society, are essential to the well-being of humans. Development of the community requires attention to these integrative structures." Other development narratives such as social capital, empowerment, and solidarity efforts parallel this type of strategy.

Conversely, development "in community" has been the traditional focus of development efforts, including economic growth, modernization, and improved social services. Community, then, is more about the social processes that happen to the parts (seen as micro-units) rather than to the whole. Community economic development is perhaps the most familiar example. The emphasis is on job creation and raising the real incomes of residents, and judging the ability of individuals or families to utilize resources efficiently. However, the order brought by the market cannot be removed from social and legal institutions in the context of recovery (Boettke et al. 2007). Narratives such as community assistance, the use of motivators, the rungs on a ladder metaphor, all boats rise with the tide (neoliberal policy), and social engineering are commonly invoked. This is not to say that development "of" and "in" community are mutually exclusive. Indeed, both strategies can work in concert (e.g., social capital creates greater job opportunities for individuals) or in conflict (social engineering may disempower specific populations). Either way, community development should be looked at as a dynamic process that encompasses both means and ends.

SUSTAIN, ACCOMPANY, GUIDE, AND EMPOWER RESETTLEMENT APPROACH

La Iglesia utilized a hybrid of the technical assistance and self-help community development approaches, drawing on the strengths of each while attempting to avoid their weaknesses. After reviewing the literature and not finding an adequate term or description, I will define this hybrid model as *sustain, accompany, guide, and empower* (SAGE) resettlement development.[8] Like the two strategies discussed above, SAGE describes the relationship between the supporting organization and resettlement citizens and institutions. Each element of the acronym will be briefly defined below and furthered described in chapter 5.

Sustain refers to a sponsoring organization's core provision of material resources to a resettlement to continue the development process. This is a common element in all of the resettlements studied, although the quantity and quality of resources varied. Some organizations provide only housing and infrastructure, such as water and electricity. Other NGOs recognized a much greater need. However, post-Mitch survivors needed more than physical capital, as they were encumbered by social and economic disarticulation and challenges, including poverty, trauma, secondary trauma, broken social networks, and vulnerability to social problems. Some NGOs, like La Iglesia, utilized their fund-raising capacity and development expertise to build the resettlement and provide residents with their basic needs as well as social resources for the collective advancement of their new community.

Accompany, defined as the continuation of the relationship between organization and resettlement over an extended period, is a clearer designation than the vague discussion of time in some technical assistance and self-help projects. A resettlement culture and a sense of community are built over years. Trust, social capital, collective efficacy, and civic engagement are also long-term processes that need regular maintenance. Both providers and recipients must be committed to investing the time and energy or risk the resettlement fracturing into competing interest groups without a sense of community. Survey and interview data highlight that residents, due in large part to their high level of vulnerability, relied on organizations for support and desired consistency. Residents of Pino Alto, for example, expressed concern that an organization might leave, creating distrust of the organization and fear of walking alone in the future, disrupting the development process.

Guide is expressed as assisting in reaching a final destination in an unfamiliar area through collaboration.[9] As will be described in chapters 5 and 6, vulnerable survivors in the new resettlements looked to the sponsoring organization for help in navigating the new social, political, and economic terrain. Guiding also signifies the organization's potential social intervention in resettlement affairs. Again, the vulnerability of residents, or the exploitation of the resettlement by external agents, may create internal conflict. Organizations can utilize their resources to ensure that the resettlement stays on its proposed development trajectory by resolving internal squabbles, removing problem households (such as those including drug dealers or gang members) from the resettlement, addressing external threats, and holding resettlement leaders accountable. La Iglesia and La Internacional followed significantly different approaches to guiding and intervening, which subsequently impacted each respective resettlement's social health outcomes.

Empower is a core element in ensuring the long-term success of the resettlement post-disaster organization involvement. I follow Craig's (2002) definition of empowerment as "the creation of sustainable structures, processes, and mechanisms, over which local communities have an increased degree of control, and from which they have a measurable impact on public and social policy affecting those communities." Like the self-help strategy, the process must ensure that resettlements develop new structures and that residents obtain new capacities to address whatever social problems they encounter in the future. By balancing sustainment and guidance with resident empowerment,[10] the resettlement will have the necessary support it needs, while it avoids long-term dependence on the organization.

The SAGE approach also views the relationship between the organization and resettlement residents and institutions as one of equals, but one in which the recipient receives much more from the relationship than the provider. A patient-doctor relationship provides an analogy—the patient (resettlement) is in need of treatment and care due to previous trauma and injury. The patient does not have the expertise to address the injury and lack of mobility, and may not understand the multiple ways in which the injury affects other parts of the body. The injured patient may be able to maintain daily activities, but due to the injury would not be able to take on new projects (like creating a sense of community in the nascent resettlement). The doctor (sponsoring organization) has a set of skills and resources and can diagnose the physical ailments and provide the patient with a plan to strengthen the body (sustain). This plan often requires multiple follow-up appointments to ensure that the correct progress is being made (accompany). Over time, the doctor gives advice, delivers different types of care depending on need, changes levels of medication, and may intervene if the plan is not working or becomes worse (guide). The doctor, as well, has a duty to encourage the patient to take a proactive role in her recovery, recognizing that a patient's health is foremost the patient's responsibility (empower).

Lastly, a SAGE development strategy bridges the technical assistance and self-help approaches. The sustain and guide aspects of SAGE are similar to the external support and intervention promoted by technical assistance. In addition, following the self-help approach, organizational influences must decrease while resident empowerment increases. All three strategies must also be reinforced for multiple years. Simply put, the SAGE strategy recommends providing a vulnerable post-disaster resettlement with resources and guidance, while empowering residents to take on increasing responsibility over time.

PARTNERSHIPS

La Internacional drew upon a partnership approach to develop Pino Alto. The partnership approach, which falls under the banner of self-help community development, has deep historical roots and is widely accepted by development INGOs. Some scholars link the policy to a 1968 World Bank Report called "Partners in Development," written by former Canadian prime minister Lester Pearson. Others believe the partnership strategy was born in the radical solidarity movements of the 1960s and 1970s in Latin America (Hailey 2000).[11]

No matter the origin, from an NGO perspective, partnerships (sometimes called self-help approach, coalition, accompaniment, and development alliances) can be summarized as: "a working relationship that is characterized by a shared sense of purpose, mutual respect and the willingness to negotiate" (Lister 2000, 228). Partnerships are considered to be more egalitarian and therefore theoretically more successful, since historical paternalistic or technical assistance relationships have unbalanced power dynamics, including the potential disempowerment of recipients. A partnership approach is seen to resolve issues of power and is considered a sustainable development strategy as well. The goal is to listen to, and base decisions and projects on, what the people themselves seek or request. Additionally, this strategy creates greater independence than many other development initiatives, which (ideally) enables future long-term sustainability.

On the organizational and local levels, Brinkerhoff (2002, 1) offers a more definitive and process-based definition of partnership approach: "organizations form partnerships not only to enhance outcomes, whether qualitatively or quantitatively, but also to produce synergistic rewards, where the outcomes of the partnership as a whole are greater than the sum of what individual partners contribute."

The partnership paradigm also has received noted critiques, many of which are similar to those of technical assistance. A 2011 article found that partnership strategies developed in poverty-reduction strategy papers did not work at the national level in Honduras because there was no real buy-in by stakeholders. The project was too focused on rational planning and not on the importance of politicking (Dijkstra 2011). Occasionally, partnerships may also fail due to infighting within a community (as happened in the Santa Fe resettlement), a lack of social development along with economic development, or an unrealistic commitment by an organization. Like the technical assistance strategy, partnerships have both benefits and drawbacks for NGOs and communities.

Chapters 5 and 6 will build upon the theoretical foundation noted above. Chapter 5 will investigate how La Iglesia utilized the SAGE strategy, a developmental technical assistance and self-help/social capital approach to building the necessary social structures that support the creation "of community." Chapter 6 will describe how La Internacional used a self-help partnership approach to develop the institutions "in community."

WEAK STATE AND STRONG NGOS IN HONDURAS

Approaches to community development cannot be decoupled from the role of external influences, such as the nation-state and organizations. Historically, the social and economic development and well-being of a nation's citizenry were the responsibility of the government, defined often as the welfare state (McMichael 2016). To be sure, there were nongovernmental organizations, mostly in the form of missionary groups or religious organizations, that addressed a community's social ills by providing immediate social services, but this typically happened in the remote regions of each state. Since the late 1970s and the scaling back of large governments due to neoliberal policies (often forcibly implemented [Robinson 2004, chapter 2]), NGOs have grown in number, size, and influence and have had an increasingly meaningful role in providing goods and services to constituents. This is no more clearly seen than in the context of disaster relief and recovery (Jackson 2005; Bolin and Stanford 1998; see also Morello-Frosch et al. 2011).

Changes in the nation-state and the role of NGOs in providing services comport well with the new neoliberal paradigm. First, Western governments and foundations that had focused their aid through nation-states were reluctant to give funds to unreliable, corrupt, or socialist governments, leaving a gap to be filled by NGOs (Craig and Mayo 1995). Donors channeled their assistance through organizations and church bodies—an "'NGO-ization of the mainline churches' (Gifford 1994) because churches in effect became NGOs involved in development programs" (Bornstein 2005, 15). Neoliberal advocates found this change refreshing, as it freed up funds to repay debt and created a competitive market for social services, which, economically speaking, should have reduced service costs. Second, debt repayment and structural adjustment programs (SAPs) have deepened inequality throughout the world, including Latin America, affecting the role of the nation-state. SAPs cut civil service jobs and work, replacing them with local and international NGOs, further weakening the state and creating greater instability. Third, for neoliberal proponents, civil society could also work through NGOs, offering citizens many positive opportunities to pressure governments for democracy and good governance. NGOs could be vehicles for development programs and empowerment of the poor, creating a smaller state (Mohan and Stokke 2000).

La Internacional is a case in point. The organization initially was reluctant to become involved with house building, as its historical strength and mission lay in emergency relief, not recovery and development. After the government petitioned the organization to build a resettlement, though, it did so, helping about 1,250 families from Tegucigalpa (and many more throughout the country). As Naomi, a top administrator for La Internacional in social projects and resettlements, explained,

> There was a commitment—La Internacional would provide housing to families, and the government committed to provide the land on which to build [and] all basic services to the population, such as education, basic health, access roads, and others. The whole process was originally going to take less than a year, but the government had to prepare the land for La Internacional to build.

The agreement seemed straightforward; however, by the time the government had acquired the land rights and had the land terraced, more than three years had passed and not a single house had been built. Additionally, the government, due in part to corruption and in part to disorganization, did not fulfill its promise to provide water for the homes. As a high-level waterworks employee in Pino Alto, Don Roberto explained that after years of waiting, La Internacional finally gave up on the government services promised and asked a partner organization in the United States to build a water system for the resettlement, which it subsequently did. The same issues occurred with building a school, a clinic, a police station, a library, roads, and a community center—

all of which were constructed by La Internacional in partnership with other NGOs. Without state support or guidance, La Iglesia and La Internacional were obliged to complete the entire construction, resettlement, and development on their own.[12]

Like many poor global-south nation-states, Honduras did not have the national apparatus, capacity, or legitimacy to address citizen need during or after the disaster. No disaster relief and recovery plan was in place when Mitch arrived, leaving the state without direction, let alone specific steps to facilitate moving forward. Government services were already stretched and understaffed due to a significant lack in funding.

The Honduran government's inability to confront the enormity of the disaster forced government officials to hand over much of the recovery and reconstruction efforts to national and international NGOs (Jackson 2005; Alaniz 2012). This was not a new phenomenon. In 1974, Hurricane Fifi roared through Honduras, killing several thousand people and displacing hundreds of thousands. While not as devastating as Mitch, Fifi was at that time the most devastating natural disaster the country had experienced. Unlike the nation-state of today, the Honduran government then was able to create some resettlements that were as successful as those created by organizations (Snarr and Brown 1978). Due to changes in the international political economy discussed above as well as poor governance of the country, Honduras no longer had the funding or institutional capacity to address an even larger disaster.

Throughout my interviews with NGO staff, I repeatedly heard complaints about the lack of government involvement and support in the community-building process. Organizations were encouraged to take full responsibility for their projects—issues such as waterworks, road construction, schools, and housing were handed over by the state to the participating NGOs. The government promised to take care of some infrastructure (putting in sewer lines, roads, schools, clinics, police stations, electricity, potable water, etc.), but rarely, and only after significant persistence and time (or for political gain), were some of these basic services finally provided.

Campo Cielo is another example. The NGO's job was to build homes and move people in, while the government was to provide basic plumbing and electricity. Although the resettlement was the first built in El Valle, it was one of the last to obtain these services, precisely because they had to wait for the government to build the system. Nearly twelve years after Mitch and ten years after initial habitation, Campo Cielo waterworks are not up to par with many of the other post-Mitch resettlements in El Valle.

Due to its inability to address the titanic aftermath of Mitch, many citizens understandably did not trust the government. Years of corruption and cronyism left citizens looking toward churches and civic organizations, rather than to the national government, for help. Officials—lacking money, public trust, and institutional capacity—had no option but to ask national and global NGOs to take over much of the recovery and reconstruction efforts (Jackson 2005; see Klein 2007 and Edwards 1999 for other examples), even when the NGOs did not feel suited to do the work (Gray, Bebbington, and Collison 2006). According to one NGO social worker, the government begged organizations to manage its temporary shelters and eventually build new resettlements for survivors even when the organizations did not want that responsibility.

In sum, the newly empowered and burdened NGOs were asked to move beyond their specialties and engage in the resettlement process of hundreds or even thousands of families. No organization had any idea of the complexity of such an undertaking. Most were funded to provide houses and build infrastructure, which they did fairly successfully. Few were funded for or planned to do long-term development and support the creation of a sense of community. Deciphering how NGO support and community development strategies led to long-term outcomes requires a flexible theory that can incorporate change over time. In the next section I outline the theory of path dependence and its salience in tracking the trajectories of community development projects as a dialectical process leading to particular outcomes.

PATH DEPENDENCE: A FRAMEWORK FOR UNDERSTANDING COMMUNITY SOCIAL DEVELOPMENT

Ultimately, the success of post-disaster reconstruction [and resettlement] is much more than a matter of delivering and constructing houses and towns. It is as much a matter of how it is done as it is of what, or how much, is done. (Oliver-Smith 1991, 20)

Tying the long-term outcomes of a resettlement to the complicated process of community social development necessitates an elastic framework accounting for the creation of social structures and resident agency over time. The theory of path dependence offers guidance in this area, identifying the key processes that set a resettlement on one particular trajectory rather than another and singling out what can sustain or interrupt movement along that development path (Aminzade 1992, 2013). It can take into account both the process of community development and the difficulty agents have in making change once a resettlement begins down a particular road.[13]

Path dependence is a theoretical framework that can explain how past choices and external events shape subsequent development paths and current outcomes (David 1985; see Thelen 1999 for a review). The framework has been found to have faults (Page 2006; Goldstone 1998), such as the broad critique that path dependence only illustrates that "history matters," but refining the framework to a narrower conception can reliably parse out which events in history were likely critical junctures in path divergence. Many scholars have found value in the framework, notably Aminzade (1992), David (2000), and Pierson (2000). Of the multiple components used in various path dependence explanations, I will focus on four: (1) the initial conditions and critical juncture, (2) the mechanisms that set the development process moving, (3) key processes that sustain movement along the path, and (4) processes that provide increasing returns (Aminzade 1992, 462–463; Pierson 2000). Path dependence will also be discussed in further depth in chapter 7 to explain how initial differences and key processes sent each resettlement on a divergent trajectory.

A metaphor may clarify this point. Established communities have a cultural impetus, a way of doing things, a path they follow. Like snowballs rolling down a hill, over time they gain momentum and size, requiring significant force to change trajectory. The culture is deeply embedded in the hearts and minds of residents and is likely represented in the physical attributes of the area. New heterogeneous resettlements, initially, are similar to small snowballs at the top of a hill. They have yet to create their own culture, and it has not been ingrained in residents. However, once resettlements choose a cultural path and begin to roll down the hill, they pick up speed. The social practices and values are socially constructed and reinforced, narrowing and straightening the path. It becomes increasingly difficult to push resettlements toward a different cultural milieu as their inertia grows.

The seven resettlements' development can be captured by this metaphor. Initial conditions matter—setting a path, providing momentum, and preventing divergence through return mechanisms, self-reinforcing processes, and positive feedback loops (Pierson 2000, 252). Much of the long-term social health of each resettlement can be traced back to early efforts to develop and maintain a community culture, such as a common vision and set of social norms (Turner and Killian 1972). As these attributes became embedded within the resettlement, residents who arrived later[14] were socialized into the "normal" behavior of the resettlement. A particular path for each resettlement was created and reinforced.

This conceptual chronological figure exhibits how the process of path dependence occurred in each resettlement (figure 3.1). Four periods mark development from resettlement to community. The initial conditions (I) are the similarities between the two resettlements. At the very beginning, each re-

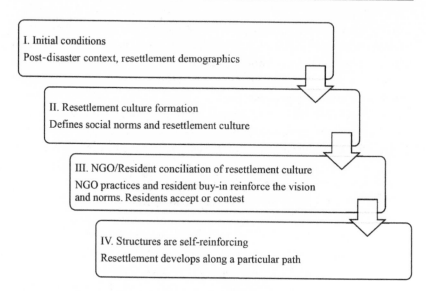

FIGURE 3.1. Path Creation and Reinforcement over Time

settlement has an opportunity to take any number of paths that will lead to particular outcomes (Pierson 2000). This critical juncture, a moment when multiple paths can be taken and are not predetermined by previous structures, has been rightly criticized for being a rarity (Thelen 1999, 385). However, creating a resettlement culture among a heterogeneous population is as close to a blank slate as one finds in the social world. For Suyapa and Pino Alto, their similarity as intentional, new, post-disaster heterogeneous resettlements with survivors of similar trauma and socioeconomic status meant that their paths were not predefined by previous structures (they had not yet been defined) or initial characteristics, but rather were created over time. Their direct comparison can, in fact, serve as a guide for identifying choices that contributed to or deterred social health over time.[15]

The second time period (II) is defined by the formation of community culture. For brevity, I will discuss only two features of community culture—collective vision and social norms. Collective vision refers to the values, beliefs, and common identity of a given group. Social norms are formal or informal rules that define expected, acceptable, or required behavior in particular circumstances, and they are learned through social interaction (NSNI 2014). Unlike established communities, heterogeneous resettlements do not begin with a common community culture. NGOs and resident leadership must draw together the disparate household understandings of community into a common, unifying vision. They must then encourage and sanction the social norms to reinforce this vision.

Community culture exists in a direct relationship with social health—the development of particular norms, like looking out for one's neighbor or the degree to which sanctions are imposed, directly impacts the social health of the resettlement. Without the formation of community structures that provide guidance to a resettlement, the data suggests that residents return to their previously known community culture, that of Tegucigalpa, which had significant social health issues. The absence of government support and no overarching theory of community development meant that the process of creating a new culture was facilitated by NGOs, which caused a different set of issues, such as diverse behavior expectations. Each NGO administered its own approach, created unique resettlement cultures, and obtained different social health outcomes.

With varying degrees of resident participation and negotiation, organizations implemented a vision and social norms (III—Conciliation).[16] Each resident had to decide whether, and how much, they would buy in to the goals developed by the NGO for the resettlement. Conflict began immediately. In both Suyapa and Pino Alto, many different visions and many sets of norms were proposed, and residents split over which they supported. The ensuing conflict and negotiation shaped what residents came to know as *their* community culture, *their* vision for community and the acceptable behaviors therein.

Once the community vision and social norms have been internalized by residents, they begin to take on a life of their own in a process of increasing returns (IV). "Increasing returns" refers to the stabilization and self-reinforcing nature of culture. Pierson (1993, 602) notes that "policy feedback is likely to be most consequential in issue-areas . . . where interest group activity is not yet well established." This is particularly relevant in the liminality of resettlement social life. Pierson goes on to articulate that small influences at crucial junctures can make profound differences. If the values of trust, social cohesion, and collective efficacy are developed and reinforced through practice (activities and informal and formal sanctions), positive social health outcomes can result. Once a social norm such as high trust is created, it will continue to reproduce trust because untrustworthy behavior is negatively sanctioned (Coleman 1988). Additionally, the cost of changing culture, for better or worse, is high as residents invest in a specific institutional arrangement. Krasner (1988, 83) describes this as a self-reinforcing feedback loop (see also Thelen 1999).

An example from Suyapa and Pino Alto may clarify this process. La Iglesia's and La Internacional's vision for Suyapa and Pino Alto was a model resettlement that could guide future post-disaster resettlement efforts around the world. This belief was shared among residents initially. In Suyapa, the belief was supported by a strong NGO that intervened to prevent gang entry into the resettlement, removed drug dealers, and set high behavior expectations. Residents accepted this vision, recognized the work of La Iglesia, and decided to work toward creating a model community. This vision, accepted and reproduced by both the NGO and the residents, became embedded in Suyapa culture.

In Pino Alto, the vision was also provided to residents, but La Internacional did not intervene in resettlement affairs. Since the organization did not maintain the structures to create a model community, it became increasingly difficult for the large, diverse population to maintain a common vision themselves. Other elements, such as gangs and problematic residents, destabilized the fragile social fabric of the resettlement and led to the vision's disintegration. Each household retrenched into their own understanding of what community should be, often based on the problematic Tegucigalpa neighborhoods from which they came.

Collective vision and social norms not only affect current residents of a resettlement but are immediately passed on to new residents moving in. Finnemore and Sikkink (1998, 292–293) point out "how agreement among a critical mass of actors on some emergent norm can create a tipping point after which agreement becomes widespread." The timing and type of training of a critical mass of initial families (between twenty and two hundred, depending on the resettlement) was crucial in the success of the El Valle resettlements. These residents accepted and reinforced, changed, or rejected norms promoted by the NGO. As a result, future ramifications evolved for the norm expectations of the next cohort (in this case, think of a cohort as simply a subsequent population group in the same resettlement). Resettlement children also internalize the social practices of the resettlement, not having experienced anything else. As history has shown, each generation inherits a socially constructed reality as reality. It is much easier to maintain than to change the current system and social organization.

To conclude, heterogeneous resettlements differ significantly from established community reconstruction or homogeneous resettlements. Community development efforts must recognize these differences and utilize flexible theories to address the special challenges resettlement residents face. Path dependence theory offers a template that addresses these issues, such as the opportunity of a new and intentional resettlement, the interaction between organization and residents, and how social practices shape development over time. The following chapters will discuss how to measure changes in resettlement vis-à-vis social health, and later go into detail about the two main case studies as examples of divergent community development processes in heterogeneous resettlements.

CHAPTER 4

MEASURING SUCCESSFUL RESETTLEMENT

Contemporary definitions of successful resettlement are often articulated as placement in a safe structure. Yet a resettlement is not necessarily a community. Ironically, the women and children in Campo Cielo (from the preface story) were much better off living in the impoverished conditions of the temporary shelters than the beautiful and newly built houses only thirty kilometers away. If a successful resettlement cannot be defined by the number of structures built, then how can it be measured? The following chapter will provide an overview of the measure of social health and its usefulness as a metric for long-term resettlement.

WHY RESETTLEMENT SOCIAL HEALTH?

Social health provides a measure that is an alternative to, and more appropriate than, the current emphasis on infrastructure and livelihoods still employed in the literature discussing post-disaster recovery, resettlement, and community development. As Brenchin, West, and Associates describe in their work on human displacement in the creation of national parks,

> What is too little understood both by professionals and scholars alike is the social impact of displacement and relocation. When resident peoples are forced to move, certain general impacts can be expected. But the collective social impact on the community or other social organizations differs widely from case to case; to date no model exists to predict the cumulative effect. (1991:17, cited in Cernea 2000)

The lack of a model to explain the collective social impact of resettlement continues to prevent scholars and practitioners from having a deeper understanding of the development of resettlement toward community. This is due in part to the time-consuming data collection process (obtaining quantitative and qualitative data of a population over time) and the complicated nature of the data. The metrics must be relevant to resettlement members, clearly define the collective experience, take into account the interactions of multiple agents and social structures, and consider development as both a process and an outcome. This chapter attempts to unravel the collective social experience and its cumulative impact through the use of social health characteristics.

There are many ways to measure successful recovery in resettlement. The following five examples, from some of the largest organizations in the world, showcase what is and is not prioritized in current recovery and resettlement praxis. The US Federal Emergency Management Agency, the largest emergency management organization in the world, defines its guiding recovery principles as housing, infrastructure, business, public health (including emotional and psychological), and mitigation (FEMA 2011). The United Nations International Strategy for Disaster Reduction classifies disaster recovery as "the restoration and improvement where appropriate, of facilities, livelihoods and living conditions of disaster-affected communities, including efforts to reduce disaster risk factors" (UNISDR 2012). Similarly, the United Nations Development Programme defines it as encompassing "the restoration of basic services, livelihoods, shelter, governance, security and rule of law, environment and social dimensions, including the reintegration of displaced populations" (UNDP 2008, 7). The International Federation of the Red Cross and Red Crescent describes their recovery goals as the construction of shelter and housing, livelihoods for survivors, capacity building, and physical health (IFRC 2006). Additionally, under the guidance of Michael Cernea (1997; 2000), the World Bank has promoted the impoverishment risks and reconstruction framework, which promotes a multifaceted approach to addressing eight clear risks of resettlement based on an "economics of recovery" (Cernea 2000, 14). Recently, however, the World Bank admitted that its resettlement efforts since 1990 have had "serious shortcomings" in multiple areas of implementation, data collection, and tracking (World Bank 2014, 2015b).

What is noticeable in these definitions is that the goals and measures of success in disaster recovery and resettlement are, for the most part, focused on infrastructure and economic development. This is a critical and necessary part of recovery, yet there continues to be debate as to what recovery means (Olshansky and Chang 2009), especially in the context of resettlement (Cernea 2003). Tradition and measurement can both be blamed for this misplaced emphasis. In the development industry, it is widely believed that if average income in a post-disaster resettlement rises 4 percent each year, then the resettlement is developing and therefore successful. Much of the development literature critiques this type of research, yet it continues.[1]

Finally, the recent publication by the Institute of Medicine provides a comprehensive discussion of community health, resilience, and sustainability. Its expanded definition of a healthy community is worth quoting at length.

> A healthy community is one in which a diverse group of stakeholders collaborate to use their expertise and local knowledge to create a community that is socially and physically conducive to health. Community members are empowered and civically engaged, assuring that all local policies consider health. The community has the capacity to identify, address, and evaluate their own health concerns on an ongoing basis, using data to guide and benchmark efforts. As a result, a healthy community is safe, economically secure, and environmentally sound, as all residents have equal access to high quality educational and employment opportunities, transportation and housing options, prevention and healthcare services, and healthy food and physical activity opportunities. (2015, ix–x; see also chapter 2)

This holistic definition underscores the social and physical ideals and metrics of community health. As discussed below, I utilize many of the same metrics. However, in the context of resettlement in an impoverished and weak state, some of the ideals are tempered by the limitations of the supporting NGO or government.

As discussed in chapter 2, resettled residents have particular challenges and opportunities. It is at this juncture—where recovery as resettlement turns into the development of a community—that I hope to discuss the mechanisms that can encourage social health as it applies to new intentional resettlements composed of traumatized, displaced, and poor disaster survivors. In sum, how can we measure the social success of a resettlement project as it moves toward community? And for survivors, when and how do strangers become neighbors?

RESETTLEMENT SOCIAL HEALTH: A DEFINITION

Infrastructure constitutes an important measurement of recovery, but it can be appended by indicators of social health. The number of families in new homes, how many schools have been built, the number of people receiving clean water—are all much easier to quantify. These characteristics are also more immediately and easily understood by donors than long-term social development, which takes years if not decades to observe. Solidly built, structurally sound homes are undeniably important. That said, in the case of the Campo Cielo gang takeover, if residents are afraid and exploited, a hurricane-proof roof barely matters. Resettlement social health offers an important measure that supplements traditional evaluations of recovery success by going beyond mere appearances.

The social science literature and government initiatives provide multiple definitions of the unwieldy measure of community health. Reports—quality-of-life reports, scorecards, portraits, profiles, compasses, vital signs, community vitality, community well-being, road maps, gross national happiness, social development initiatives, and so on—each define community slightly differently and with various metrics. Whichever social indicators are in place, researchers use the results as guiding principles for future development strategies, city plans (IISP 2011), government national plans (Scott 2010; CMCD 2010; Bhutan 2016), and even the Healthy Cities Initiative promoted by the World Health Organization (2003). The reports can be narrow, focusing only on economic or physical health indicators, or as broad as measuring numerous characteristics from all aspects of community or national life. Costa Rica, for example, draws upon some common social indicators (such as civic participation) but also includes economic, education, and health indicators (MPNPE 2007). Panama, in its 2006 community social well-being report, highlighted issues of social exclusion, conflict, social infrastructure (health and education), and access to basic services as issues preventing social health in communities (República de Panamá 2006). One of the most comprehensive social well-being reports is the recent Canadian study entitled "Community Vitality: A Report of the Canadian Index of Wellbeing" (Scott 2010). The study pinpoints specific social health indicators emphasized in the academic literature (Chambers 1997; Edwards and Hulme 1996; Mohan and Stokke 2000; Plunkett 1995; Putnam 2000; Sampson, Raudenbush, and Earls 1997; Smith and Wenger 2007).

With international policy and academic literature as a foundation, I interviewed resettlement residents and NGO staff about their understanding of and desires for their community. Across the groups, similar characteristics arose—including feelings of trust, security, working together, and a common set of values and goals. Combining academic and practitioners' perspectives with local context, I developed the resettlement social health index that captures five different but interwoven aspects of social life: crime, social capital, collective efficacy, community participation, and vision.

These indicators also take into account the Honduran political and economic context (similar to many global south nations) and social ills that plague its cities (high crime and social isolation), as well as the general circumstances of post-disaster resettlement residents (trauma and broken social networks). Furthermore, the particular nature of these heterogeneous resettle-

Table 4.1. Social Health Indicators, Metrics, and Literature Citations

Indicator	Metrics	Citation
Crime	Survey, interviews, police records	Shaw and McKay 1942; Kawachi, Kennedy, and Wilkinson et al. 1999
Social Capital	Survey, interviews, participant observation	Coleman 1988; Putnam 2000; Nakagawa and Shaw 2004; Aldrich 2012a
Collective Efficacy	Survey, interviews, participant observation	Sampson and Wilson 1995; Sampson, Raudenbush, and Earls 1997; Alesch, Arendt, and Holly 2009
Community Participation	Survey, interviews, participant observation	De Tocqueville, 1835; Chambers 1997; Mohan and Stokke 2000; Scott 2010
Vision	Survey, interviews, documents	Smith and Wenger 2007; Chamlee-Wright and Storr 2011

ments offers an opportunity to understand development in a unique way. Not all resettlement projects have such significant challenges, like the high levels of violence, as found in Honduras. El Valle provides a baseline, illustrating that if these resettlements with major social hurdles can develop into a community, perhaps others can as well.

These five are by no means the only metrics from which to gauge resettlement success. I attempted to obtain other indicators, such as community resilience, democratic processes, economic development, and bridging and linking social capital among NGOs and residents; however, the data was either not available or not sufficient for analysis. These issues *are* important, and some will be touched upon. Still, the goal of this book is to provide indicators that can reveal the broader well-being of a community over time, without being anchored to traditional and incomplete definitions of successful development that fail to account for the characteristics that make a place worth living in. In this way, social health prioritizes strategies and resources to develop civic participation, protect citizens from crime, build a collective culture to address delinquency, create bonding social capital among residents, and construct a positive and coherent outlook for the future. The five characteristics engender opportunities for other beneficial outcomes—increased hazard resiliency, collective political agency, and economic development, among others. The metric is also meant to supplement existing models by Scudder and Colson (1982) and Cernea (1997) with social characteristics.

The division between the indicators is only theoretical since no measure can be decoupled from any other. They must be seen as part of a holistic model. This is also a drawback of many of the previously discussed studies that only examine one or two of the five metrics. For example, although social capital is critical, social capital without participation or a common vision may be ineffectual. By discussing multiple indicators, I hope to put forth a more comprehensive understanding of the disaster resettlement process that does not neglect the multidimensional and integrated nature of social life.

THE SOCIAL HEALTH OF ORIGINATING TEGUCIGALPA NEIGHBORHOODS

Tegucigalpa, the capital of Honduras, was originally a mining town for the riches of gold and silver coveted by international mining companies. Founded in the late sixteenth century on the site of a native settlement alongside the Choluteca River, the city remained small, due in large part to a lack of economic growth once the valuable metals disappeared. At its peak, the city was beautiful, with large colonial buildings, well-cared-for parks, and ornate churches. Indeed, the geometric outline so representative of Spanish design, the tight streets better suited for horse and carriage than bus and taxi, and subtle reminders of history—a statue, elaborate architecture, or the restored palatial homes of the upper class—give visitors a taste of a bygone era.

The capital's center, Parque Central (central park), sits two blocks east of the river, bounded by Cathedral San Miguel to the south, a pedestrian walkway to the north, businesses to the east, and government buildings of congress to the west. From the Parque Central, one of the lowest parts of the valley, the city spreads in all directions up the mountainsides. Most of the growth has been over the last three decades, as economic hardship and environmental challenges (such as drought) in rural areas forced people, predominantly men, to migrate from the hinterlands looking for work.

Ideally, as a measure, resettlement social health must also be compared to the neighborhoods of origin insofar as possible. The question as to whether Suyapa, Pino Alto, or both are outliers compared to other Honduran communities, particularly the Tegucigalpa *colonias* from which residents arrived, is central. After all, it provides the primary basis of comparison. If the resettlements have higher social health than the rebuilt *colonias*, and residents have a better life than before Mitch, then success can justifiably be claimed. The opposite is also true. However, of the five characteristics that I use to define social health, concrete data is only available at the neighborhood level for crime.[2]

How do Suyapa and Pino Alto compare to their Tegucigalpa neighborhoods of origin? While a full answer to this question lies outside the purview of this manuscript, crime and homicide rates provide the most comparable and definitive measure of resettlement success. First, Honduras continues to have a very high crime rate, especially in and around major cities (UNDP 2007; UNODC 2007, 2011, 2015). Since 1996, the nation has also had some of the highest intentional-homicide rates in the world, ranking in the top three nearly every year since 1997[3] (Leyva 2001; UNODC 2016; World Bank 2016). The prevalence of crime and violence guides how people act, when they can move about the city, whom they can interact with and trust, where they can go, and what types of work they can accomplish. In short, crime dominates the Honduran urban culture and mentality. Second, Tegucigalpa, where nearly all resettled community members are from, is a hub of high crime. The Tegucigalpa metro area is considered the fifth-most-violent city in the world (SJP 2014) and second-most in Honduras (after San Pedro Sula). Finally, as both longitudinal and social data are hard to come by in Honduras, crime statistics (specifically homicide[4]) are one of the few concrete measures available. It is the only characteristic that can be used for comparison without conducting surveys and interviews in Tegucigalpa neighborhoods—an inherently dangerous, difficult, and time-consuming proposal.

The *colonias* and barrios (neighborhoods) of Tegucigalpa are as diverse as they are numerous. As in most cities, some local areas are fairly intimate, where people know and look out for one another, while other districts have high residential turnover and are extraordinarily dangerous, and residents tend not to know each other at all. A history of gang problems in the city, an unreliable and corrupt police force, and high crime (Call 2000) have forced residents into voluntary seclusion in their homes protected by steel garage doors, high walls with razor wire or broken glass shards embedded in the cement, and grated windows. As one Honduran friend explained to me after returning from her first visit to the United States, "The thing that surprised me the most in Los Angeles is that there are no walls around people's houses." Finding a home without high levels of security and protection is rare in Tegucigalpa.

The general experience in Tegucigalpa, whether as a foreigner or resident, is similar. During the day, people are aware of their surroundings and where the nearest safe place is, whether it be a restaurant, a business, or even the middle of the street.[5] At night, the streets are quiet. I know of no one who walks the streets in Tegucigalpa for any reason. Day or night, the city is dangerous. My friends have been robbed at gunpoint in taxis, accosted and then chased into restaurants, shot at while driving, kidnapped for their debit card, raped, and, as mentioned earlier, even murdered. In 2012, the Peace Corps evacuated all 157 volunteers due to security concerns, and as of this writing, have yet to reinstate the program. A 2008 investigation found that 27 percent of Tegucigalpa residents have been a victim of crime, a rate more than 1.5 times higher than any other city or area in the country (Coleman and Argueta 2008). Recent anecdotal evidence suggests the crime rate has grown in the city since then.

The seclusion necessitated by the high crime and murder rates makes social capital almost nonexistent in many Tegucigalpa *colonias*. People who have lived next to each other for years may know their neighbors' faces and perhaps their names and occupations but are otherwise strangers. There are few examples of community gatherings, celebrations, barbeques, or even sports teams based on geographic proximity, in part because of the necessity of long hours of work leading to little leisure time and in part because it is dangerous to be out at night. Rather, social capital is built and maintained mainly on religious affiliation and family more than other social networks. In my experience, Tegucigalpa residents spend their time with family, work associates, or members of the same church, but rarely with their neighbors.

The same goes for other social health metrics, such as collective efficacy, community vision, civic participation, and even political or local agency to create change. Fear of crime and distrust of law enforcement contribute to social isolation, as citizens are forced to race from a fortified home to behind the secure walls at work to the defended (with armed guards) shopping centers and finally back to a fortified home. This social isolation and anomie (Durkheim 1984 [1893]) of the city (that existed both pre- and post-Mitch) contrast starkly with how members speak about their new resettlements. Highlighting these differences will illustrate where residents came from and where they end up, in terms of local social health.

Another Tegucigalpa resident, Bella, noted that in her upper-middle-class neighborhood (Alta Miramontes), she did not really know any of her neighbors, even after living there for ten years. When asked about them, she replied, "Next door is a journalist, but we believe he had to leave [the country] for political reasons. Across the street, we don't know him but they have many [social] parties. On the other side of us is a small family, I don't know their name. The rest of the houses I don't know either."

Bella also maintains a family home that is standard for their neighborhood. The front gate is solid steel, about four meters high with electrified wire above. The walls of their home abut those of the two homes next to theirs, which also have electrified wire alongside the top of each cement wall. In addition, they share a back wall with a neighbor on another street, and shards of metal and glass are inlaid in the cement of the five-meter-high wall. Finally, a watchman roams the two-hundred-meter street twenty-four hours a day with a machete and cell phone in case there are any problems. Although there are differences depending on neighborhood (the wealthier homes also include security cameras and guards with automatic weapons, while the poor may only have bars on the windows), the message is the same—crime and violence are rampant and security is of the highest priority.

ARE RESIDENTS BETTER OFF IN RESETTLEMENTS THAN IN TEGUCIGALPA?

A primary question is how resettlements stand in comparison to residents' neighborhood of origin. Relocation can be a blessing or a curse, depending on where someone came from and where they end up. Drawing on household surveys from the seven post-Mitch resettlements, I find that the vast majority of residents believe their life has improved in terms of lower crime, increased civic participation, more trust, equal or improved employment opportunities, and more satisfaction with their life.

When resettlement residents were asked to compare their lives before the hurricane to their lives at the time of the survey (eleven years later), most residents claimed that their lives and the social aspects of their new resettlement were either equal to or better than in their previous neighborhood in Tegucigalpa. In regard to delinquency, which could arguably be the most important characteristic, given the national crisis, 93 percent of residents from the seven resettlements believe that delinquency is lower than or the same as in their previous community. This is a significant improvement in comparison to Tegucigalpa. Suyapa, where 95 percent of residents now see less crime than previously, especially showcases progress in comparison to the average resettlement (80 percent) and Pino Alto (68 percent).

Most resident participation has either increased or stayed the same. Community participation has been found to have numerous benefits for society, including decreased crime, higher social cohesion, and greater involvement in politics. When residents were asked to compare their participation now to in their pre-Mitch neighborhood, Pino Alto has a similar response rate to the average of the five other resettlements, 39 percent and 34 percent, respectively. In contrast, nearly two-thirds of the Suyapa residents participate more than they had previously.

Overall, these are encouraging statistics in that many residents are participating more often than they had before. A very large difference also exists between the increase in Suyapa and the similar Pino Alto and average resettlement.

Table 4.2. Differences in Participation Pre-Mitch (1998) and
2009–2010

*In comparison to the community where you lived before Mitch,
your participation in the community is: less, equal, or more?*

	less	*equal*	*more*
Suyapa	8 percent**	29 percent**	63 percent**
Pino Alto	28 percent	33 percent**	39 percent
Avg. 5 coms.	23 percent	43 percent	34 percent

Z score: **.01.

This difference is striking. One would imagine that variables like living in a much smaller area that is removed from the city, experiencing less violence, and having additional support from the sponsoring NGO could be correlated with a difference in participation among residents. This difference can be seen more as a commentary on the anomie in Tegucigalpa than on the strengths of these communities. Across the board, most residents increased their participation, illustrating that they have a desire to do so but may have felt constrained from acting on that desire as Tegucigalpa residents under those particular conditions.

Putnam observes (2000, 402) that "creating (or re-creating) social capital is no simple task. It would be eased by a palpable national crisis, like war or depression or natural disaster." Indeed, Hurricane Mitch and the resettlement process increased trust among neighbors for at least 40 percent of each resettlement, and more than 80 percent of residents said their trust was equal to or greater than in their community of origin. This is a substantial improvement. Suyapa again is distinguished, as nearly 60 percent of residents in Suyapa trust their neighbors more now than previously, compared to 40 percent for Pino Alto and 43 percent for the average resettlement. This much higher number likely positively affects other social health variables, such as participation and lower crime.

This trust also appeared in the resettlements. Compared to the neighborhoods in which I spent time in Tegucigalpa, there was a great sense of people's knowing and trusting one another. Residents would wave to one another, have neighbors watch the kids while they ran to the store, or share goods when times were tough. The markets and informal stores (*pulperías*) provide another good example, as people would often buy on credit from vendors. In Tegucigalpa, this was much less the case, possibly due to the high crime and violence barriers forcing people to live behind walls and barred windows (see Pine 2008, chapter 1).

Employment as well is equal or better for most, despite the fact that 1997 (3.2 percent) and 1998 (4.0 percent) had lower unemployment rates than 2009 (4.6 percent), when the survey was given (Econstats 2010). Suyapa stands out by experiencing better employment: 43 percent, while 25 percent of Pino Alto residents and 23 percent of the average resettlement residents had the same experience. In Pino Alto, 41 percent of inhabitants responded that their employment was worse, compared to 34 percent for the average resettlement and 30 percent for Suyapa. Possible reasons for the decline relate to the international recession and the location of resettlements. Since each resettlement was built outside of Tegucigalpa in a rural area, there are significantly fewer opportunities for low-skilled workers.

THE SOCIAL HEALTH OF PINO ALTO AND SUYAPA

As noted earlier, crime levels in Honduras are high, both in Tegucigalpa and nationally. The question, then, is whether Pino Alto, Suyapa, and the five other resettlements have similar levels. One would expect that new resettlements could go in either direction. With significant support from NGOs, it seems that resettlements could break the mold and live more peacefully than their established neighbors. Or, without support, a resettlement could find itself embroiled in internal conflict and lose the ability to self-govern or control residents (as happened in Campo Cielo). The following section will compare the social health outcomes of Pino Alto and Suyapa and the average of the five resettlements.

CRIME

According to Don Ricardo, a well-respected community leader, Pino Alto suffers from *mala fama* (a bad reputation). As I was speaking with friends and other professionals in Tegucigalpa concerning my work, many expressly forbade me from interviewing and surveying in El Valle. I was told that it was too dangerous for anyone, let alone a foreigner, to enter these resettlements, especially Campo Cielo and Pino Alto. In fact, the only way my sponsoring organization permitted me to first visit these resettlements was if I was accompanied by someone who was well known throughout the area for her participation in the Catholic Church.

The fear was not unjustified. The Pino Alto resettlement has suffered more than its share of criminal activity, including gang violence. Two incidents stand out: the first was a story told by residents and confirmed by the police. A woman was caught up in drugs, possibly with her boyfriend. To make an example out of her, gang members killed her, cut her into little pieces, and attempted to flush her down a toilet. Officer Valdez, a police officer posted in Pino Alto, shared the second story. He described a situation in Pino Alto in which the police received complaints about a loud party late at night. One officer went to check out the problem, leaving the other officer at the station. When the officer approached the door where the party was located, he was accosted by a drunken man, also the homeowner. As the officer began to take the man away to the station, the drunken man's family members surrounded the officer, and the son of the drunken man stabbed the officer in the back. None of the family was ever charged with a crime. "Now," Valdez added, "we don't go anywhere by ourselves." Indeed, anytime I saw the officers outside of the station, they wore bulletproof vests, carried handguns, and on occasion were also armed with semiautomatic or automatic rifles. Other homicides in the resettlement include a double murder, an intentional drowning, massive trauma to the head with a blunt object, and shootings (Pino Alto police reports 2004–2010). All told, there had been twenty-eight murders between 2004 and January 2010.

Upon arriving and spending time in Pino Alto, I realized the *mala fama* that Don Ricardo had described was not as bad as I had been led to believe. During the day, the city itself is quiet, with kids playing soccer in the street and women walking to visit friends, holding colorful umbrellas to protect them from the sun. Walking the perimeter, up and down almost every street, and interviewing individuals from throughout the resettlement, I felt comfortable in Pino Alto almost all of the time. Notwithstanding the story above, even Officer Valdez admitted that "people say Pino Alto is much worse than it actually is." Padre Eduardo and Padre Carlitos echoed this sentiment. Eduardo, a Christian minister, lived in the *macro-albergues* with the people and moved to Pino Alto with them. He explained that due to his sociability, his occupation, and his coaching of local soccer teams, he has never had a problem with any residents. Similarly, the Catholic priest Padre Carlitos has always felt comfortable, even arriving late at night to visit someone dying or leaving late after being invited to dinner. "When they see my car . . . all of the youth [say,] 'Here comes Father,' 'See you later, Father,' 'Give me a ride, Father,' and so I am not afraid. . . . When I go to Pino Alto, sometimes I arrive at eleven [p.m.] . . . and no, I have not been afraid." Don Rudy, the director of the waterworks in Pino Alto, and Don Pablo, a leather artisan in Pino Alto, also feel *tranquilo* (calm) in the resettlement. When asked about crime, they both mentioned that they have always felt safe in the resettlement.

The survey confirms the existence of *mala fama*. When residents were asked whether they or a family member had been a victim of a crime in their resettlement, no statistical difference appeared between Suyapa (7 percent), Pino Alto (10 percent), and the average of the five resettlements (10 percent). However, over a six- to eight-year period, this number remains high. Although there were more crime events per capita in Pino Alto, there was no statistical difference between Suyapa, Pino Alto, and the average of the other post-Mitch resettlements.[6] This finding is intriguing, as one would expect the victim rate to be higher in Pino Alto, as they have had a higher reported crime rate. It remains to be explained why the victim rate would be the same while feelings of security would be so different. One reason may be reporting differences by resettlement (discussed in chapter 6).

My 2011 visit to Pino Alto reaffirmed the feeling. My friend Ernesto accompanied me to the town on a weekday afternoon. He is a security guard in Suyapa but has lived most of his life in one of the nearby villages in El Valle. I had asked him to join me in the trip because I would be driving there in another friend's car, and Pastor Eduardo (Pino Alto's Methodist minister) and other valley residents had warned that the resettlement had become even more dangerous since I was last there in May 2010 (following the national trend). The visit took me through about 60 percent of the town as I located friends and interviewees, as well as taking photographs. More than once, Ernesto would tell me in a low voice to "be careful" or "look out for those guys" as we walked between meetings. It was clear that he was much more uncomfortable than I was. Whether this was due to my ignorance and his wisdom or my familiarity and his belief in the *mala fama* of Pino Alto was difficult to tell.

In comparison, Suyapa was not well known outside the valley, due in part to its smaller size and in part because it did not have the international fanfare of Pino Alto.[7] According to residents in the valley, Suyapa was thought of as a nicer and wealthier resettlement, even though most respondents had never visited. Having spent time in the resettlement five years earlier, and being reassured by La Iglesia that things had not changed, I felt very comfortable returning to Suyapa and using it as my home base for the nine-month-long ethnographic portion of the study.

One of my first activities in the resettlement was to speak with the police. I found the station and police officers to be significantly different from those of Pino Alto. In Pino Alto, the police station was set apart from the resettlement and had a foreboding feel. A two-and-a-half-meter-high chain-link fence surrounded the compound. In order to obtain the attention of the officers, a resident had to bang the chain lock against the fence, and an officer would come out to hear the problem and possibly unlock the gate to let the person in. In Suyapa, the approximate location of the station was similar to in Pino Alto—

not in the center of town, but not on the periphery either. The station, though, had no fence around it, and the front door was often left wide open, even when the police were out on patrol. More than once I found myself sitting inside the front room for a half hour before an officer returned. The actions of the officers in the resettlement were also different. Only about half of the times that I ran into an officer in Suyapa was he (there were only male officers) armed with a handgun. I also only rarely saw them in bulletproof vests (and usually only the new officers wore them). As one resident remarked to me with humor, "The only thing the police do around here is flirt with our girls."

The social psyche of Suyapa was noticeably different as well. There had been no homicides in the resettlement, a fact in which residents took great pride. There were no back alleys and no extended threatening glances from groups of young men. My female partner also felt very comfortable taking walks around the resettlement with our six-month-old multiple times day and night. She only once had a negative encounter with a bus employee, who was high on drugs at the time. In contrast, I would have not have been at ease if they walked unaccompanied or been out at night in Pino Alto. Indeed, I would not have done so myself even after months of working in Pino Alto.

As for the question concerning how secure residents feel in the resettlement, Pino Alto inhabitants do not differ much from those in the average resettlement; they feel they are likely better off than Tegucigalpa residents and much better off than the national average.[8] By contrast, residents in Suyapa feel significantly safer, with four-fifths of residents feeling very secure and almost everyone else feeling somewhat secure. In one of the most violent nations in the world, this state of affairs is a noteworthy achievement.

Similarly, whether people are afraid to go out at night is revealing. Again, Suyapa residents feel safer in their resettlement than Pino Alto residents and residents of the other resettlements. This is worth calling attention to in light of the fact that almost no difference in crime victimization exists. Even with similar levels of crime, one explanation of the difference in feelings of security could be the types of crime committed in each resettlement, as seen in the next section.

Turning to the actual crime statistics of Suyapa and Pino Alto, there is also a significant difference between resettlements. Pino Alto has a much higher crime rate in general than Suyapa, except for theft and kidnapping. Homicide is the crime that stands out. Suyapa residents recognize that their resettlement is an outlier in this regard, and I heard it repeated at almost every town gathering I attended. Leaders would announce at almost every meeting, "We have yet to have a violent death in our community," as a point in favor of voting, community building, or paying a special tax to fix the road. Absence of homicide

Table 4.3. Resident Feelings of Security in the Resettlement

Survey questions	Suyapa	Pino Alto	Avg. of 5 com.
How do you feel in the community:			
Not secure	2 percent	6 percent	6 percent
Somewhat secure	17 percent**	30 percent	33 percent
Very secure	80 percent**	64 percent	61 percent
Are you afraid to go out at night [in your community]?			
(Yes)	6 percent**	24 percent*	19 percent
In comparison to the community where you lived before Mitch, is the delinquency in the community:			
less	95 percent**	68 percent**	80 percent
equal	4 percent**	19 percent*	13 percent
more	1 percent**	13 percent*	6 percent

Z-test significance: *.05, **.01 compared to avg. of 5 resettlements.

was a source of pride, cohesion, and motivation to continue doing whatever necessary to keep the community free of violent crime.

Pino Alto residents, however, felt very differently. I spent, on average, one day a week in Pino Alto, and there were streets and areas that I would actively circumvent, even after dozens of visits. I was told by residents to avoid these streets—streets with young men gambling at the side of a house and the smell of marijuana. Whether the danger was real or perceived, I steered clear of those areas. Interestingly, Nina, a resident of Pino Alto who shared a home with her mother, sister, and nephew, explained to me that since living in the resettlement, they have never left their home unoccupied. Someone was always at the house. The family believed that leaving the house empty was an invitation to thieves to enter and take the little that they owned. The fear was not unfounded; after Nina's next-door neighbor moved out, the house was stripped bare—electrical wires, faucets, roof tiles—anything not cemented down. Although many neighbors know who stole these resources, no one called the police for fear of retribution. The police in Pino Alto explained that this fear likely led to lower reporting rates.

While Suyapa has less crime statistically, it is not completely immune. In a 2010 case, residents moved out due to a marriage in the family, and within a week the vacant house was stripped of electrical wire, windows, and tubing. To protect public buildings from the same fate, La Iglesia hired twenty-four-hour security to protect the resettlement vocational workshops.

Table 4.4. Reported Criminal Activity in Suyapa and Pino Alto, January 2004 to December 2009 (Actual number of events in parentheses)

	# of crimes per 1,000 people	Average # of crimes per year	Murders per 1,000	Kidnappings per 1,000	Rapes per 1,000	Thefts per 1,000
Suyapa	95.4**	42**	0.0**	0.7**	0.7**	12.1**
			(0)	(2)	(2)	(34)
Pino Alto	270.7	116	3.42+	0.514	1.37	8.9
			(28)	(3)	(8)	(52)

Z-test significance: **.01.

+The homicide rate in Pino Alto (.49) averaged annually is still half of that in Tegucigalpa (1.13) (*Honduras Weekly* 2011), and nationally (.821) (*Washington Post* 2011).

In the five other resettlements, either no police records were available, police records had been lost or were incomplete, or police record requests were denied.

Other delinquency concerns appear in the survey. When asked whether young people causing trouble is a large problem, 41 percent of Suyapa and 69 percent of Pino Alto residents agree, a statistically significant finding compared to the average resettlement (52 percent). As has been well documented, delinquency follows a skewed bell curve over a person's lifetime, peaking in the late twenties and declining after age thirty (FBI 2011). Concern with young people causing problems illustrates that there may be underlying structural issues not being addressed, such as unemployment or low levels of resettlement social control.

This notable difference is one that affects more than crime victims; it affects the entire atmosphere of a resettlement. When nearly 70 percent of Pino Alto residents see young people (*jóvenes*) as a large problem, it changes interactions between older residents, families, and youth. As Sampson and Groves (1989) describe, this may also have an effect on the social organization of community structures, creating a cycle of distrust, broken social networks, crime, and further distrust and crime.

Similarly, drugs, alcohol (illegal in all resettlements), and graffiti also point to deeper social issues and the potential for further social disorder (Keizer, Lindenberg, and Steg 2008). In Suyapa, 61 percent of residents think the selling of drugs and alcohol is a large problem, while 89 percent of Pino Alto and 78 percent of other resettlement inhabitants think so. Concerns about graffiti follow suit. In answer to the same question, 65 percent of Suyapa, 82 percent of Pino Alto, and 77 percent of the other resettlement residents believe graffiti is a large problem. My ethnographic work supports these opinions. I observed men who were under the influence of drugs or alcohol much more often in Pino Alto than in Suyapa, and, although alcohol was obtainable in either resettlement, it was much more visible and easily purchased in Pino Alto.

POLICE, CORRUPTION, AND REPORTING

The statistics above must also be taken in context. One would expect there to be less crime in a resettlement with more police per capita, which was often the case in Suyapa. One might also expect that the likelihood of crime reporting would also rise due to a larger police presence, which is not the case. A previous study by the Bureau of Justice Statistics has shown that violent crime is more likely to be reported than nonviolent or property crime (Hart and Rennison 2003). Other studies have noted, in contrast, that rape is often underreported (Koss and Gidycz 1985; Koss 1992).

Crime in El Valle, though, is rarely reported. According to Officer Valdez, "There is at least seven times more crime than actually is reported. The crimes that are reported are usually the less significant crimes. People do not want to offend anyone, as the police might tell the criminal who reported them and the criminal would take revenge." Even with this perspective, Suyapa residents (86 percent) feel much more comfortable reporting crime than Pino Alto residents (62 percent). This large difference (24 percent) in feeling comfortable reporting implies likely underreporting in Pino Alto. In light of this underreporting and concerns about retribution, Pino Alto's crime may actually be considerably higher than the data shows.

This sentiment was confirmed by many interviewees. A friend and Honduran engineer who has worked on projects in most of the El Valle resettlements, Santiago, was hired to build a new structure in a remote post-Mitch resettlement called Santa Clara. He had worked in Santa Clara dozens of times over the previous five years and had visited once a week over the previous two months to check on the construction of a soccer field for the resettlement. In April 2010, as he was leaving the resettlement, a man stood in the middle of the road pointing a gun at the windshield. Rather than stop and likely be robbed of everything, including his car, Santiago hit the gas and the man shot at him twice, missing both times. Santiago decided not to go to the police for fear that the man would find out and come looking for him (see also Consultoría 2011).

This was not a unique incident. Multiple residents from each resettlement had little to no faith in the police, fearing, with good reason (Kahn 2013), that they are "*en la cama*" (in bed) with the criminals. To illustrate the reality of this concern, in November 2011, 176 top Honduran police officers were fired and a half dozen put into custody for charges connected to corruption and theft of government property, including three hundred automatic rifles with ammunition (BBC 2011). As noted earlier, in 2010, the LAPOP survey found that when Hondurans were asked about their level of confidence in the police, 68 percent said they had little to no confidence (Latinobarometro 2011a).

Finally, to check whether perceptions of crime and security were a community effect, I also asked residents to compare current delinquency to the delinquency in their pre-Mitch Tegucigalpa neighborhood. This question enables a better comparison of current perceptions, as many of the residents from Suyapa and Pino Alto came from the same pre-Mitch neighborhoods in Tegucigalpa. The difference is astounding. In Suyapa, 96 percent of residents are convinced that their resettlement has less delinquency, while only 68 percent in Pino Alto and 80 percent in the five other resettlements hold similar views. The opposite is also revealing. Only 1 percent of residents in Suyapa believe there is now more delinquency, compared to 13 percent in Pino Alto and 6 percent in the average of the five other resettlements.

In sum, average Suyapa residents feel considerably safer in their resettlement than do average Pino Alto residents. They have experienced less crime, the crime they do have is less severe, and they feel more comfortable reporting crimes—all of which may have a multiplying effect on future security and crime issues.

SOCIAL CAPITAL

As described in chapter 3, social capital has been found to be beneficial in many areas by encouraging mutual trust and reciprocity in relationships. In the seven resettlements, trust increased over time for at least 40 percent of each resettlement, and more than 80 percent of residents said their trust was equal to or greater than that in their community of origin. This is a substantial improvement. Yet, Suyapa again is distinguished, as nearly 60 percent of residents trust their neighbors more now, while only 40 percent of Pino Alto and 43 percent of the five other resettlements can say the same. Suyapa's high trust likely positively impacts other social health metrics, such as participation and lower crime.

Another proxy for social capital is value sharing, which can lead to increased connection and social cohesion among residents. Pino Alto, in this case, is the outlier. Less than a third of Pino Alto residents believe they share the same values as their neighbors; more than half of the control group and Suyapa residents agree that their neighbors share their values. This important question displays the sense of identity and, by extension, trust (Gillespie and Mann 2004) within each resettlement. Moreover, in terms of trust, the surveys revealed that 57 percent of Suyapa residents have *mucho* (a lot) of trust in their neighbors, while only 38 percent of Pino Alto and 39 percent of the control group have similar feelings. As noted, the ramifications of the lack of trust could play a major role in how residents work together for the betterment of the community. Social capital will be further discussed within each case.

COLLECTIVE EFFICACY

Drawing on Sampson, Raudenbush, and Earls (1997, 918), collective efficacy can be defined as "social cohesion among neighbors combined with their willingness to intervene on behalf of the common good." Thomas (2007) defines the value and necessary characteristics of collective efficacy at the neighborhood level:

> The willingness of local residents to intervene for the common good depends in large part on conditions of mutual trust and solidarity among neighbors. Indeed, one is unlikely to intervene in a neighborhood context in which the rules are unclear and people mistrust or fear one another. It follows that socially cohesive neighborhoods will prove the most fertile contexts for the realization of informal social control. In sum, it is the linkage of mutual trust and the willingness to intervene for the common good that defines the neighborhood context of collective efficacy.

Collective efficacy, then, has an inverse relationship to crime and corruption. One would expect that the creation of cohesive neighborhoods and communal efforts of informal social control would produce less criminal activity. In the cases of Suyapa and Pino Alto, a clear pattern appears; as collective efficacy increases, crime decreases.

Beginning with the ideas of community social cohesion and trust, Sampson, Raudenbush, and Earls (1997) describe the concept as represented by five related items. Utilizing questions similar to those in their seminal Chicago crime study, they surveyed resettlement residents about their beliefs concerning shared values by neighbors, recognition of neighbors, recognition of strangers, unity of the community, and neighbors' willingness to help others. The results are revealing.

Major differences exist in the ability to recognize neighbors and strangers between the resettlements. In Suyapa, 84 percent of residents find it easy or very easy to recognize someone from the resettlement; only 54 percent in Pino Alto and 69 percent in the other resettlements feel the same. Likewise, 80 percent of Suyapa residents find it easy or very easy to spot a stranger, while 37 percent of Pino Alto residents and 55 percent of the control group believe it is difficult to recognize a nonresident within the boundaries of the resettlement.

It should be remembered that Pino Alto has twice the residents of Suyapa and up to fifteen times the residents of the smallest resettlement, Cerro Viejo, in the study. However, there was no clear correlation between size and resident recognition across the various resettlements.

Familiarity among neighbors can stimulate cooperation and social capital as well as help create stability and future crime prevention (Bursik and Webb 1982). Similar to a US neighborhood watch group (NCPC 2016), crime can be prevented or delinquents caught if residents can identify when strangers are in the resettlement. The difference in resident recognition is also supported by my own observations of the resettlements, where residents often acknowledged their neighbors by name, while in Pino Alto and the other resettlements this occurred less often.[9] Collective efficacy is also measured by the feeling of service to one's neighbor and the feelings of unity within the community. In terms of neighbors helping neighbors, nearly 90 percent of Suyapa residents, 75 percent of Pino Alto residents, and 84 percent of the control group believe their neighbors would help them. Community unity also displays the socially integrated environment created in Suyapa. Most significantly, a much higher number of Suyapa residents (89 percent) believe the community is semi- or very united compared to Pino Alto (69 percent) and the control group (69 percent). The repercussions of high collective efficacy have been found to impact crime levels (Sampson, Raudenbuesh, and Earls 1997; Sampson and Raudenbush 1999), and likely positively impact social capital and civic participation.

Moreover, residents were asked about the likelihood of their own or their neighbor's willingness to work on behalf of or for the benefit of the resettlement, especially through the use of informal social control mechanisms. Informal social control is represented by questions that concerned resettlement life in general: How do neighbors control their children? Do they send them to school? And are neighbors willing to intervene on behalf of others? Each question had similar response rates; responses to two of the questions will be described below.

Respondents were asked, "If someone was trying to sell drugs to your children or other children in the community, would your neighbors stop them?" and "If a thief entered your house, do you think a neighbor would do something to stop them?" Answers to both questions were nearly identical for each resettlement, with 85 percent of Suyapa residents responding in the affirmative compared to Pino Alto (66 percent) and the average resettlement (79 percent). This large difference, in which nearly one-fifth more residents believe their neighbors are willing to stop a drug dealer or a thief, underscores the greater collective trust and cohesion Suyapa residents have in their neighbors, further evidencing the divergent process and outcomes of each resettlement.

Table 4.5. Civic Participation

Survey questions	Suyapa	Pino Alto	Avg. of 5 resettlements
Do you vote? (Yes)	72 percent**	56 percent	58 percent
Do you participate in any community organization? (Yes)	36 percent**	16 percent	13 percent
Do you participate in the church? (Yes)	49 percent**	43 percent**	57 percent
Are you involved in classes, projects or activities in the community? (Yes)	37 percent**	17 percent	17 percent

Z score: **.01 compared to the average community.

CIVIC PARTICIPATION

Resident civic participation also differs among resettlements. On all four measures—voting, organizational participation, church involvement, and community service—Suyapa exhibits higher engagement than the others. Pino Alto is comparable to the average, except for lower levels of church participation.

These four measures corroborate that Suyapa has greater civic participation than do Pino Alto and the control group—which has ramifications in other areas. Greater participation can lead to increased social capital, collective efficacy, and political voice in shaping the resettlement's development. Higher levels of engagement may also reduce crime, as residents are more engaged in resettlement affairs and want to ensure its future success.

SHARED VISION

The importance of a resettlement vision with respect to development toward community cannot be underestimated. Indeed, the development of almost any organization, bureaucracy, political structure, or community necessitates a common vision for progress to be possible. Not only must this vision of "community" be agreed upon, it must also continually be reproduced to function (Weber [1947] 2009; Morello-Frosh et al. 2011). The following section will discuss selected proxy measures to compare the collective vision of the resettlements.

Each resettlement NGO announced its intention to "build back better" and improve the lives of survivors. In all seven resettlements, nearly two-thirds of residents (63 percent) agree that twelve years after Hurricane Mitch, their lives are better now.[10] Indeed, when asked to compare their life in general before Mitch and their life today, 73 percent of residents in Suyapa and 53 percent in

Pino Alto said their life was better. Only 8 percent in Suyapa and 16 percent in Pino Alto expressed that their life was worse (the rest noted it was the same). This is a positive sign for development workers and NGOs. In general, residents see the relocation as a net positive.

Other survey questions support these encouraging results. Both La Iglesia and La Internacional publicly announced that they had built "model" resettlements that could serve as exemplars for the rest of the nation and even the world. Residents moving in were made aware of this fact from the very beginning by the NGO. The importance of the collective narrative (Chamlee-Wright and Storr 2011) was understood by NGO leadership and shared with residents even before they set foot in their new homes. To ascertain the success of this endeavor, I asked residents whether they believed they lived in a "model community."[11] A majority of residents in Suyapa (88 percent) and Pino Alto (72 percent) agreed. This was a statistically significant difference between the two resettlements as well as with the control group, wherein 46 percent agreed.

While the figures above demonstrate resident beliefs about their current state, the following question asked respondents about their future outlook. One would assume that the higher the percentage of residents believing the resettlement was headed down a good path, the more invested they are in a common vision. When asked whether their "community is headed on a bad (*mal*), good (*bien*), or very good (*muy bien*) path," residents overwhelmingly answered "good path": 62 percent of Suyapa, 69 percent of Pino Alto, and 67 percent of the average residents agreed. They are not pessimistic about the future but are not overly optimistic about it either. The largest difference was in the very good category. Again, Suyapa has the highest response, with more than a quarter of residents (27 percent) agreeing their community was on a very good path. Pino Alto follows with 10 percent, just above the five other resettlements at 7 percent.

Notwithstanding Suyapa, the six other resettlements' perspective on the future was parallel to national opinion polls on the progress of the nation. LAPOP (LatinoBarometro 2011b) asked Hondurans about their perception of the progress of the country. Is it progressing, standing still, or declining? In 2008 only 11 percent of Hondurans thought their nation was progressing, while 34 percent believed the country was on the decline. Comparatively, resettlement residents are more confident in their resettlement's development than that of their nation, affirming the relative success of the projects.

The examples above reveal how Suyapa residents hold a more positive association with their resettlement than do residents of Pino Alto and the control resettlements. This optimistic outlook may reflect Suyapa's social cohesion and clearer vision for the movement of the resettlement toward community. As will be discussed in the following two chapters, the resettlement vision consti-tuted part of a clear strategy by La Iglesia to implement a SAGE development approach to create a resettlement culture that would empower residents to aspire to and achieve a better future.

CONCLUSIONS AND QUESTIONS

The analysis above offers a variety of insights and questions for resettlement theorists and practitioners. Generally, most residents are content in their cur-rent living circumstances and feel that they live better than they did before Hurricane Mitch. According to national crime and opinion statistics, these perceptions are accurate, and residents have a reason to be grateful for the dif-ficult relocation when compared to their neighborhoods in Tegucigalpa. They are generally safer, have a more positive outlook on the future, think their community is on the right track, and have access to better infrastructure than they did in previous Tegucigalpa neighborhoods.

Conversely, significant differences are present between the resettlements in terms of social health, particularly in terms of crime, social capital, collective efficacy, civic participation, and collective vision. This development stratifi-cation (wherein the resettlements began with similar starting points but have followed significantly different trajectories, increasing their differences) poses a number of theoretical and practical questions. The umbrella question is "why?" How did certain resident and NGO development strategies guide the development path? How did these strategies create a cycle of positive or nega-tive increasing returns? The following two chapters will describe the two case studies, Suyapa and Pino Alto, respectively. This detailed analysis will high-light the development strategies in each resettlement and their corresponding outcomes. The final chapter will analyze how these differences contributed to the particular trajectory of each resettlement.

CHAPTER 5

SUYAPA

Driving out of Tegucigalpa, the road eventually descends into a beautiful valley bowl. Thousands of pine trees, green scrub brush, and pockets of identical houses are scattered about the hillsides. Billows of smoke rise from the two coffee-processing plants. On a calm day, the scent is particularly inviting. Soon the lowest part of the valley appears, where the dirt roads wind their way up into mountains well worn by foot, tire, and hoof. The last road on the left, the one before heading up the mountain on the other side of the valley, climbs around a cow pasture bordered by a drainage ditch on the right side and thorny branches on the left. It is wise to drive slowly or hold onto something to avoid hitting one's head on the roof due to the dips and bumps. Following the sign up the hill to Suyapa, workers cutting grass will stop and wave to travelers, wondering who is entering their community. If they know the person, they will shout with a raised hand *"Compa"* or *"Tío,"* endearments that remind one of friendships among neighbors. Drivers must watch for skinny dogs and roaming cattle on the road. The resettlement is a microcosm of the glory and sadness that is Honduras: people laughing alongside burning trash, kids playing barefoot with a flat soccer ball on a dirt field, abandoned cars alongside beautiful gardens, and gentle smiles that turn into frowns when the conversation veers to politics.

In the center of town just beyond the central park, the Catholic church holds a commanding presence. It is the largest building in town by far, but is simply built, with a red-tile roof and a dozen trees surrounding the cement structure. To the left of the brick building is the old preschool, once run by Capuchin nuns. They moved to another community a few years ago, and the place has been closed ever since, to the great dismay of the resettlement.

Suyapa is a resettlement built by La Iglesia to serve survivors of Hurricane Mitch using donated funds from international organizations and churches. Building began in 1999, only a few months after the October 1998 disaster, and has continued, to a limited extent, into the present. The original plan was ambitious, with the goal of constructing 800 homes. Limited by funding and geographic space, La Iglesia settled on 583 homes, most of which have been continually inhabited since late 2001.

This chapter provides an in-depth description of the resettlement and non-governmental organization, as well as an analysis of the interaction between them. To provide a holistic picture of the resettlement, various elements will be discussed, starting literally from the ground up. The material aspects of Suyapa—its land use, infrastructure, and urban design—will lay a foundation for understanding how the entire resettlement developed. A description of the residents will follow, specifying their livelihoods and leadership as well as the role of religion and religiosity in the resettlement.

The second half of the chapter will consider La Iglesia and its role in the development of Suyapa. Starting with a brief background of the organization, I will then discuss La Iglesia's community development philosophy and practices. Importantly, the organization's SAGE (sustain, accompany, guide, and empower) resettlement-to-community development approach will be described in detail to highlight how particular interventions directed Suyapa but also led to conflict between the organization and residents.

LAND USE AND INFRASTRUCTURE

The map and key in figure 5.1 show all of the homes and most of the terrain of Suyapa, with each number illustrating a point of interest within the resettlement. First, notice how the main road enters the resettlement and the center of town. Taking the bus (#5)—the most common commuting mode of transportation—means that people pass through half the town, only meters away from their neighbors' houses. All roads lead to the main road (#1), which sees the first bus depart at four-thirty a.m. and the last one return at eight p.m. Suyapa residents are almost the sole users of this part of the road, as neighbor villagers take a different road home. Due in part to the few cars owned by residents and by the low outside traffic the resettlement experiences, residents will take a hard look at an unfamiliar car or motorcycle passing through town.

In addition, due to the main road being the only convenient way in or out of the resettlement, a resident sees the same people every day. Near the market, ninety-two-year-old Don Oscar rests regularly beneath the same tree each morning, watching people and waving to the cars. It is not uncommon to see him fall asleep midday. Farther down the road, the mentally ill young man, Lionel, sits at the edge of town all day staring at the mountains; the neighborhood women walk the same routes from home to the market and back; and the same boys set up their soccer game in the middle of the street. The main road then becomes a place of familiarity, safety, and collective efficacy. For better or

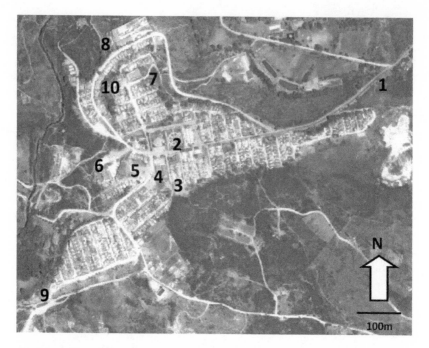

FIGURE 5.1. Map of Suyapa
Map Data ©2016 Google

1 Main road to highway. A dirt road that floods and creates traffic problems.
2 Central Square. This area includes the market on the right, the central park center, and the Catholic church on the left.
3 This is La Iglesia's office. It is a combination of two houses.
4 Elementary school. Just north of the school is the old day care that is now a community hall.
5 Bus station.
6 Workshops. This large building houses four workshops where adolescents and adults took vocational classes. Connected to the building were the living quarters of the four nuns who ran the workshop for six years. Now used for small group meetings.
7 Multisports complex. Usually used for small-sided soccer games. It has changing rooms, bathrooms (that do not work), and stadium-type seating. Also used for large votes.
8 Middle and high school buildings.
9 Road to a neighboring community and the only nearby bar (100 meters beyond Suyapa limits).
10 Police station.

worse, it also provides a fishbowl environment where everyone in the resettlement knows everyone else's business.

Following numerical order, #2 pinpoints the heart of the resettlement. The lively market, open seven days a week from six a.m. until six p.m., has forty-four of its fifty-two stalls filled with vendors selling everything from hardware to groceries, hot lunches, school supplies, DVDs, clothing, and services such as haircuts and bike repair. The central park is beside the market and boasts beautiful red-brick paths, well-groomed brush and flowers, and a four-meter-tall water fountain. Set up in the shape of a small amphitheater, the east (market side) area has a large concrete platform that acts as a stage for speakers, dance troupes, and other community events. Also on the east side lies a plaque in gratitude to La Iglesia, the sponsoring organization, for founding the resettlement. Every evening, men gather to play cards or dominoes (occasionally for money) on small concrete slabs nearby. The men collected enough money among themselves to put up a roof and fix the seating so that they could play in the rain and out of the heat of the sun.

Interestingly, although the central park was originally designed by La Iglesia, La Iglesia promised to provide the materials if residents reciprocated by providing the labor. This is one of the proud partnerships between residents and the NGO. Both consider it a success, as residents are able to enjoy the fruit of their labor and La Iglesia is satisfied with the joint effort. Throughout the dry season, the park attracts much foot traffic. For older residents and families with children, the park is often a destination for evening strolls or an opportunity to catch up with friends. For adolescents, the park offers just enough dark corners to sneak in a romantic moment with a partner. On weekend evenings, about twice a month, the park is used for many types of outdoor activities, including concerts, dance competitions, prayer meetings, fund-raisers, and talent shows for children.

Next to the park is the Roman Catholic church, the largest building in the resettlement apart from the schools. Standing prominently in front of the day care and elementary school (#4), and close to the bus stop (#5), it acts as the hub of the resettlement. The church also maintains a large open space for parking on Sundays, though during the week the kids use it for soccer or bicycling, and townswomen use it to sell oranges and *catrachas* (a fried tortilla with beans, cheese, and salsa on top). Farther down the street stands La Iglesia's office, a quiet building made up of two combined houses, fitting in nicely with the surrounding homes. Far from ostentatious, a small covered patio with simple blue tiles and metal chairs invites visitors to sit and wait to meet with the accountant, engineer, or social worker.

On the periphery of the town lie four important destinations, though important for significantly different reasons. Locations #6 and #8 pinpoint the vocational school (now closed due to a lack of funds) and the high school, respectively. Location #7 represents the miniature concrete soccer field where youth play throughout the day. Here, young kids are able to play from two until four, when the adolescents and young men gather and play until dark. More recently, the resettlement came together and, with some funds donated by a US NGO, repaired the fences and lights, so that tournaments could be held at night.

Point #10 is the police station. The small four-room concrete building—a greeting area with two chairs, a small desk and a nonworking telephone, two small holding cells, and a back bedroom for the night police officer—is yellow with a bright department insignia painted on the front. It is occupied only about half of the time; the other half the officers spend walking the resettlement. The police expressed how peaceful Suyapa is in comparison to surrounding resettlements and communities. Both Officer Ramírez in Suyapa and Officer Valdez in Pino Alto agree that they would rather be in El Valle than in Tegucigalpa, and in Suyapa rather than Pino Alto, due to safer working conditions.

Finally, location #9 represents the western boundary of the resettlement and a small trail that leads into Río Frío. This area is often referred to jokingly as sector *diez* (ten). There are only nine sectors in the resettlement, but men often go to sector *diez*, where an original inhabitant of the area turned part of his house into the only nearby bar. As one Suyapa resident warned me, "Ryan, you should never go to sector ten at night. Bad things happen there. People get drunk and get into fights. Sometimes people get stabbed." While this may have been true at some point, according to police records a stabbing has never been reported. Talking with other men in the resettlement, it was considered a shady place, viewed with a hint of both disdain and appeal. My own experience both during the day and at night was that this small bar was unthreatening, as were the men who frequented the locale. Indeed, the only thing that differentiated the bar from any other house in the area was a small dirt patio with some wood benches and a hand-painted sign advertising Imperial, one of the national beer manufacturers.

RESETTLEMENT DESIGN

Geographers, urban planners, engineers, and architects continually remind us of the impact of space and design upon the dynamics of a resettlement. This factor is perhaps even more critical in creating a new resettlement, built with international funds, for survivors who are brought together through necessity and without strong networks of support. Infrastructure blueprints could encourage or discourage the building of community among residents. In Suyapa, as the map illustrates, the plan encourages constant social interaction between residents. No matter which sector a resident lives in, she cannot escape running into resettlement members, through bringing her children to school, going to church, buying food at the market, or catching a bus.

Suyapa's layout was designed by a group of Honduran architects and urban planners who maintained a number of resettlement-appropriate cultural elements, like building homes that look traditional, have adequate space indoors (taking into account the average family size), are designed with input from the future residents, have utilities (water, electricity, sewer), and offer residents both a little private backyard and a small public front yard (CESAL 2008, 54). Although the property space surrounding the home would be considered very small for someone arriving from a rural area, it felt spacious to someone from Tegucigalpa. From my interviews, most residents appreciated the size and design of both the house and the space surrounding it.

Unlike those in other resettlements, Suyapa residents did not participate in the construction of their homes. Rather, La Iglesia hired professional firms to build the homes to a specific standard and residents were to "buy" the house via a fifteen-year loan held by the NGO. Although they did not construct where they were going to live, they were involved in the building of much of the infrastructure, including the roads, the central park, and the community meeting space and soccer field.

According to CESAL (2008, 53), a Spanish INGO that supported the building of many houses in El Valle through financing from the Spanish government, the housing was designed to achieve six objectives shaping the culture of the resettlement:

1. Avoid creating dependency. Materials should be easily attainable. The home should be a means, not an end in itself [to self-sustainability].
2. The homes are built in a manner that fits with local skill sets and are more economical than technical.
3. The homes are respectful of the sociocultural reality, understanding that the process is constantly evolving. There is a focus on practicality and not nostalgia.
4. The homes should be acceptable to future residents.
5. The homes should permit local adaptation, should be easy to understand, and should favor resident adaptation rather than a one-size-fits-all model.
6. The homes should be built to a standard that resembles the economic level of the region.

Discussed below is an example of a home that addresses all six of these criteria. The house is made of cinder block, common and inexpensive for most

Hondurans. Fixing a problem or building onto the existing structure is relatively straightforward and can be done by most people. Both the building and the grounds allow residents to make the structure their own. Some residents' yards feature gardens or garages, while others are barren or used for storage. The homes also fit aesthetically within El Valle; there are houses that are grander and more beautiful, and there are others that are smaller and made of mud brick. The new homes are within both the economic and sociocultural standards of the area.

Strolling along the dusty roads of the resettlement, familial socioeconomic status is easily discerned. Those with less wealth lack the resources to improve their home and terrain. Unpainted walls, an open unfenced green space, and general emptiness characterize these homes. Most residents, however, have been able to make some improvements. Many families have painted their home with vibrant colors, others have put up walls or fences around their home (perhaps a cultural return to living in Tegucigalpa), and still others have added on rooms and even second stories to their houses. Based on a physical attributes survey, approximately 75 percent of houses exhibit considerable enhancement.

Similar to all of the other post-disaster resettlements, but unlike established neighboring communities, Suyapa has electricity in each home, running water two to three days a week, indoor plumbing, a waste-treatment plant, and trash collection. The electricity is on approximately 95 percent of the time. During thunderstorms, the electricity will often go down not only for Suyapa but for the entire valley. A great amenity for Suyapa residents is running water in the home, even though it only runs for a few hours two to three times a week. Residents fill a *pila* or large tub to provide them with water in the interim. A waste-management plant is also used for black and gray water, filtering solids from the water before it enters the local river. Finally, although the municipality-level trash agency picks up trash twice weekly, the resettlement continues to discard trash on the sides of roads and in green areas due to its cultural acceptability.

LIVELIHOODS

As noted earlier, a marketplace flourishes in the central square of Suyapa. According to the market manager, since 2002, when the market opened, occupancy has never dropped below 75 percent of total stalls. The marketplace is the largest within a five-kilometer radius and therefore attracts residents from local communities and people who live in villages in the surrounding hills.

There is also a prospering informal economy in Suyapa. As part of the physical and social disorder survey, I identified the number of streets with at least one *pulpería*. *Pulperías* are illegal in both Suyapa and Pino Alto, as each sponsoring organization wanted to promote a central market. *Pulperías* popped up, however, to address the demands of consumers for small goods like snacks, drinks, and toiletries and services like adding call minutes to a cellular phone. These stores have low start-up costs, signs are usually provided by different companies, and owners can make a small fortune through the sheer quantity of sundries sold. About 60 percent of Suyapa streets have at least one *pulpería*; that is comparable to the average of the other five resettlements. In comparison to Pino Alto's 89 percent, Suyapa had a much lower rate of streets with informal stores, possibly as a result of maintaining a stronger central market.

As income is not usually generated in the resettlement (except from locals from other communities who buy foodstuffs at the market), most of the revenue that enters Suyapa derives from those who work in the valley or in Tegucigalpa and a small amount of remittances from abroad. Those who work outside the resettlement tend to have either blue-collar jobs in the valley (construction, brick making, and general manual labor) or in Tegucigalpa (housecleaning, selling newspapers on the street, selling water or "cure-alls" on buses). A few have white-collar jobs in the capital city in business, government, the health field (nurses), teaching, or law (there is one lawyer in Suyapa). About a third of Suyapa residents receive no remittances, 60 percent receive between 1 and 10 percent of their total monthly salary as remittances, and 10 percent rely more heavily on the subsidy, obtaining more than 10 percent of their income from relatives abroad.

For those who commute to Tegucigalpa, most either take the bus or request a ride with one of the few families in the resettlement who have cars. As noted, buses in Suyapa run every thirty minutes from four-thirty a.m. on, with the last bus arriving at seven-thirty p.m. The morning buses are consistently full until seven a.m., by which time most residents need to be at work in the city. Since the bus ride lasts between fifty minutes and two hours depending on traffic, residents who work in town participate less often in the political processes or social activities of the resettlement, except on weekends. In fact, the 2010 president of the Comité Cívico Social (CCS), who is employed by the national electric company, after being elected admitted to the board that he would do his best but would be frequently absent due to work. Like all of the resettlements studied, many of the best, brightest, and most energetic residents in Suyapa cannot participate in the resettlement development process because they are too busy working.

Obtaining an accurate account of employment for residents is challenging.

While residents were asked about occupation before and after Mitch, the surveyors mostly interviewed residents who were at home during the day, usually women. The only accurate data available was a 2004 self-study by La Iglesia and a Spanish NGO. The study provides some insight into the general means of attaining money for families based on employment status and type.

Most Suyapa residents over twelve years old are employed in manual labor (41 percent), approximately a third maintain permanent employment, and a quarter are self-employed. These figures show that Suyapa may have had a slightly stronger economy, as 10 percent more of its residents have permanent work than do residents of Pino Alto (La Iglesia and CESAL 2004, 29–34; La Internacional and Pino Alto 2007). A possible explanation of the inverse relationship between self-employment and manual labor is that when a family member (usually a man) engages in manual labor, another family member (usually the woman) can focus more on taking care of the children and household. On the other hand, when a man cannot find work, the woman of the house begins to find ways to help support the family through self-employment, such as selling tortillas or opening a *pulpería*. If the business is successful, the man may then focus his energy on this informal work, which is easier than laying brick or digging ditches. In all of the resettlements I studied, residents believed that the man should try to make enough money for his spouse to be able to stay home and care for the children. This traditional family practice is maintained by both economic and social factors. From my observations, jobs tend to go to men no matter the skill level—except for such jobs as secretary, office assistant, teacher, or nurse. Socially, as noted earlier, family is central to Honduran culture and life. The idea of having two parents working is seen as less than ideal, and women have been socialized to have fewer career ambitions and opportunities than they would in a country like the United States.

RESIDENTS AND LEADERSHIP

Even though Mitch stories differ in their details, Doña Mariana has a fairly common tale of hardship and relief. When Mitch hit, she was a single mother with three children who worked cleaning the homes of wealthy Hondurans. Her house washed away, and she remembers, with great emotion and distress, sleeping under a bridge with her three children, concerned about food, their safety, and where they would go. After the storm, the family made its way to one of the larger temporary shelters (*macro-albergues*). She was grateful, in hindsight, that the shelter she ended up at was among the safer ones. They lived together in a three- by five-meter space, protected by four walls of plastic and wood beams. She volunteered in the temporary shelter, took classes,

Table 5.1. 2010 Monthly Cost of Living in Suyapa for Don Bernardo

Monthly income and expenses	Lempiras	US dollars
Minimum wage income for Don Bernardo	5,500	289
Household water	–150	7
Household electricity	–100	5
Household mortgage	–1,388	73
Transportation for one person to the city (e.g., high school, groceries, etc.)	–1,175	61
Leftover income after the above	=2,697	=142
If leftover income is spent on food per person (six in total)	450 per person	24 per person
Education, health, travel, savings, home repairs, sports, etc.	0	0

and raised her children. When she learned about the various projects, she was drawn to Suyapa. "I chose to live in the community for my kids. I believed it would give them better opportunities in the future. I knew there would be a major sacrifice on my part, though, to work to pay the mortgage." Indeed, she has sacrificed. Now with four children, Doña Mariana has to work seven days a week cleaning homes in the capital. She often leaves at four-thirty a.m. to arrive at her employer's home by seven, and although she commonly leaves the city around five or six, the two-hour bus ride returns her home for only a couple of hours of rest and relaxation before going to sleep in the same four-by-five-meter bedroom with four children. Doña Mariana has managed to continually make her mortgage payments each month, and is encouraged that three of her four children have stayed in school. When asked directly about her experience in Suyapa, she simply replies, "I like it very much."

Living up the hill about two hundred meters away, Don Bernardo is short in stature but large in humility. He has a dark complexion; deep, kind brown eyes; and jet-black hair. Married, with four daughters, Don Bernie (as he is affectionately known) is not a leader, does not put much thought into politics, goes to church every Sunday, and loves soccer. He is one of the few residents who work for La Iglesia; as a guard of the workshop grounds, his hours are six a.m. to six p.m. six days a week on odd weeks, and six p.m. to six a.m. seven days a week on even weeks. He makes the national minimum wage of 5,500 lempiras (~$289 in 2010 US dollars) a month but has been active in setting up a microenterprise tilapia farm with some other residents to make a little extra money. His wife takes care of their daughters, who are between eight and eighteen.

As for their opinions about the resettlement, residents almost unanimously liked living in Suyapa. According to the resettlement census, about 90 percent of residents believed that their resettlement was a model community for other post-disaster settlements. This sentiment provides compelling evidence that despite their different backgrounds, residents seem to have found a place they want to live and raise their children.

Don Bernie, like Doña Mariana and Don Francisco (discussed below), offers the reader an idea of what type of residents La Iglesia was looking for: financially self-sufficient, moral, hardworking, service-minded, committed to the well-being of the community, and, ideally, Catholic. They found many families through their strict selection process, namely those who were willing to take advantage of new opportunities to get ahead.

RELIGION AND RELIGIOSITY

Religion and religiosity in both resettlements is an important feature. Due to the complexity of the topic, a deep analysis is beyond the scope of this book. What follows is a brief overview of Suyapa's faith.

The statistics in Table 5.2 are fascinating in both how the resettlements do not fit standard evaluations (the CIA World Factbook [2015] classifies 97% of Hondurans as Catholic) and how Suyapa's Catholicism (61 percent) is so far above the average of the five resettlements (28 percent). La Iglesia may have had greater success negotiating this process due to its Catholic philosophy, structure, and SAGE practices, which provided the organization a certain degree of legitimacy, in part due to shared religious convictions. Indeed, according to informal discussion with residents throughout the valley, Suyapa is known as the most Catholic resettlement in the area. It has the largest Catholic church in El Valle, and the only priest who celebrates mass for the valley lives in Suyapa. Additionally, in 2010, the cardinal built a large two-story house for three priests in Suyapa, which they will use as their home base to serve the rest of the valley. As will be discussed below, La Iglesia initially made a con-

Table 5.2. Religion by Resettlement

	Catholic	Protestant	Evangelical	None	Other
Suyapa	61 percent**	0 percent	29 percent**	10 percent**	0 percent
Pino Alto	23 percent	2 percent	45 percent	29 percent*	1 percent
Avg. 5 resettlements	28 percent	1 percent	47 percent	22 percent	2 percent

Z score: *.05, **.01 (Comparison group—Avg. 5 resettlements).

Table 5.3. Religiosity by Resettlement

	Do not attend	Attend on holidays	Attend every week	Attend two or more times each week
Suyapa	13 percent**	20 percent	32 percent**	36 percent
Pino Alto	32 percent**	16 percent	17 percent**	35 percent
Average of 5 resettlements	26 percent	18 percent	24 percent	33 percent

Z score: **.01 (The average of the 5 resettlements is the comparison group).

certed effort to attract an applicant pool that was Catholic or sympathetic to Catholic values.

Suyapa residents are also outliers in their religiosity, as measured by church attendance. According to the survey, only 13 percent of residents never attend services, even on major holidays. This figure is twice as high in the other resettlements and nearly three times as high in Pino Alto. There is no statistically significant difference between those who attend only on holidays. Still, the difference between religions is highlighted in how often per week residents attend services: 32 percent of Suyapa residents attend every week, and 36 percent attend twice a week or more.

Another figure of interest is the relatively high number of Catholics and low number of nonbelievers in Suyapa. This is the reverse for Pino Alto. Fittingly, religious attendance in Pino Alto is also significantly lower, creating less opportunity for social interaction. As originally theorized by Emile Durkheim, this difference could have played a major role in the ability of each resettlement to create and maintain social cohesion, an agreed-upon culture, and even social control (1979 [1897]; 1995 [1912]).

LEADERSHIP

Don Francisco is perhaps the most well-known and well-respected person in Suyapa. The regal and handsome seventy-two-year-old maintains an impeccable appearance. He is often dressed in khaki pants and a collared white shirt that contrasts against his dark-brown skin, and maintains a perfectly trimmed white mustache. He walks slowly and with care, the same manner with which he speaks to children and adults. He is widowed as of 2008, when cancer took his wife, but has an adolescent grandson who now lives with him to keep him company. He spends his days involved in various community organizations, especially those connected with the Catholic Church. He takes walks with friends and helps those he sees in need. As another resident shared with me, if there was one person who could unite the resettlement, it would be Don Francisco. In many ways, his role in the resettlement rivals that of Doña Rosa, vice president of La Iglesia, although he would be too humble to admit to it.

Don Francisco's role has been multifaceted. After Mitch, his house was deemed to be in an at-risk area, forcing him and his wife to move into one of the local church shelters. As a beloved elder of the Church, he was called upon by the priest to organize and support the temporary relocation of thousands of families in different parishes. Similar to a social worker, he would listen to the needs of particular families and then match them with resources in other parishes or with other organizations. When La Iglesia began its recruitment via local priests, Don Francisco was asked whether he would be interested in relocating to Suyapa. He accepted and began helping La Iglesia find families in need who would fit the criteria to live in the resettlement.

Don Francisco was also one of the first members of the CCS. Unlike the *patronato*,[1] a political patronage system that is common throughout Honduras, the CCS is made up of three equal powers—the Church, La Iglesia, and the resettlement. The Church receives two voting members, La Iglesia has two voting members (including the president and the attorney), and the resettlement maintains four voting members. Decisions are made by a simple majority, with ties broken by a representative of La Iglesia's president. Easily recognizable in this political structure are the power and influence both La Iglesia and the Church have in resettlement decision-making. The power distribution offers checks and balances among the three entities, but as many residents shared with me, it gives too much influence to the NGO and the Church. Indeed, since the CCS was instituted, in 2002, there have been occasional resident protests against it with the hope of implementing a *patronato*. This trend continued in 2010, when residents called for a referendum on the CCS (though there was never an official vote). It did, however, push La Iglesia to move more quickly to separate the organization from the resettlement. By July of 2011 the organization and the resettlement were legally separated (six years earlier than anticipated), although the Church itself would maintain a voice in the CCS. Over time the influence of each group has ebbed and flowed, but the majority of decision-making power had been consistently held by La Iglesia until the separation. The CCS will be discussed further in the section on La Iglesia.

Under the purview of the Tegucigalpa municipality, all of the resettlements in El Valle have a similar peripheral relationship with the local government. According to multiple interviews, after Hurricane Mitch the Tegucigalpa mayor was overwhelmed by the city's problems and had little time to deal with El Valle. Today, the relationship has changed little. The small number of

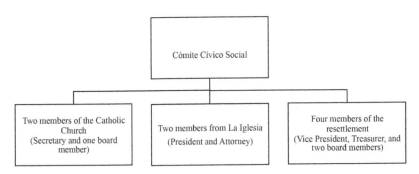

FIGURE 5.2. The Structure of the Comité Cívico Social

residents in El Valle compared to the capital city place them as a low political priority; its rural location on the other side of the hills may provoke a feeling of out of sight, out of mind for politicians. In addition, as highlighted in chapter 4, El Valle has a lower crime level than the city. From a political standpoint, the resettlements appear to need less support than the Tegucigalpa metro area. Residents shared with me that the only time politicians visit or support the needs of a community is right before an election.

The organizations also negotiated the political landscape in a similar fashion. Both La Iglesia and La Internacional recognized that favoritism and nepotism dominated Honduran politics. La Iglesia dealt with this by asking important and well-known socialites and professionals on both the political left and the right to sit on the board of directors. This ensured that the Suyapa resettlement would be relatively protected from shifts in national governance. Similarly, La Internacional also cultivated political allies in the National and Liberal parties. Its international reputation also provided it with a high level of respect and influence on multiple layers of government.

LA IGLESIA

La Iglesia was originally founded not for social purposes, but rather as an organization to build a national monument. In 1997, in preparation for the Roman Catholic–proclaimed Year of Jubilee, 2000, a high-ranking Catholic clergy member wanted to create a monument for the country that would represent faith, love, and family unity. He brought together key elite Hondurans to raise money and build a thirty-meter statue. To legitimate the process and fund-raising, this group created an organization called La Iglesia. In January of 1998, seven months after initial construction, the monument was inaugurated and continues to be a major landmark and tourist attraction standing above the city of Tegucigalpa.

Nine months later, Hurricane Mitch devastated the country, particularly Tegucigalpa. Recognizing the need, La Iglesia's board of directors decided to build a resettlement for survivors. The mission was to "return to the most vulnerable [survivors] the possibility of recovering their normal life, as well as transform them using a holistic vision, oriented toward strengthening education and evangelism with the end result of generating a new type of citizen with a sensitivity to solidarity and community well-being" (La Iglesia and CESAL 2004, 1). Within a month of the disaster, the organization was already fund-raising for, designing, and planning the resettlement. The organization was supported initially by national and international donations, most often through other Catholic churches and dioceses in the global north. However, once Suyapa was built, the organization would be supported through Suyapa mortgage payments to cover repairs and maintenance, further community growth, and a small support staff (director, engineer, social worker, accountant, and secretary). Since the houses were built not by future residents but by different construction companies, Suyapa had the first 300 houses up within twenty-one months (July 2000) of the disaster, and all 583 homes completed four and a half years after Mitch, in March of 2003. La Iglesia was also able to move residents in by 2001, three years before the Pino Alto residents settled in their homes.

To understand the role of La Iglesia in the development of Suyapa as a resettlement qua community, four aspects of the organization and its influence must be understood. By painting a broad landscape of organization intervention and engagement, how the actions taken by La Iglesia enabled Suyapa to develop from a resettlement into a community comes into relief.

LA IGLESIA COMMUNITY DEVELOPMENT
PHILOSOPHY AND PRACTICE

Doña Rosa is a powerful elderly woman who can shift from a stern look to a broad smile almost instantaneously. She is tenacious and passionate, especially about the well-being of Suyapa. An original member of La Iglesia, her background as a social worker and her desire to help the survivors of Mitch nudged the organization in the direction of community building, raising her status to vice president of La Iglesia, subordinate only to the symbolic president. Doña Rosa was the key figure in designing the selection process. She waded through thousands of applications to select the first few hundred families. She gave capacity-building classes before residents moved into the resettlement, found social workers to assist the resettlement, and played a pivotal role in shaping the social design of Suyapa. To understand La Iglesia's role in Suyapa necessitates understanding Doña Rosa.

Her reputation preceded my first of many interviews with her—I was told she is direct, has high expectations of others, and is *the* person to speak to about the development of Suyapa, at least from La Iglesia's perspective. If she approved of my work, I would be granted access to anything La Iglesia had—documents, resources, and contacts, including a potential interview with the high-ranking clergy. If she disapproved, I would need to find another resettlement.

Doña Rosa lived up to her reputation. Arriving at an upscale home in Tegucigalpa, I was greeted by the executive director of La Iglesia and brought into a comfortable living room with pictures of family and a small coffee table with petite dessert snacks. Although she is small in stature and was laid up on the couch with a broken leg, her presence was overwhelming. After a short, cordial introduction and a gift of fancy chocolates from the United States, I began my interview. I was quickly interrupted. "Tell me again what you are studying and how this will be of benefit to La Iglesia and Suyapa," she demanded, in excellent English. Surprised and humbled, I quickly reiterated the goals of my research and the importance of Suyapa as a case study. Only after a few more critical and probing questions was she satisfied, and she opened up to the interview process. Although I was able to ask the questions I needed about La Iglesia and development of Suyapa, I knew who was in charge and who needed to be grateful for this opportunity.

Indeed, I believe my interaction with Doña Rosa is a suitable starting point to describe the philosophy of La Iglesia and its relationship to Suyapa. As is often found in development work, the difference between development provider and development recipient is highly discernible. Doña Rosa did not need me; I needed her—and the situation was evident to both parties. Similarly, La Iglesia did not need Suyapa, but the residents needed La Iglesia. The negotiation of this unequal power relationship over decision-making, control of resources, vision, and so forth, was often highly contentious and led to conflict between the organization and residents.

The line espoused by Doña Rosa and other La Iglesia staff is that Suyapa was created to be a self-governed and sustainable model community. More specifically, the objective of La Iglesia in founding Suyapa was "to create a project in support of and to accompany families and communities in their process of adaptation, social organization, and capacity for self-governance" (La Iglesia and CESAL 2004, 14). Unlike other projects, which focused almost solely on material recovery, such as housing, infrastructure, and employment, La Iglesia saw its role as transforming residents' understanding of self and community and building the resettlement into a model community.

Transformation is never a short-term project. La Iglesia planned on maintaining an office and a significant presence within the resettlement for fifteen years. The assumption is that it would take this amount of time for a group of strangers to develop the capacity and skills necessary to run the resettlement on its own, and to develop into a community. Although La Iglesia's long-term presence generated some problems that will be discussed below, it also offered a stability that many residents wanted and needed, especially in the early years.

SUSTAIN, ACCOMPANY, GUIDE, EMPOWER DEVELOPMENT MODEL

La Iglesia developed its own resettlement development model, a hybrid of technical assistance and self-help, introduced in chapter 3 as SAGE—sustain, accompany, guide and empower. *Sustain*, as described in chapter 3, is the most commonly recognized type of development—the provision of resources. So far, this chapter has discussed a few of the many ways in which the organization sustained Suyapa, such as providing houses and infrastructure, leadership, and support for livelihood development. The following paragraphs will describe some of the strategies La Iglesia implemented to accompany, guide, and empower Suyapa residents.

ACCOMPANY

A major difference between La Iglesia and the other sponsoring NGOs was the commitment to accompany the resettlement for fifteen years. The importance of this assurance cannot be overstated. First, this pledge sustained the infrastructure development process. In other resettlements, for example, residents had little engineering support to fix a defunct well pump or connect the sewer to individual houses. They were also left on their own to fight with government bureaucracies to pave a road or find NGO sponsorship to build a computer center for the youth. La Iglesia worked hand in hand with Suyapa to address these and many other issues. In 2015, for example, La Iglesia found an international donor to pay for a new piping system to bring water from a river five kilometers away. Suyapa residents matched the funds with sweat equity, digging a ditch the entire length of the pipeline.

Second, unlike other NGOs, La Iglesia also intervened in resettlement social affairs over time. The organizational influence was necessarily heavier in the beginning, as residents required extra support to develop resettlement cohesion, collective efficacy, social capital, and a new culture. However, residents recognized that if problems were to arise, they could count on La Iglesia to help find residents social service resources, negotiate neighborly conflicts, and protect against gangs. As will be described in chapter 7, the lack of consistent support in other resettlements may have led to larger social problems, political nepotism, and infighting, leading to lower social health outcomes.

Third, as demonstrated by Pino Alto in chapter 6, a changing NGO withdrawal timeline leads to distrust of the organization and broader social anxiety. La Internacional employees shared with me how some residents came to regard the organization as untrustworthy, since the organization expressed to residents that it would leave on a particular date yet continued to stay. Some residents became even more dependent on the NGO, believing that if they continued to request help, the organization would continue to stay despite promises to leave. This was not the case with Suyapa.

Finally, drawing on survey results, more than half of the residents in all resettlements wanted the sponsoring organization to have played a greater role in community affairs.[2] While some organizations left within months or a few years, La Iglesia was the only organization to accompany a resettlement for more than ten years. As further explained in chapter 7, long-term accompaniment also enabled La Iglesia to reinforce a particular culture in Suyapa that, once ingrained among residents, became self-reinforcing.

GUIDE

Chapter 2 laid out the social disarticulation and trauma of Hurricane Mitch survivors and future resettlement residents. It can be argued that due to these challenges, many survivors may have had a diminished capacity to engage in the development project of transforming a resettlement of strangers into a community of neighbors. La Iglesia recognized this characteristic among residents and took proactive steps to guide the resettlement process early on, relinquishing decision-making over time as residents became politically and socially empowered. Although the organization intervened in many ways, three prominent efforts will be discussed here: resident selection, governance, and social control.

RESIDENT SELECTION AND TRAINING   In all cases, resettlement required acceptance by the resident and the organization. On the one hand, survivors had many motivations for choosing one resettlement over another. Interviews with residents from all seven resettlements demonstrate that families prioritized different values in deciding on a resettlement. Some looked to keep extended family together and so chose the same resettlement as their relatives. Others wanted to move out of the *macro-albergues* as quickly as possible, choosing the first available home. Some families decided to work a certain number of weeks on the project rather than pay a long-term mortgage. Still others desired to be in a resettlement where their faith was of central importance.

On the other hand, each NGO created its own criteria and selection process for future residents. Some organizations selected families based on need, such as choosing to bring in single mothers with children. Others drew upon recommendations from partner organizations or churches. Lastly, most had an application process, trying to find survivors who were in need and would be a good fit for the future resettlement.

La Iglesia had one of the most stringent application processes, looking for heads of households who were dependable, who were willing to pay a fifteen-year mortgage to finance their home, who wanted to be civically engaged, and—at least in the initial years—who were willing to live by Catholic values. A second set of standards was also investigated in order to avoid what were seen as potentially problematic residents, such as those with gang affiliations or criminal records,[3] those who were unwilling to pay a mortgage, or those who would cause social disruptions in the resettlement. The section below describes La Iglesia's selection process and how it likely influenced the type of residents who ended up relocating to Suyapa.

First, La Iglesia targeted networks in affected Catholic parishes first, before looking for residents in *macro-albergues*. This method provided a possible difference between residents. Both *macro-albergues* and churches would take anyone who was in need, but it is likely that those who attended a particular church would go there for help.[4] Since the Church has prestige and some influence over its members, certain groups, such as gang members, would actively avoid churches for assistance and find help where they had more autonomy (Wolseth 2008). As the churches already had embedded social capital due to shared beliefs, drawing future residents from these groups may have increased the initial level of trust and connection among residents.

Second, La Iglesia wanted to prepare the first two hundred families before they arrived in the resettlement in order to instill particular expectations, beliefs, and a collective vision. Every Friday from five-thirty to nine p.m., La Iglesia held classes taught by Catholic clergy, social workers, or respected members of the future resettlement. Topics ranged from basic logistical information concerning mortgage payments and the design of the resettlement to more interpretive matters, such as how to live as neighbors. These classes were held throughout the city in different parish centers, totaling twenty-four capacity-building classes. Not attending more than a few classes would forfeit the chance of obtaining a home.

The capacity building of the first two hundred families also shaped the community development process and future trajectory. La Iglesia did not know how much money it would receive to build the new resettlement. Money that had been promised did not always materialize, and fund-raising was difficult for a Honduran organization without many international ties. Neverthe-less, Doña Rosa advocated for excellent training of the first families, believing they would be the initial resettlement leaders and would set high standards for future residents. These meetings were a nexus for social interaction and relationship building. Survivors were no longer swimming in a sea of the un-known; they had begun to form relationships with other survivors and future neighbors. The social aspect of the resettlement was being built, and La Iglesia was encouraging each new resident to take responsibility in creating a model community. This process also impacted the creation and conciliation of re-settlement culture, as explained in chapter 7.

Third, during the capacity-building practicum, prospective residents were vetted through a strict selection and application process. Doña Rosa, work-ing closely with numerous other organizations and La Iglesia board mem-bers, created a formal selection process for potential candidates. Once the applicants had been vetted and the list narrowed, La Iglesia had prospective residents fill out a six-page application form detailing family demographics, employment and housing history, and corresponding aptitudes for living in community—such as having volunteered in a neighborhood organization, worked in the Church or a cooperative, or been involved in sports or poli-tics, as well as other manual or professional skills the candidate maintained. There was also a particular religious bent to the applications. One of the nine sections of the questionnaire, entitled "Religion," solicited responses to three questions: "What is your religion?"; "How are we able to know that you are Catholic?"; and "Parish Name." The questionnaire ended by asking the resi-dent for three references and a description of why he or she wanted to live in the new resettlement. Once complete, the applications were followed up on by social workers who checked the backgrounds of residents and their children and reviewed the veracity of the application, for example, whether family members owned another home or had criminal records or gang af-filiations.[5] After the pool of applicants was distilled based on the criteria above, each head of household was interviewed by a social worker, with the interviewer's impressions subsequently noted in the application. Thousands of applications were sorted through to draft the right candidates for Suyapa (CESAL 2008, 64).

Albeit rigorous, the selection was far from perfect. La Iglesia unknowingly selected a family that sold various illegal drugs in Suyapa. They also selected a few residents with serious mental illnesses who subsequently caused problems in the resettlement, residents who were anti-Catholic and anti–La Iglesia, resi-dents who quickly rented out their home to others and moved away, residents who did not pay the mortgage, and residents who were incapable of making payments due to a disability. Selecting residents is not as straightforward as it may seem and, in a resettlement as large as 583 families, a statistical likelihood of some deviant residents cannot be avoided.

GOVERNANCE   The traditional Honduran *patronato* system has been criticized by many for being undemocratic and nepotistic. It also gave resident leaders nearly total legal power in running the resettlement. La Iglesia, concerned that handing over total control initially would not be in the best interest of all resettlement residents, especially the most vulnerable, designed and implemented a new political structure called the CCS, or Social Civic Committee. Impossible in a *patronato*, the Catholic Church and La Iglesia together were provided with half the official decision-making power (four of eight votes) within the resettlement.

In many ways, this move from the common *patronato* system to the CCS had major repercussions for the type of presence La Iglesia maintained within the resettlement. Not only were residents moving into an entirely new resettlement with new neighbors, new rules, and new expectations, they also had an entirely new form of governance. The change from traditional authority based on patronage to one of rational-legal authority (Weber 1968) afforded La Iglesia considerable influence over the resettlement, enabling it to shape the collective vision, protect the resettlement from political gridlock, address large social problems with residents, and find funding for resettlement projects. The goal always, however, was that residents would take on more and more responsibility and leadership over time. It was also the hope of the organization that the new CCS could avoid the nepotism common in *patronato* systems by having residents vote for each individual candidate, rather than voting for a winner-take-all slate of candidates.

La Iglesia held power politically (one-quarter of the CCS) and financially (via mortgages) and wielded this power in formal and informal ways to ensure that Suyapa followed a particular path. The organization believed that residents were initially vulnerable—because of their survivor status, trauma, poverty, and previous experience of "community" in Tegucigalpa—and needed support in overcoming these challenges. Doña Rosa used the metaphor of a parent caring for her child to define the NGO-resettlement relationship: "The parent had to raise the child, teach the child right, accept the pushback of the child, and eventually let the child go." It was the role of the organization to use its influence (formal and informal means of social control) to develop residents' capability to become a well-run and independent community based on Catholic values. Suyapa residents had to be encouraged (and in some cases taught how) to live in community—leaving it to residents would, in the minds of La Iglesia, lead to a relapse to previous values and norms held in Tegucigalpa—a state of poverty, violence, distrust, lack of civic participation, and crime. The organization expected that if a clear vision and healthy culture could be created in the first few years, it would be able to leave Suyapa to continue independently.

To encourage residents to develop their own social norms, La Iglesia and CCS initiated the development of a "Manual of Conduct and Community Coexistence." The four-page document, developed by the first two hundred families and approved by La Iglesia, had to be signed by each head of household. In brief, the manual spells out twenty community-specific rules. Below are some of the most striking:

2. The Comité Cívico Social has the ability to evict residents for very grave infractions. The determination of these infractions will be decided upon by the *comité*.

3. There is no selling of alcohol or informal business practices in Suyapa.

11. A person may lose their home for continued bad behavior, including physical or verbal abuse toward family members, neighbors, or project authorities.

13. The head of household is responsible for all people within his or her household.

15. It is strictly prohibited to gamble using cards, dice, roosters, or anything else (2002).

When I asked Doña Xela, one of the original residents and recent secretary for the CCS, about whether there was any pushback from residents, she noted that some residents believed they should be able to do whatever they wanted to their home, such as kick the door and break it in anger. Despite this concern, the rules were accepted unanimously by the first two hundred families.

While these appear to be fair rules for a model community, some members believed they undermined the autonomy of Suyapa members. After all, it was La Iglesia, not residents, who could enforce the toughest sanctions, such as legally taking away a home. Later residents had to agree to these rules to obtain a home in the resettlement, but they had no voice in their development and no way to change, adjust, or eliminate the rules other than to object through formal channels. Moreover, La Iglesia has acted on this code of conduct unilaterally by evicting more than ten families for both behavior and large mortgage debt. In these evictions, residents are reminded of the expected conduct in Suyapa.

SOCIAL CONTROL   Residents know the rules and live by them. La Iglesia was considered *estricto* (strict or inflexible) by residents due in part to its removing residents from Suyapa. Each removal was justified by law (multiple years of no mortgage payments) and the code of conduct; one person was re-moved for selling drugs in Suyapa, others for domestic violence, and others for not paying their mortgage and inciting others to not pay their mortgage. The remainder were asked to leave because they had income but were unwill-ing to pay their mortgage.

Don Paolo was also punished by La Iglesia for his behavior. In his late fifties, Don Paolo appears to be much older due to his dark-brown, wizened skin, weather-beaten and damaged by the sun. He and his family were one of the first two hundred families to move into Suyapa, and he has worked for La Iglesia intermittently through the years, doing various jobs, mostly in construction. In 2008, Don Paolo's wife accused him of physical abuse. Although he denies the charges, the assault claim went to court and he was convicted of domestic violence. He was required to pay his spouse a monthly stipend as mandated by the court, but La Iglesia went a step further and told him that he could no longer live in his home, though his wife and children could stay.

For La Iglesia, mortgages were a means of keeping residents in line. In con-trast to other resettlements whose residents provided "sweat equity" for their home by putting in months of labor, Suyapa households are required to pay 750 lempiras (~$45; 16.5 lempiras to the US dollar in 2002) every month for fifteen years (with an annual increase of 8 percent to account for inflation). From the standpoint of La Iglesia, paying a mortgage had three intrinsic bene-fits: resident stability, social control, and a revenue stream to fund future de-velopment projects.[6] The NGO was convinced that the process of buying a home, not just outright home ownership, would promote greater residential stability[7] and give residents a larger stake in their community over the long term. Suyapa has seen a much smaller turnover of residents compared to other resettlements. Monthly house payments also force residents to find ways of making a living in order to keep their home.

In addition, La Iglesia used mortgage payments to remove residents legally. The broken Honduran criminal justice system made the removal of anyone very difficult. However, if the organization could prove that someone was not paying his or her mortgage, it streamlined the legal process. It turns out that drug dealers often do not pay their mortgages; this became the leverage for removing criminals from Suyapa. Although it happened rarely—only ten of the sixty families that left the project were forced to leave—it did set the clear standard that residents were to comply with the rules that La Iglesia had estab-lished or risk losing their home. Smesler's (1998) description of ambivalence captures how the residents felt: they loved what La Iglesia had done for them but did not always appreciate the social control it exerted over their lives.

Other rules are also selectively enforced. Ernesto, who worked six days a

Table 5.4. Mortgages

Initial mortgage payment per month in 2002 *slightly more for two-bedroom homes	750 lempiras ($45)
Yearly mortgage interest increase per year (matches average inflation)	8 percent
Mortgage length	15 years
Percentage of homes paid off in 2010	0 percent, 4 percent debt forgiven[+]
Percentage of homes behind on the mortgage— 0–3 months (2010)	72 percent
Percentage of homes behind on the mortgage— 4 or more months (2010)	28 percent

(Statistics gathered from internal La Iglesia documents)
[+] The La Iglesia president forgave the debt of a handful of families whose head of household could not work due to a disability or illness.

week in Suyapa as a guard, explained to me in 2010, "There *is* a cantina in town [Suyapa]. It is a secret. But if you like, I will get you some *aguardiente* [hard alcohol]." While Ernesto was willing to get the alcohol for me, he hesitated to take me to the home for fear that La Iglesia might find out and the residents would lose their house.

Another example of the social control strategies implemented by La Iglesia is the decision-making process about how development funds (financed by resident mortgage payments) and land are to be used. These two items were under the control not of the Comité Cívico Social or residents but of La Iglesia's board of directors. The board chooses how to spend the money without direct community input, leaving residents wondering where exactly all their payments are going. This lack of transparency also causes frustration concerning the acres of green space that are part of the resettlement but left unused. One three-acre parcel in particular was originally designated for more housing but remained vacant for eight years. Many residents have the same feelings as Don Paolo: "They should just give us the land." La Iglesia responds in kind. When I asked the director about it, she explained that the organization was willing to give the land to the people if they were willing to do something useful with it. According to her, they had yet to come up with a viable proposal, so in 2009 the land was put up for sale.

Finally, La Iglesia interceded in the affairs of the resettlement, usually for the benefit of the resettlement, on nearly a daily basis from 2002 until 2015, when the NGO departed.[8] During the work week, the organization had between four and six employees working in the office, a hundred meters from the central park. The employees—a project director, a secretary, an accountant, an engineer, and two social workers—were constantly working on projects for the resettlement. The accountant interacted with each head of household on a monthly basis as they came to the office to pay their mortgage, and the engineer was constantly running throughout the resettlement in his Toyota 4Runner directing the repair of a water pipe here, building a new fence there, or designing a new soccer field for the high school on the other side of town. Belkis and Luis, the social workers, not only acted as intermediaries between La Iglesia and residents, but also solved problems (such as arguments between neighbors, fighting adolescents, or political rivalries), initiated new capacity-building classes, and encouraged civic participation. In addition to the full-time staff, La Iglesia brought in a number of specialists to encourage startups of microenterprises over the years. From tortilla-making to sewing to welding to growing and selling *pastes* (loofah-like sponges), the NGO has worked closely with other organizations to bring in economic opportunities for residents. In sum, La Iglesia guided the resettlement development through the selection of and interactions with residents. This is an important step in the formation and conciliation of resettlement culture over time.

EMPOWERMENT OF RESIDENTS

The empowerment of residents can be seen in three areas of La Iglesia's guidance strategy—the encouragement of social interaction among residents, the transition of decision-making power, and the challenges that were borne in the process. Although the process was difficult, the data underscores the great success residents have had in creating a socially healthy resettlement with a clear and resilient path for the future.

SOCIAL INTERACTION   On any given Suyapa evening, as long as it is not raining, no less than a hundred adult residents are out and about the resettlement visiting friends; attending church, civic, or sports meetings; buying ingredients from the local *pulpería*; or just taking a walk after the temperature has cooled. Children and adolescents chase one another through the streets, run errands for parents, or play in one of at least six small-sided soccer games that are going on under the streetlamps. The type of semidense housing and isolation designed by La Iglesia creates a social environment where it is almost impossible to not socially interact. For most residents, it is difficult to move from one's house to the store, the soccer field, or the church without running into an acquaintance or friend and having a brief conversation. The resettlement also boasts dozens of clubs, organizations, sports teams, Bible studies, self-help groups such as Alcoholics Anonymous, and three churches. Many of these groups are sponsored in part by La Iglesia, with mortgage payments directed back into resettlement social activities. Besides groups, festival parades and holiday events were also financially supported by the organization. Each of the nine sectors hold meetings to discuss issues in its area, and each has a political representative that would meet with the CCS by request.

Other collaborations strengthened the resettlement as well. As previously described, Suyapa infrastructure projects, such as laying pavers down the main road to decrease dirt and dust, building the central park, and digging the five-kilometer pipeline, were funded by La Iglesia but built by residents. These and many other partnerships encouraged residents to work together on projects as well.

According to Javier, a Suyapa resident since 2001, it took nearly two and a half years for the construction and posting of the police station, which was completed in March 2002. Before then, in order to maintain the social order that was developing within the resettlement and prevent crime, Suyapa residents were proactive in its self-defense. Due to the initial influx of new residents, no one was sure who belonged and who did not, and theft from homes became a major problem. Residents then came together, under the leadership of the CCS, to create a neighborhood-watch group to patrol at night. About once a month, each household would take a turn providing a man or woman who would stay up all night walking the resettlement armed with a whistle. If the volunteer watchperson saw a problem, she would whistle, and all neighbors would come out of their houses armed with machetes, sticks, farm tools, or other weapons they might have. Also, each sector raised funds to put up a chain across peripheral roads. This was done to prevent a car from pulling up in front of a home and loading up with stolen goods. The system was highly successful at decreasing crime, and residents continue to speak about the experience with a sense of pride.

Once the police station was built, a second vote was taken to implement a resettlement-wide curfew at ten p.m. After ten p.m., the police would stop and question anyone out wandering in the resettlement. If you had a good reason, you were led home. If you did not, you were either told to leave or put behind bars until morning. Residents had democratically mandated that those particular social control mechanisms were in the best interest of the resettlement, and all residents submitted to the regulations and social practices (discussed in chapter 7).

TRANSITION OF DECISION-MAKING   La Iglesia recognized the vulnerability of survivors arriving in the new resettlement; most struggled to put food on the table and did not have the time, energy, or resources to create community. It was the job of the organization, then, to provide sustainment and guidance early on, slowly handing over responsibility as time progressed. Doña Rosa expressed this timeline as a fifteen-year process, demonstrated in figure 5.3. La Iglesia hoped to provide technical assistance in the first years of the resettlement, when residents were most vulnerable. As residents settled

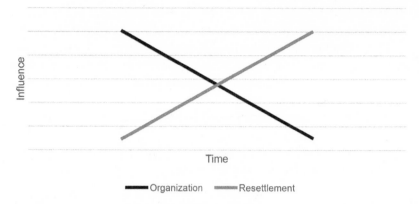

FIGURE 5.3. Influence in Resettlement Affairs over Time

into their life in the new location and gained further capacities and resources to lead, they would take over increasing decision-making power. This would both protect the neophyte resettlement from external and internal threats and empower residents to create a community independent of the NGO.

CHALLENGES WITH A SAGE MODEL

No development strategy or process is without problems. In particular, the relationship and role of a sponsoring organization and the people being served can be quite contentious. To investigate the drawbacks of the different community development strategies comparatively, the survey asked three questions: "Do residents want the NGO to have less, equal, or more influence?"; "Have residents had problems with the organization?"; and "Are residents concerned the NGO can take their home?" The results are instructive.

More Suyapa residents wish that La Iglesia had less influence within the resettlement than the average of the six other resettlements. This sentiment is supported by many informal conversations I had with members, who feel La Iglesia has interfered unnecessarily in resettlement affairs or overstayed its welcome and should move on. However, almost half of all residents wished the organization had greater influence in resettlement affairs, illustrating just how important social intervention in resettlement affairs is.

Similarly, a greater number of Suyapa residents (9 percent) have had problems with La Iglesia than in Pino Alto (2 percent) and the average of resettlements (4 percent). While this could happen for any number of reasons, the most common explanation I heard from members involved having to pay the mortgage when they had no money, the lack of transparency by the organization in its financial accounting, and the poor treatment of some residents by La

Iglesia, especially those who have been evicted. Though the SAGE approach did frustrate some residents, more than 90 percent of residents had no issue with the organization.

Finally, La Iglesia's social intervention in shaping resident behavior had a strong impact on Suyapa residents. When asked, "Are you concerned that the organization can take away your home for your poor behavior in the community?" almost three-quarters (72 percent) of the community responded in the affirmative, in contrast to 60 percent of Pino Alto residents and just over half (51 percent) of other residents in the average of resettlements. These results show that the minimal enforcement of the social contract (removing 10 of a total of 583 families for behavior and debt) significantly reinforced Suyapa social norms. As discussed in chapter 7, encouraging a common vision and discussing a set of values and behaviors were not enough to guarantee buy-in by residents. In the case of Suyapa, the additional application of penalties ensured greater commitment to the accepted code of conduct.

According to Doña Rosa, La Iglesia's approach should not be confused with being patronizing. La Iglesia staff tried to nurture the social health of the resettlement through intervention without an air of superiority. Yet a few board members and NGO staff held a belief that they were "better" (e.g., more cultured, more educated, wealthier) than the residents, and that residents needed to change (*mejorar*). As will be discussed, there has been an underlying internal tension in the organization about whether the resettlement received "toda en la boca" (everything provided for them) and La Iglesia should end its involvement, as opposed to continuing to support the social and economic development of the resettlement and maintaining its influence.

In sum, La Iglesia implemented a SAGE approach in Suyapa, sustaining, accompanying, and guiding resettlement affairs initially but slowly relinquishing control and empowering residents to take on increasing leadership roles

Table 5.5. Opinions about the NGO

Do you wish the NGO, in the last few years, had:

	Left as soon as possible	Had less influence	Had the same influence	Had greater influence
Suyapa	7 percent	13 percent**	34 percent	46 percent**
Pino Alto	7 percent	5 percent	29 percent	60 percent
Avg. of five resettlements	7 percent	4 percent	33 percent	56 percent

Z-test significance: **.01 (Avg. is the comparison group).

over time. The organization interceded in the political, social, and economic aspects of Suyapa's development until 2012, when formal ties were cut. For La Iglesia, intervention and technical assistance were viewed as necessary to support the vulnerable population and laid the foundation for residents to take on self-help development. From the residents' perspective, Suyapa did need La Iglesia's help, but the support came with high expectations and clear rules.

More objectively, La Iglesia's SAGE approach is likely one of the most significant factors in the long-term social health of Suyapa. By creating clear social norms and a collective vision subscribed to by residents, a new resettlement culture became ingrained. With sustained resources, the development of a healthy culture, and La Iglesia staff's consistent encouragement for residents to take on increasing responsibility, the resettlement had the foundation and momentum to develop in a positive direction.

CONFLICT

Approximately sixty families (about 10 percent) have left the Suyapa project since its inception in 2002. Most of these families, according to a top-level La Iglesia employee, Myra, left of their own volition. Some left for family reasons, some because they were far behind on their mortgage, and others for reasons that remain unknown. La Iglesia bought homes for and moved five families to other resettlements in El Valle on request of the president, as they were in particular need and could not work to pay their mortgage due to disabilities or long-term illnesses.

Ten families (less than 2 percent) were forced out of the resettlement by La Iglesia. There were several reasons for this. In all of the cases, the family had defaulted on their mortgage for years. Belkis, a La Iglesia social worker, explained:

> La Iglesia had realized that it was losing money on Suyapa and that the project was not self-sustaining in part because a number of community members were not paying their rent or their water bill. Because it was in the red, two things happened. First, La Iglesia created a list of people who had defaulted on their mortgage and then selected out those who could not pay due to their post-Mitch experiences. They sent letters to those who had defaulted on their payment but who they knew could pay but did not want to.[9] La Iglesia told the people that they had signed an agreement in which they promised to pay their mortgage.

As noted above, mortgage default was used as a social control mechanism to remove problematic residents. Residents observed that getting out of line could lead to losing one's home. What surprised La Iglesia was the pushback it received for removing residents.

A movement led by a charismatic Suyapa resident claimed that because the houses were donated using international aid, residents should not have to pay for them. As part of their critique, movement members claimed that the Comité Cívico Social was only a puppet for La Iglesia and that Suyapa would do better to return to a *patronato*—a *patronato* that could eliminate the payment of mortgages altogether. In protest, a number of families marched through the resettlement and shut down the major highway between Tegucigalpa and San Pedro Sula, even surrounding the church so that the priest (as a representative of the Catholic organization) could not leave his residence. After a long legal dispute, the courts ruled in favor of La Iglesia, and the tenants who had stopped paying their mortgage and were causing a great deal of division in the resettlement were evicted in 2006 (*El Heraldo* 2006).

Still, the conflict continued. Drawing on post-Mitch sympathies for survivors, the families slandered the reputation of La Iglesia, claiming that they were kicked out for political reasons rather than for not paying their mortgage.[10] Residents who remained pointed to this experience to exemplify La Iglesia's mismanagement of the resettlement and as a touchstone for a multitude of other complaints.

Suyapa was not the only resettlement impacted by mortgage default issues. About the same time, five miles south lay La Tierra, another post-Mitch resettlement built by a Catholic organization. In many ways similar to La Iglesia, this organization likewise paid close attention to the social, political, and spiritual development of the resettlement's five hundred families. Much of the responsibility for addressing conflict lay with the priest, who lived in the resettlement as well, and worked out any issues with resettlement leaders.

La Tierra residents shared the same frustration those in Suyapa had with paying mortgages. Why should they have to pay when other resettlement residents in El Valle do not? In anger at the organization for not responding to their requests for an elimination of resident debts, La Tierra families surrounded the priest's home to prevent him from leaving for multiple days. Terrified for his safety, the priest left, never to return, and the organization turned homes over to the *patronato*, washing their hands of the project.

In the case of Suyapa, the vast majority of residents want to pay their mortgage. Yet in Honduras, a crippled economy, political nepotism, a large unskilled labor pool, and a small labor market inevitably produce unemployment. Two large textile plants closed in 2008, laying off hundreds of El Valle workers (including many from Suyapa and Pino Alto). Residents often cannot pay, not because they do not want to, but because there is no work available. The entrepreneurial spirit is strong within all of the resettlements I studied. Suyapa boasted a successful tortilla-making business, two large ponds where half a dozen men diverted river water to grow tilapia, a small organic farm, an internet café, and a thriving central market. But the need far outweighs the opportunities.

As one La Iglesia employee noted, the organization finds itself between heaven and earth, between God's compassion for human frailty and the necessity of holding people responsible for their commitments, such as paying their mortgages. La Iglesia recognized the difficulty of finding work, and understood, based on daily interactions with residents, which families were really trying hard to succeed and which were free riders. So how does an NGO maintain its obligation to treat people fairly (sustainment, accompaniment, and guidance) while encouraging all residents to take responsibility for their lives (empowerment)? Belkis, a La Iglesia social worker, explained how La Iglesia must put on two faces: "We are both God and the Devil. We want to promote God's love and compassion but we are also the ones pushing people to pay even when it is very difficult for them to pay." Indeed, La Iglesia's strategy and Doña Rosa's parent-child analogy fits this model of God and the Devil. The organization insists it must provide support and at the same time maintain accountability in order to develop the resettlement into a socially healthy model community.

FINDING BALANCE

The great risk of too much developmental technical assistance and social intervention is creating dependency and subsequently disempowering residents. The risk of too much self-help in resettlements is that vulnerable residents may not have the assets, skills, or resources necessary to invest in the difficult development of a community. While not perfect, La Iglesia offers one example of how the implementation of a SAGE model can provide the technical assistance necessary to create a foundation for a resettlement self-help development. Suyapa's path was far from linear; it has been closer to "three steps forward, two steps back." The dialectical relationship between La Iglesia and Suyapa residents showcases the nuances and idiosyncrasies of resettlement development as well as its patterns and processes. It also highlights the great risk of the SAGE model—conflict between resettlement residents and the sponsoring NGO. La Iglesia, through its SAGE strategy, walked a fine line between guiding resident norm formation and disempowering residents in the process. The following chapter examines a second post-Mitch resettlement, Pino Alto (built less than four kilometers from Suyapa), to compare and contrast the development processes that led both locales to such divergent outcomes.

CHAPTER 6

PINO ALTO

POEMA A PINO ALTO

Por El Barrio
Somos Naciones Unidas.
Pino Alto, nueva ideal
La mirada en el futuro
Ha empezado su gestar.
Pino Alto
Hace que el hombre
Se sienta en libertad.
Construyendo en todo el orbe
Una gran fraternidad.
Del amor la ley triunfante.
Lazos de odio romperá.
El esfuerzo y sacrificio
Que La Internacional nos brindo
Y nos brindará.
Al hacer juntos Pino Alto
La vida nos cambio
Sublimando al hombre
Difundiendo amistad.
Con fé humana y esperanza
Pino Alto hará la
Hermandad y prosperidad.

A POEM TO PINO ALTO

To the Barrio
We are the United Nations.
Pino Alto, new ideal

Looking into the future
You have begun your quest.
Pino Alto
You make the person
Feel freedom.
Building around the world
A great fraternity.
The law of love triumphant.
Links of hate will be broken.
The effort and sacrifice
that La Internacional offered us
And may offer us.
To work together Pino Alto
Life changes us
Refining the person
Spreading friendship.
With human faith and hope
Pino Alto will create
Brotherhood and prosperity.
LA INTERNACIONAL (2007)

The half-paved, half-dirt road winds its way up a mountain of pine and shrub. Cornfields and spotted cattle dot the landscape. The road gets worse, then better, then worse again. At one point around a bend, the street drops fifteen meters to cross a creek and rises another thirty meters before maintaining a less acute angle. Near the creek, brightly colored clothes are hung to dry on the fence posts and barbed wire in front of adobe homes. The ride is longer than to Suyapa, as Pino Alto is higher in the hills, with a steeper climb and more turns. The feel is also more rural. Ascending the hillside through the pine forest, one can no longer see the major highway that cuts through the valley or hear the mechanical sounds of cars or factories. All is quiet except for the rustling of leaves. If one is standing at the top of the western slope, Pino Alto's vista is spectacular, affording a panorama of the valley, where the mountains slide gradually into the valley floor.

Arriving in Pino Alto, one notices that although there are 1,250 homes, the environment feels spacious and light. The resettlement was built in a large basin on the edge of the mountains. At the bottom of the basin are the main offices, the soccer fields, and the central park. The houses are built outward and up the hills in all directions. There are broad sidewalks between the rows of homes that are intentionally too narrow for cars. Each home has a small front and backyard, enabling residents to plant fruit trees or flowers or to personalize the space to their liking. Pine trees line the hills surrounding the resettlement, interspersed with tall grass and the occasional scrub brush. The air is pure, and on the outskirts of town the wind is refreshing.

This chapter will provide a rich description of Pino Alto and La Internacional, as well as the interface between them. To begin, I will describe the important material characteristics of Pino Alto, including its land use, infrastructure, and design. Then the human aspects of the resettlement will be covered—the livelihoods, residents, leadership, religion and religiosity, and social interactions that take place within Pino Alto. The third section will sketch Pino Alto's historical roots and mission and the role La Internacional played in the development of the resettlement. La Internacional's development strategy, a partnership approach, will be introduced, along with ways that the practice of partnership may have had unintended consequences for the organization and residents. The section will conclude with the departure of La Internacional and its continued influence on Pino Alto.

RESETTLEMENT LAND USE AND INFRASTRUCTURE

The six-kilometer distance between the main highway and Pino Alto generally takes between fifteen and twenty minutes by bus depending on the motivation of the driver. The center of Pino Alto is the last stop (#5); as the bus enters, a cloud of dust arises from the town's dirt roads. Doctor Berto, a Cuban who worked for three years in Pino Alto and six months in Suyapa, found that the greatest problem in both towns, but especially Pino Alto, was the dust. The dirt in Pino Alto is fine, and the town has no paved streets. Dust is kicked up from bus traffic, from the wind, and even from cattle grazing on the weeds of the soccer field. Berto found that respiratory problems were the most serious physical hazard in the resettlement, from both dust particles in the air and families cooking with wood fires inside or too near the home.

The roads and major walkways more or less segregate the ten barrios in Pino Alto. Each has its own political representative, who works with the *patronato*, and its own sense of identity. In most of the barrios, residents were provided with houses next to people whom they had never met. In a few others, a large group of survivors from the same neighborhood arrived together, retaining previous social networks and bonding social capital.

Just before the entrance to the resettlement (not shown on the map) are two large buildings meant to be used for either industry or vocational workshops (#6). Adjacent is a large white building with eighty-eight stalls for vendors; according to residents, only four have been open consistently since 2005. La

FIGURE 6.1. Map of Pino Alto
Map Data ©2016 Google

1 Main road to highway. It is a dirt road, although before elections it is often leveled.
2 Central square. The area has a cement foundation and benches, but few trees for shade. A full-sized soccer field lies to the east, and a library sits across the street to the north.
3 This was the La Internacional office. It is a building with eight rooms. A small community center sits to the north, and the waterworks to the south, of the office.
4 Elementary school.
5 Bus station.
6 Workshops and marketplace.
7 Multisports complex. Usually used for small-sided soccer games.
8 Middle and high school buildings.
9 The closest legal bar.
10 Police station.
11 Senior center.

Internacional had hoped this would be a bustling center of microenterprise supported by residents and the nearby communities. The large market was fairly successful until 2006, when a tragedy occurred,[1] and the market never regained its momentum. Behind the market is a cultural center that is also used for youth group meetings.

Between the market and vocational workshops and just outside of Pino Alto proper lies a brightly painted blue and yellow building with a small patio and multiple windows through which to serve customers (#9). When open, this general store and bar will serve anything from a cold bag of water on a hot day, to chips and plantains, to one's beer of choice. On the edge of Pino Alto but within the neighboring town boundaries, the bar does not have to follow Pino Alto's rule that no alcohol be sold.

Entering the central park of the resettlement (#2), houses spiral in all directions quite beautifully. Unfortunately, with high humidity and temperatures reaching into the nineties Fahrenheit or higher in the dry season, residents are discouraged from gathering together there. North, across the street from the park, is the closed library. Alejandro, a previous president of the waterworks and the highest-ranking elected official in Pino Alto (since there was no functioning *patronato* at the time), explained its closure. La Internacional, after providing capacity- and leadership-building classes to a group of youth, handed the running of the library over to them. Although it was initially successful, the library was closed by La Internacional after allegations that the youth were "doing bad things" in the library.

On the east side of the park is the multisports complex (#7) with basketball hoops and soccer goals. The concrete floor is bounded by one-meter-high concrete walls, which are extended another two meters by a chain-link fence. This enclosed field is popular in Latin America since the walls and fence keep a soccer game going indefinitely.

About two hundred meters up the road from the library sits an empty dirt lot with a small tin-roofed, open-sided wood structure. This was the space designated for the Catholic church. The structure holds plastic chairs, a table, and other necessities to hold weekly mass. A lack of interest by members to take on the difficult task of raising funds, coupled with the Catholic Church's focus elsewhere, has left the resettlement with a church roof but no building. Of the almost six thousand residents in the resettlement, only about fifty show up to any given mass.

On the south side of the park lie three important buildings: the community center, La Internacional's office (#3), and the waterworks. The community center is a small hall with a few adjacent offices. One of the offices was rented by a group of youth entrepreneurs in 2010. With a small loan and the belief that the resettlement needed internet access, they started an internet café with four computers. The La Internacional building sits empty as of early 2009, when the last social worker left, but the waterworks building has a beautiful interior courtyard with blossoming flowers and grass. Residents come here to pay their monthly water bill and to request plumbing fixes. Behind all three buildings sits the full-sized soccer field where youth and adults play on weekends.

In the mornings, children and adolescents walk north up the hill to the elementary school (#4) and high school (#8). Resettlement members built the schools. Don Ricardo explained that the first *patronato* was asked by La Internacional to organize residents for extra workdays beyond what they gave for their home. The resettlement came together and built the schools and the police station. Since that time, though, the high school has been heavily defaced by graffiti. When I visited, a significant amount of trash littered the property.

On an adjacent hill sits the senior center (#11), a popular amenity where senior citizens meet, talk, play cards, and take classes. Farther up that hill is the Pino Alto police station (#10). The station is bounded on two sides by a steep ledge that drops nearly six meters and maintains a two-and-a-half-meter-high chain-link fence around the perimeter. Many resettlement members and the police themselves park their cars inside the fence to ensure that they are protected.

RESETTLEMENT DESIGN

According to William Siembieda,[2] the author of a post-Mitch regional plan for the valley, Pino Alto was one of the best-designed resettlements in Honduras. Given the housing design, the use of space, the water system, and the location of infrastructure, it was a model for others. Indeed, there are many valuable aspects to the resettlement's design. First, there are only a few main roads, with most houses separated by a large sidewalk. Each sidewalk was paved and had gutters to prevent flooding of homes and problems with mud during the rainy season. This also improved public health. The less mud, trash, and animal waste located in and around homes, the less illness residents experienced in the resettlement, which was important given the high national infant mortality rate (19 per 1,000 [World Bank 2015a]).

Second, like Suyapa, the design followed the historical Spanish model of a central plaza surrounded by homes. A significant difference, though, was that Pino Alto's central plaza was very large, perhaps ten times the size of Suyapa's. It included a full-sized soccer field, a *cancha* (indoor concrete soccer mini-field), and a large cement common space for carnivals, temporary markets or meetings, or other resettlement activities. As in Suyapa, there were almost no trees to provide shade from the intense sun in the central park, so it was unused until late evening. There were few benches to lounge on, nothing to block the wind or dust from the dirt roads and dirt soccer field, and often trash littering the area. According to urban planners, this lack of useful, clean social space would not have been conducive to the growth and development of social capital within the resettlement (Jackson 2003).

Lastly, unlike Suyapa, the central park did not have a church or a market—just the La Internacional office, the water commission office, and a small meeting space for the *patronato*. Churches and markets are traditional gathering spaces for residents both formally (to go to mass or buy necessities) and informally (to hang out or as a meeting spot). Pino Alto's large market was outside of the resettlement, nearly a half-mile away from some members' homes, and it closed less than a year after opening. Evangelical churches are spread out throughout the resettlement, and the Catholic Church did not have a building for holding services.

A significant difference from Suyapa is how the homes are built. The goal was to "have quality construction, security against crime, and have a contemporary architectonic and aesthetic quality to encourage a better perception of the home and of the community" (La Internacional 2002). The homes are just that. La Internacional had four different models that are made of local material, are easily repaired by almost anyone, and have a steel door and bars on the windows to prevent crime. The homes themselves, in comparison to those of other resettlements, are slightly smaller but have larger lots. This would enable—perhaps even encourage—a resident to add on to her property so that extended family could also live there. From an outsider's perspective, the material and design of the homes in Pino Alto were warmer and more inviting than those of Suyapa. The red clay bricks of the walls had simple, linear indentions, giving the wall a three-dimensional look in comparison to the flat concrete cinder-block walls of Suyapa.

Additionally, rather than buying their homes like in Suyapa, Pino Alto residents build their own homes. As discussed later, residents worked for forty weeks on projects to obtain a home. After the forty weeks, the organization had a lottery system to determine which homes residents would receive.[3] This proved to be successful in empowering residents to take ownership of their resettlement. In 2004, residents came together and built the elementary school, receiving no financial compensation. One drawback of this method, though, was that La Internacional lost leverage within the resettlement, as it no longer could control what residents did with their homes (e.g., sell, rent, or abandon them). La Internacional knew houses were being sold, rented, or used as vacation homes. It did not have the long-term commitment, capacity, or funds to fight original residents legally.

The informal conversations I had with residents about their homes were positive. Like Suyapa residents, Pino Alto residents have electricity about 95 percent of the time (except during valley-wide blackouts). Pino Alto also receives trash pickup every few days and has a trash problem similar to Suyapa's, albeit on a larger scale due to its larger population. The most common positive response I received was that residents were grateful for continuous running water. Pino Alto, until 2015, was the only resettlement that received running water consistently, drawn from a mountain stream ten kilometers away through a gravity-fed system.

LIVELIHOODS

Pino Alto began with a formal economy and an official marketplace, but geographic distances and social issues precipitated a transition to a more informal economy. Initially, La Internacional renovated an old mill near the entrance of the resettlement for a general market. It was an ideal building but not an ideal site. Located between one hundred and eight hundred meters uphill from any given house (approximately a five- to twenty-minute walk), the market was not conducive to buying groceries and carrying them back home in the heat of the day.

Additionally, social conditions soon made the market unappealing. Don Pablo, a resettlement leader, related that at the outset, businesses thrived in the market. Most of the stalls were open, and there was significant entrepreneurship in the resettlement. Over time, however, businesses could not succeed, as too little money was coming into the resettlement to create a critical mass of consumers. The final blow to the market was a tragedy. According to a Pino Alto police report, on May 14, 2006, late in the evening, a vehicle was driven into Pino Alto with intent to commit homicide. Arriving from Olancho (the central eastern province of Honduras), the men inside had come to take revenge against the two guards of the market. They were successful. The next morning the guards were found dead with multiple gunshot wounds in their bodies. Pastor Eduardo (the Methodist minister) explained that the market closed down for a time after the incident and was never successfully revived. Indeed, by 2012, only four of the eighty-four stalls were in use.

With the decline of the formal market, the informal economy—specifically the *pulperías*—flourished, despite being illegal by resettlement rules. These home markets are spread throughout the resettlement, simple to initiate, and cost effective. The distance from the market encouraged residents to buy basic home supplies and foodstuffs in bulk and sell them to neighbors. This is a common practice throughout the country, and convenience created demand. The setup is simple. Unlike many countries, there is no enforced tax and no permit or zoning restrictions to dissuade the practice. A resident merely needed to put up a sign, have product, and leave someone at home to service customers (I have purchased phone minutes from elementary school children). It was also cost effective. For selling a product, a manufacturer (usually Coca-Cola or Pepsi) would paint a resident's house for free in their brand colors and with their logo. Thus, informal businesses sprang up throughout the resettlement. In my field survey, 89 percent of streets or walkways hosted informal businesses, a number significantly higher than in either Suyapa (60 percent) or the other resettlements (58 percent).

Table 6.1. Employment Type

	Self-employed	Manual labor	Permanent
Suyapa (2004)			
$N = 501$	25 percent	41 percent	34 percent
Pino Alto (2007)			
$N = 1,513$	33 percent**	34 percent*	33 percent

Z score: *.05, **.01.
Data from the same year does not exist.
(La Iglesia and CESAL 2004: 29–34; La Internacional and Pino Alto 2007)

This shift likely impacted the amount and type of interaction residents had, decreasing opportunities to build relationships that spanned the resettlement and occasions to develop social cohesion and bonding social capital (Putnam 2000). As found in other resettlements, a centrally located market facilitates the development of broad bonding social capital, as residents interact with people throughout the resettlement rather than only on their street (as with *pulperías*). For example, Santa Fe is an isolated resettlement with ten rows of twenty houses facing one another. In an effort to put survivors in homes as quickly as possible, the designers did not build a central market or central plaza, and the two churches, Catholic and evangelical, were on opposite sides of the resettlement. When residents were asked about whether they trusted their neighbors after living in the same resettlement for ten years, one older resident stated, "I trust my neighbors on this street. But down there [approximately two hundred meters away], I don't know them." Proximity does not necessarily lead to trust; social interaction must occur as well. In my conversations with Pino Alto residents, I heard similar comments: residents trusted their next-door neighbors but did not know and consequently did not trust those on the other side of the resettlement.

The best data on Pino Alto livelihoods was obtained from a self-survey by the residents (La Internacional and Pino Alto 2007, 23–29). Pino Alto's residents are equally split between three tiers of employment—working from home, working in manual labor, and permanent work other than manual labor (like owning a business and blue- or white-collar work). The numbers also reveal the type of work each gender did. Women often innovatively created self-employment initiatives at home; staying at home enabled them to care for the children and household while making a small income by selling goods from their porch (in a *pulpería*, selling tortillas, childcare for other families, etc.). Permanent work was also high for women with jobs such as cooking, cleaning, secretarial work, and nursing, outpacing the men's permanent work status, which included positions such as security guards, mechanics, and machine operators.

Without an internal market or production of goods within the resettlement, as in Suyapa, most of Pino Alto's income derives from remittances or work in Tegucigalpa. Almost all Pino Alto residents (99 percent) receive some kind of support from remittances, which is comparable to the five other resettlements but high in relation to Suyapa (69 percent). The vast majority, though, receive less than 10 percent of their income from this source. In short, these statistics illustrate that within the first few years of being resettled, residents of both resettlements had similar job categories and economic status. It is unlikely that the different social health outcomes can be attributed to economic differences initially or over time.

RESIDENTS AND LEADERSHIP

Doña Nina is a thirty-four-year-old woman who speaks briskly, asks direct questions, and is generous with her time and energy. She has long, black hair tied up above her head and a stern demeanor but laughs easily. She is constantly cooking and does not mind hollering either at her nephew or at the neighbor. She lives with her mother, sister, and nephew in a two-bedroom Pino Alto home between the library and the high school. Doña Nina is not a leader, often does not vote "porque no vale" (because it does not matter), and is trying to make it day by day selling corn tortillas and *charamuscas* (flavored frozen treats). After expenses, she earns approximately 40 lempiras ($2.10) a

Table 6.2. 2010 Monthly Cost of Living in Pino Alto for Doña Nina

Cost per month	Lempiras	US dollars
Income for Doña Nina	1,200	60
Household water	−50	2.50
Household electricity	−100	5
Household mortgage	−0	0
Transportation for one to the city (e.g., groceries, supplies, etc.)	−200	10
Leftover income after the above	=850	43
If leftover income is spent on food per person (4) per month	213	10.63
Education, health, travel, savings, home repairs, sports, etc.	0	0

day or nearly 1,200 ($63) a month, which supports the four of them.[4] She and her family are Catholic, but because there is often no mass held in Pino Alto, they do not attend church.

Similar to Suyapa, most residents like living in Pino Alto, especially in comparison to Tegucigalpa. In Pino Alto, 53 percent of respondents said that their life was better than in the capital city and another 31 percent reported that it was the same. The majority of residents also described living with less crime, with about 40 percent noting that they have engaged in more civic participation in Pino Alto. Although Pino Alto had *mala fama* in El Valle, most residents still found the resettlement a better place to live than their pre-Mitch neighborhood.

RELIGION AND RELIGIOSITY

In terms of religion and religiosity, Pino Alto is much closer to the average than Suyapa. Table 6.3 illustrates that there is no statistically significant difference between Pino Alto and the other resettlements. Unlike Suyapa, Pino Alto had no religion-based selection process. The secular La Internacional did not utilize religious frames or ideologies to justify their intervention or work. Theirs was a partnership development strategy that had the same goal of creating a model community but through very different means than La Iglesia: capacity building, leadership, organization, and excellent infrastructure.

Pino Alto was much more religiously diverse than Suyapa. The largest Methodist church in El Valle was built on the border of Pino Alto and is connected to the infrastructure of the town. The Catholic Church owns a plot of land in the resettlement, and numerous other evangelical sects have grown in the resettlement, two of which have constructed their own independent churches. Religion has been found to create a bond among followers, but it can also cause conflict between faiths (Durkheim 1995[1912]; Putnam 2000). One might venture to say that the religious homogeneity in Suyapa impacted its social health outcomes. Although the data places no statistical significance on levels of trust by different religions when controlling for resettlement, religious affiliation is still important. Indeed, religious homophily creates one of the largest divides among people (McPherson, Smith-Lovin, and Cook 2001). It was likely easier for Suyapa residents to create a common vision and develop social cohesion and social capital since a majority subscribed to the same core values already.

Another important difference is the lower religiosity of Pino Alto residents. In comparison to Suyapa, two and a half times more residents do not attend any services (concomitant to the percentage with no religious preference) and

Table 6.3. Religion by Resettlement

	Catholic	Protestant	Evangelical	None	Other
Suyapa	61 percent**	0 percent	29 percent**	10 percent**	0 percent
Pino Alto	23 percent	2 percent	45 percent	29 percent*	1 percent
Avg. 5 com.	28 percent	1 percent	47 percent	22 percent	2 percent

Z score: *.05, **.01 (Comparison group—Avg. 5 coms.).

Table 6.4. Religiosity by Resettlement

Resettlement	Do not attend	Attend on holidays	Attend every week	Attend two or more times each week
Suyapa	13 percent**	20 percent	32 percent**	36 percent
Pino Alto	32 percent**	16 percent	17 percent**	35 percent
Average of 5 resettlements	26 percent	18 percent	24 percent	33 percent

Z score: **.01 (Comparison group—Avg. 5 resettlements).

only about half as many attend weekly services. This fact also indicates that social interaction is happening either in a different arena or perhaps less often. It is also possible that the quarter of the population who are Catholic do not attend because no formal Catholic church exists. Taking a bus to attend mass in another resettlement is costly (14 lempiras [~75 cents]) and time consuming (a one-hour bus ride each way), and this likely accounts for a decline in participation and attendance.

About one hundred meters west of the main entrance of Pino Alto lies what locals referred to as "the castle." The Methodist church stands at one of the highest points of the resettlement and can be seen from almost any home. Although there are only two stories of usable space, the roof extends into the heavens another six meters. The outside is painted tan with sharp red borders. Despite being the largest church in the valley, it has only minimal attendance (around ten people a week).

La Internacional ensured that all faiths are welcome in Pino Alto. Like much of Latin America (Masci 2014), Pentecostalism is growing rapidly in the resettlement. Residents who are part of these groups often utilize a free room in someone's home to start their church. According to Pastor Eduardo, these groups are both cohesive and divisive within the resettlement. On the one hand, for participants, the group can often strengthen bonding social capital. On the other hand, these participants may view other faiths and nonbelievers with suspicion, preventing bridging social capital between sects.

LEADERSHIP

Don Ricardo is a soft-spoken, kind, and serious man. The president of the *patronato* for five years and appointed interim president of the water commission (as of August 2011), Don Ricardo is viewed by residents and by La Internacional as one of the few go-to people for action and leadership. I met him at his home, one of the largest in the resettlement, as it has a second floor. While I had an introduction from Pastor Eduardo, his solemn demeanor kept me on my toes. I was soon able to relax on his sofa as his wife brought us soda and we began our conversation. He is a heavyset man in his mid-fifties, perhaps 1.7 meters tall, and balding. He knows how to dress well when out, but today he is comfortable in a light T-shirt and shorts. He speaks clearly and with great intention, telling stories as if sharing secrets to the past and present.

His role in the resettlement has ebbed and flowed. As the first president of the *patronato*, he had to deal with the initial difficulties of a disorganized mass of persons, mostly strangers, moving in and living together. Although La Internacional was there to help, its staff left daily at four p.m. It was up to him and the other leaders to maintain order after hours, with the help of the often-ambivalent police force. He noted that the resettlement had accomplished much under his tenure. Each family contributed time and effort to the building of the schools, just as they had for the building of their homes. The process was completely self-organized, and they were able to do it with only financial support from La Internacional. In addition, when gangs became a significant problem in the resettlement, especially in 2004 and 2005, Don Ricardo spoke with government representatives to provide greater security. A special unit was brought into the resettlement under the guise of door-to-door broom salespersons, houses were pinpointed for gang residence, and one early morning all of those houses were raided and the gang members were taken to prison. According to Don Ricardo, this was a great feat and a positive change in resettlement direction. In many ways, his personality reflects that of the resettlement—serious due to the poverty and insecurity of the resettlement, but kind and generous with friends and family. What is different, though, is that Don Ricardo was willing to confront the major issue of gang violence in his resettlement, while most other residents have been resigned to accepting gangs as part of Pino Alto (as it was probably familiar to them from wherever they had lived before Mitch).

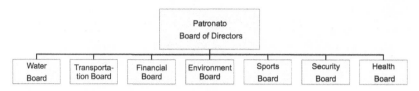

FIGURE 6.2. The Structure of the Patronato (Pino Alto 2005)

However, a single person, evenly highly motivated, cannot run a resettle-ment. Implementing the most widely used political organization in Honduras, Pino Alto residents selected a *patronato* (similar to a board of directors) to guide their resettlement. As described by the "Statutes of the *Patronato* of Pino Alto" (2005), the board of directors comprises nine officials elected as a slate and includes the president, vice president, general secretary, deputy secretary, tax counselor, treasurer, and three representatives. Like the CCS in Suyapa, the *patronato* also has a number of subgroups that manage specific affairs in the resettlement.

As one compares the statutes of the Comité Cívico Social to those of the *patronato*, differences between the SAGE and partnership development strate-gies become apparent. While the CCS document is full of references to La Iglesia and members sitting on the CCS, the Pino Alto statutes make no refer-ence to La Internacional, and the organization has no vote or power within the political system.

La Internacional also helped to put into place an additional political sys-tem, the committees for local development (comités de desarrollo locales, CODELES). CODELES consist of twenty-six democratically elected repre-sentatives. Each of the ten barrios elects between two and ten representatives, depending on population. The representatives work as intermediaries between the broader population and the *patronato*, sharing information and needs in both directions (CODELES 2005). Although the concept was superb, the practice left much to be desired after only a few years. The causes for its de-cline remain disputed. For some residents, the CODELES needed more sup-port from La Internacional in capacity building and being held accountable. For La Internacional, a representative explained to me, residents were not willing to put in the work, nor did they have the motivation to continue the project.

As reviewed in the introduction, the idea of partnership is often applauded for its empowerment of residents (Craig and Mayo 1995; Mohan and Stokke 2000; Ellerman 2007). Yet, based on the evidence, a post-disaster heteroge-neous resettlement like Pino Alto may not have been ready for such a system, as a general malaise and corruption soon plagued the administration. Don Ricardo confided that the current appointed officials have done little to improve the resettlement. This sentiment was echoed by multiple other residents and was anchored by the fact that while the *patronato* was supposed to hold elections in 2008, they were not initiated until June 2011. Members of the *patronato* were caught embezzling from the resettlement coffers in 2006 and from the waterworks fund in 2009–2010. In 2012, the problem occurred again. The water director and his niece, the waterworks secretary, absconded with hundreds of thousands of lempiras that were to pay for the electricity to pump water to resident homes.

These examples show the stark differences in the role La Iglesia played in Suyapa's leadership and that played by La Internacional in Pino Alto. Suyapa's CCS was heavily influenced by La Iglesia, and this oversight prevented significant corruption while also holding leaders accountable. The *patronato* had a different experience. It was far less dependent on an outside organization for resources and guidance, but without the strong support of an outside organization or institution, the resettlement had trouble managing multiple conflicting interests and a culture of corruption, a likely holdover from Tegucigalpa.

SOCIAL INTERACTION

Pino Alto also had a different social atmosphere than Suyapa. Its population, more than twice that of Suyapa, was also more heterogeneous, most clearly in terms of religious preference and neighborhood of origin in Tegucigalpa. The geography and planning of the resettlement, which is much more spread out than the others and lacks a central market or accommodating central park, also influenced the ways in which residents interacted throughout the ten barrios. Yet members found ways to connect.

Proximity breeds familiarity. Without a doubt, Pino Alto residents were much more trusting of their neighbors nearby than those in another barrio. Like Suyapa and its religious networks, the most successful barrios in Pino Alto were those with previous neighborhood social ties. One entire Tegucigalpa neighborhood had to be resettled, and approximately 317 of the families came to Pino Alto (Belli 2008). This group had embedded bonding social capital as well as a common identity, one that encouraged them to name their barrio after their previous neighborhood, Manzanita. Among the various barrios, Manzanita was recognized as much more organized and having the least delinquency. Indeed, when asked about the barrio, one resident said "they live better and think they are better over there." In creating a barrio identity, from an outsider perspective, those in the Manzanita section may have developed a collective vision and culture that bonded the barrio residents. Since this vision was not shared by other barrios, internal divisions were created within the Pino Alto resettlement.

Even though the *patronato* was a problematic institution, it did accomplish two meaningful goals. The first, as discussed earlier, was the construction of other resettlement buildings. Without financial incentive, residents came together under the *patronato* and spent months building the schools and police station, knowing they would benefit the resettlement as a whole. Don Ricardo mentioned that it was one of his proudest moments, to see Pino Alto residents, as a team, erect the elementary school. The second was the development of eleven committees for community development (comités de desarrollo comunitario, CODECOS). CODECOS differ from CODELES in that they are not political but rather social groups, including Alcoholics Anonymous, youth groups, a soccer league, and so forth (La Internacional 2007). The most successful of these, and the only one that has been consistent over time, is Mujeres al Rescate, or Women to the Rescue. This group was formed so that women could share their experience and provide mutual support to one another. A cross between a self-help group and a voluntary organization, the participants meet weekly and talk, as well as plan various activities to help the resettlement. In sum, like Suyapa, Pino Alto has high social interaction; however, it is more tied to the local barrio than to the entire resettlement. Over time, this may have led to commitment to barrio, rather than the development of broader sense of community.

LA INTERNACIONAL

La Internacional is one of the oldest international relief organizations in the world, with its Honduras chapter founded in 1937. Since then, the organization has grown to forty-five branch offices in all sixteen departments of the country. It is funded by national individual and corporate donations and, after Hurricane Mitch, international donations from sister organizations in other nations.[5] The current focus of the national organization is on emergency relief, such as "disaster preparedness and response, and blood donor recruitment, pre-hospital emergency, community (physical) health, housing, water and sanitation, principles and values, and education for community development." The most significant challenge and achievement in the history of La Internacional was the relief and recovery of the country after Hurricane Mitch (La Internacional 2011).

During and immediately after Hurricane Mitch, La Internacional was one of the largest organizations working with survivors. Building temporary shelters, distributing food, and organizing logistics throughout the country, La Internacional and its partners were successful in accomplishing its mission of emergency relief. What the organization did not expect, at that time, was that someday it would be building entire resettlements for survivors.

As days turned into weeks and weeks into months, the organization constructed the large *macro-albergues* for displaced survivors. These wood and plastic shelters became home to tens of thousands in the major cities. While working on the *macro-albergues*, La Internacional was asked by the national government to build a new housing settlement for survivors in and around the Tegucigalpa metro area. Naomi, the La Internacional social director, explained that the organization initially refused because it was not La Internacional's mission to do community development—indeed, it was beyond their capability. However, faced with such overwhelming need, La Internacional eventually agreed and spoke with its international partners in Spain, Switzerland, and the United States. Over time, La Internacional also found numerous other NGO and INGO partners. With this alliance procuring funding, skillful leadership, and land donated by the government in El Valle, Pino Alto was born (La Internacional 2004).

The resettlement was heralded as a model community (Lloyd 2005) for future resettlements and, as one Spanish newspaper described it, "a miracle" in El Valle (Ortega Dolz 2002). With completely new infrastructure, some of the best waterworks in the country, the promise of factory employment, and a well-designed resettlement, residents were hopeful that their new community would indeed fulfill the promises made to them. Pino Alto was held up as the best example of a "disaster reduction initiative" to date (Sutherland 2004).

LA INTERNACIONAL COMMUNITY DEVELOPMENT PHILOSOPHY

Infrastructure is one thing, but building a community in people's minds is another.
IGNACIO, LA INTERNACIONAL OFFICIAL IN
CHARGE OF PLANNING IN PINO ALTO

Naomi, like her Suyapa counterpart Doña Rosa, is a powerful woman. In her late forties, with kind eyes, a sharp intellect, and deep compassion, Naomi was the coordinator of social projects for La Internacional. She had worked there many years, learning the ins and outs of the organization, and she loved the projects she worked on. Second only to the president of La Internacional in Honduras, Naomi was the most knowledgeable employee—having literally worked in the construction of the project alongside Pino Alto residents.

Although she was chosen to lead social development throughout the country after Hurricane Mitch, her particular focus was on Pino Alto. The multiple interviews I conducted with her provided invaluable insight into how La Internacional approached the Pino Alto project.

Like Naomi—busy, overworked, and with projects that spanned the nation—La Internacional lacked the resources it needed to help all those affected. One report from La Internacional's Spain chapter found that the organization had been involved in over 169 projects throughout the country, including 10 housing projects with a total of 1,955 homes, 71 schools, and dozens of specific development projects in the areas of health, economic development, agriculture, and water and sanitation (La Internacional and Pino Alto 2007).

Lacking government support, La Internacional had to continually change its timeframe, its goals, and therefore its community development approach based on survivors' needs. According to Naomi, La Internacional agreed to build Pino Alto on the condition that the government itself or another organization would take over the role of community developer. In actuality, once the infrastructure was completed and La Internacional was ready to move on to other projects, the government requested that La Internacional remain for two more years to oversee the first stages of community development. After those two years, resettlement residents pleaded with La Internacional administration to remain, which they did, for another three years. In contrast to La Iglesia's fifteen-year pledge made during the initial months of planning, La Internacional staffers were forced to continually shift their development agenda, resources, and goals due to the uncertainty of the commitment by the government and other organizations, which precluded them from creating an intentional long-term vision.

PARTNERSHIP STRATEGY

Before resident arrival, La Internacional authored a clear partnership strategy for Pino Alto. The 2002 Pino Alto Plan explained that the goal of the organization was "a comprehensive intervention aimed at developing a new, safe, and healthy sustainable community" for survivors of Hurricane Mitch. More specifically,

> the near future vision of Pino Alto is a self-managing community that
> addresses its own problems and goals, whose residents live together peace-
> fully, and with opportunities for training, caring for personal health, and
> economic improvement. This is what guides La Internacional, along with the
> construction of housing and other basic infrastructure. The implementation

of projects is aimed at community empowerment; the promotion of health in the family and community; a holistic approach to education through support of the schools, community, family, and people of all ages; and improving the income potential of families in Pino Alto. All this, with an expectation of participation to work with and for the community. (La Internacional, Spain 2002, 9; translation by author)

Each point above underscores the partnership and participatory nature of La Internacional's strategy.

The organization focused on empowerment and capacity building, offering dozens of classes that provided different types of employable skills to survivors, such as tourism, client services, and human relations. Once the infrastructure was built and residents resettled, La Internacional made a deliberate effort to step back and not be part of the decision-making processes, respecting the autonomy of the resettlement in managing itself. As Naomi explained, "We only give them [Pino Alto] the orientation of how to do it and where to go [for help]. If they need something, advice, support, well, we give it to them, but we are not over them. We only provide them little by little because the community is relatively young." She goes on to explain that La Internacional's aim was an independent and self-sustainable community. La Internacional could not continue to play such an active role in the resettlement over the long term due to various time and financial constraints, which furthered the organization's objective of handing over power and responsibility as quickly as possible in the name of self-sufficiency.

According to Fiona, a La Internacional social worker and staffer in Pino Alto for the entirety of the development process, "We wanted residents to come to us for help. But we were not going to help them. We were only going to show them which other doors [e.g., government departments] they needed to knock on." Knowing that the organization was not going to be present indefinitely, La Internacional focused on breaking any sense of dependency the resettlement may have developed over the years. Its minimal intervention in public affairs attempted to place the responsibility back onto the residents, especially leadership, with varying degrees of success.

La Internacional's objective was always resident participation and resettlement independence with limited support of the organization, to empower the residents and facilitate a self-managing community. As mentioned in chapter 2, this fits the model of development "in" the community rather than "of" the community. After all, the focus was to build on family and individual capacity, with the creation of larger social structures, vision, and community culture a secondary concern.

Another noticeable partnership practice was the decision by La Internacional to use a participatory model of home ownership. Unlike the La Iglesia model in Suyapa, in which residents take on a fifteen-year mortgage paid to La Iglesia, one resident from each household committed forty hours a week for forty weeks to constructing homes and infrastructure in Pino Alto. By asking residents to literally build the resettlement from the ground up, La Internacional expected that residents would maintain a deeper commitment to the resettlement. In this way, residents also avoided incurring debt. La Internacional hoped that with the increased disposable income from not paying a mortgage, residents would build savings and spend on living essentials or their children's health and well-being. Once the work was completed, residents would be given the keys to their new home through a lottery system. Part of the requirement of receiving a home was that residents could not sell their homes; the homes were meant to be patrimony for their children.[6]

La Internacional staff also had different expectations than La Iglesia concerning their role in the resettlement process. Naomi and her coworker Ignacio, who also ran social programs in Pino Alto, explained that La Internacional did not necessarily want to be involved in community development projects. The organization was involved in multiple housing projects throughout the country, and its limited resources were already stretched thin. In fact, after Hurricane Mitch, the different international arms of La Internacional had worked in over five hundred projects helping more than a million citizens from 1998 to 2008 (La Internacional 2008). Unlike La Iglesia, which directed its energies at only one project, La Internacional was overcommitted, compromising its ability to be actively involved in multiple resettlements and projects.

The La Internacional partnership approach manifested itself in the type of social development efforts that emphasized individual achievement rather than a collective vision. La Internacional offered dozens of courses and capacity-building classes for those wanting to engage in self-development. One woman, Doña Julia, explained that she had a "stack of diplomas" from La Internacional in self-esteem, tourism, client service, and human relations, but they did not really help her find a job. Other than the CODECOS mentioned above, the few services provided by the organization (fixing infrastructure, helping residents find jobs, connecting the *patronato* to government agencies, etc.) gave residents the sustainment that they needed but did not create a sense of community throughout the resettlement.

RESIDENT SELECTION

In comparison to La Iglesia, the selection process by La Internacional had different challenges. In the years following Mitch, people in Tegucigalpa coped with being homeless by either renting, living with friends or family members, or, most commonly, living in the *macro-albergues*. As resettlements were being built, word was passed among informal networks about various housing opportunities for Mitch survivors. Due to a number of extraneous factors (finding land, government inefficiencies, inexperienced residents as builders, an overstretched NGO managing multiple projects, etc.), La Internacional started resettling survivors four years after Mitch, concluding two years later, in 2004. Between 1999 and 2004, many survivors had already been placed in resettlements, enticed by the option to leave the *macro-albergues* as soon as possible.

When asked how they became aware of the resettlement, the vast majority of residents in Pino Alto said they had heard about it through an organization, likely La Internacional, as many of them were living in La Internacional-sponsored *macro-albergues*. This occurrence resembles what many other resettlement residents experienced but is in sharp contrast to the experiences of Suyapa residents. Most Suyapa residents learned about the resettlement through the Catholic Church. How this affected the selection process by residents is unclear, but following theories on immigration, the stronger the social network, the more likely one is to move to a particular locale (MacDonald and MacDonald 1964). In the case of Pino Alto, La Internacional was a known quantity, an ally in the *albergues*, and thus there was a widespread belief that moving to a La Internacional–sponsored resettlement would be a positive choice.

GOVERNANCE

La Internacional had a policy of noninterference with Pino Alto leadership. Since the *patronato* system was the traditional political structure, the organization never directed the resettlement once it was built. La Internacional also made it clear to both the resettlement and the government that it did not want to be running Pino Alto or have influence in the resettlement's political development. As it was, La Internacional already felt obliged to work with the resettlement for far longer than it had planned, without knowing where future funding would come from. Thus, the NGO did not try to direct, control, or otherwise influence the politics, providing advice and support only when asked and enforcing political decisions made solely by the *patronato*.

The evidence suggests that residents did not have the assets and capacity to run the resettlement on their own. As described earlier, the patronato found itself involved in issues of corruption, nepotism, theft of resettlement property, and eventually dissolution, leaving Pino Alto without functioning leadership for years. Furthermore, without any leadership, the vulnerable resettlement had a vacuum of power, which was exploited by external entities, such as gangs. Had La Internacional maintained a strong presence and influence in the resettlement, at least during the first few years, this would have provided leaders and the *patronato* time to strengthen the institution, obtain greater legitimacy, and recognize internal and external resources. With this increased capacity, the *patronato* would have had a better chance of addressing the crime and other social ills that beleaguered Pino Alto.

SOCIAL CONTROL

With significantly less engagement in Pino Alto than La Iglesia had in Suyapa, La Internacional also had less power to guide the direction of the budding community. This phenomenon is most clearly observable in the immediate provision of land title to residents after their service, as well as in La Internacional's hands-off role in shaping the resettlement culture.

La Internacional's decision to give residents ownership of their homes immediately had mixed results. Once Pino Alto residents owned their home, it could not be taken away from them. According to many residents, this was a dream come true, as they had never believed they would own a real home. It was also a more financially empowering model at the individual level than that of La Iglesia, as residents were not burdened with rent or a mortgage. Finally, La Internacional staff believed, as did many other organizations in El Valle, that physically contributing to building the resettlement would strengthen residents' commitment to the community itself.

La Internacional did not, at the time, recognize three major disadvantages of giving residents immediate ownership. First, resident capabilities to self-govern were not fully understood. As discussed in chapter 3, residents were highly vulnerable, and most had no training or very little training in running a community. All of these problems existed in the context of a fragile state that had limited capacity to serve the needs of the resettlement (Alaniz 2012).

Second, once a family legally owned a home, it could not be taken away. La Internacional realized that there were deviants within the resettlement, such as gang members, drug dealers, and mentally unstable residents, but they had no power to address these problems. The unreliable and corrupt police force and anemic judicial system also permitted not only the continuation but the actual growth of social problems, as criminals began to utilize the resettlement as a base of operation.

Lastly, La Internacional did not have a continuous revenue stream to maintain its programming and operations in the resettlement. Aside from the original timeline, a second major reason La Internacional needed to leave Pino Alto was the huge annual expenditure. For the first few years after Hurricane Mitch, major NGOs were flush with cash for projects. As donor attention turned to ever more current disasters, funding dried up for long-term

social development. La Internacional began withdrawing its projects and resources in 2002, leaving only two support staff by 2007. In 2009, with only
one full-time staff member, the Pino Alto office finally closed, mainly for financial reasons.

As with most NGOs that built resettlements, development of community
was a secondary priority to La Internacional after infrastructure. The organization did not plan to remain in Pino Alto after construction was completed, it
had little experience in community development as a national organization, and
it followed a partnership approach that focused on the individual. Without the
intentional support of La Internacional in building social structure, it makes
sense that the Pino Alto resettlement would develop without a collective vision
or common culture. As one member of the Pino Alto *patronato* reported to me,

> La Internacional did not work in the social area. They worked in construc-
> tions, all of the infrastructure but not in the social area. They came to work
> in the social area the last two years, after all of the things had been accom-
> plished. [At that point] it was almost impossible to make people think in a
> different way.

By the time La Internacional finally became aware of the serious problems in
Pino Alto—high rates of crime and violence, gang issues, and a divided resettlement—it was too late. The culture had developed in a particular way,
and altering its direction would take time and enormous resources—neither
of which La Internacional possessed.

La Internacional, in the words of Naomi, did the best it could with what
it had. But the ambitious goals for Pino Alto may not have been attainable
employing a short-term partnership approach. If the desire was for a "self-
managing community that addresses its own problems and goals, whose residents live together peacefully," the vulnerable disaster survivors who moved
into Pino Alto may not have had the assets necessary, at that particular moment, to create that community without the intervention and support of external agents. Without strong oversight, long-term involvement, significant engagement in multiple aspects of resettlement life, and a strong social control
mechanism to deal with problem residents, La Internacional could not prevent
the encroachment of violence and crime into the resettlement, despite its best
efforts. These ideas will be further developed in chapter 7.

CONFLICT

Compared to Suyapa, Pino Alto residents wanted much more intervention in
their resettlement by La Internacional. In fact, the representative survey re-

veals that almost 90 percent of residents wanted the organization to have the same or even greater influence in resettlement affairs. Except for the leadership of Pino Alto, who were disappointed by the work of the NGO, almost all of the residents I spoke with wished that La Internacional had not left. As Doña Julia put it, "My experience was good with La Internacional. . . . They worked for our well-being. . . . They offered tools for the people to better themselves and they saw the need for development within the community." I also asked her about what La Internacional did not do so well. Doña Julia explained, "They left us to walk alone."

Although at least a few residents felt abandoned, La Internacional continued to peripherally support community development efforts through 2010. The organization brought in other NGOs to provide services to the resettlement; many organizations to this day continue to work in the resettlement. However, most work on individual projects with youth, with women, with the elderly, in sports, and so forth. They do not attempt to build a broad-based sense of community or community culture. While the CODELES were not as successful as La Internacional had hoped, other groups were. Some of the CODECOS, as noted above, continue today—as do youth dance groups and sports and cultural events.

Along the same lines, only about 2 percent of households had experienced any problem with La Internacional (as opposed to 9 percent with La Iglesia). The organization maintained positive relationships with people and was generally respected and well regarded. Likewise, residents were less afraid of losing their homes. In Pino Alto, 60 percent of households were concerned that they could be evicted (compared to 72 percent in Suyapa and 51 percent of the average). This is a surprisingly high number since no one had actually ever been evicted. I believe it was not due to fear of La Internacional taking away homes, but rather due to a lack of land and home titles being settled (due to government incompetence, according to La Internacional employees). Pino Alto folks were more likely than most to desire more support from their sponsoring NGO if it had been available (see table 5.5).

Like La Iglesia, La Internacional knew of the illegal renting and selling of properties, which in turn forced them to place large signs up near the main road, in the central square, and throughout the resettlement. The signs read:

La Internacional, Honduras
General notice to the population.
Residents should remember that the constructed homes in Pino Alto are for the exclusive use of the family with title. Therefore, the home is a family asset, which you may not sell. Selling is illegal, and those who do so will be brought to court.

Unlike La Iglesia, however, La Internacional did not take any real action against any of the residents who sold or rented their home, nor could it. Of course La Internacional knew these practices were happening, but lacking the mechanism of mortgages and considering the weak judicial system and the organization's desire to move on to other projects, it was powerless to curb the problem. The lack of oversight of the resettlement; a corrupt, dysfunctional, or absent *patronato*; and the resettlement's *mala fama* led to a shifting demographics of residents, most visible in the number of criminals.

FINDING BALANCE

The poem at the beginning of the chapter reminds us that resettlements often begin with high hopes to create "brotherhood and prosperity" through effort and struggle. The success of this process is due in large part to the people and the sponsoring organization. La Internacional chose community development strategies that fit its philosophy and resources. Like La Iglesia, its approach had strengths and weaknesses. On the one hand, Pino Alto is a more independent resettlement than Suyapa and may be able to work with government institutions more effectively inasmuch as its leaders have more experience doing so. On the other hand, the social health outcomes are much poorer than those of Suyapa, in part a result of the lack of organizational support in creating community. La Internacional's partnership approach—an organizational presence external to the resettlement especially in the social arena, a lack of long-term community development planning, and few if any social control mechanisms (e.g., mortgages)—could not guide the collective community-building process. Ignacio, a head social worker of Pino Alto, recalled,

> We start from the *macro-albergues*, we were there four years. Of those four years, two of the years we maintained a very paternalistic attitude. Since 2001, we began the process of working more in different subjects to address the more general problem of the community—the topics of education and health. The community itself saw its own problems and began seeking advice and solutions with our support. But we did not do things for them. This process of metamorphosis is not easy. [Residents would say,] "I'm comfortable here [being provided for], I do not want to walk alone." The process was not easy.
>
> Now they come to the community and have another view that they are not going to receive everything. In fact, when we were there, [they would say,] "I broke a light bulb" [expecting La Internacional to fix it]. If they have problems with water, there is the water board, the same organization they composed themselves. When there is no light, there is ENEE [national electric company]. We would teach that good resources are available and that you just

have to go get them, but not necessarily from La Internacional. We provided guidance and advice, as facilitator. But we stopped giving residents chewed-up bits to swallow.

Ignacio's insight highlights the risk of too much technical assistance and La Internacional's desire for residents to take responsibility for their community. His analysis misses a key component—without a sense of community, residents may not have the capability to work together to solve community problems. His perspective is also reminiscent of the development "in community," rather than "of community." With this focus on individual capacity building, residents may not have had the support to develop social cohesion, bonding social capital, a common vision, or a broad sense of collective efficacy.

CHAPTER 7

FROM STRANGERS TO NEIGHBORS:
THE DEVELOPMENT OF COMMUNITY

Lao Tsu, writing more than 2,400 years ago, affirms the challenge of supporting and empowering others without creating dependence.

> Go to the people; live among them; love them; learn from them; start from where they are; work with them; build on what they have.
> But of the best leaders, when the task is accomplished, the work completed, the people will remark: "We have done it ourselves." (Tao Te Ching, chapter 17 [CEC 2014])

Applied to the building of infrastructure and social structures necessary for the long-term social health of a resettlement, it is imperative that organizations begin by meeting survivors where they are, which is often a place of high vulnerability. NGOs and governments must begin by addressing vulnerability, building capacity among individuals, and developing a collective culture that will lead to social health. Finally, through a long-term, sustained process, organizations must retract from the place of power and management while simultaneously making possible the ascent of residents into leadership positions. The development of healthy social characteristics—civic participation, social capital, collective efficacy, a common vision, and low crime—will generate a sense of community and foundational culture that will be positively self-reinforcing. Residents will no longer be strangers; they will be neighbors.

Creating community in a resettlement is both a process and an outcome. As a process, it can be seen in the slow, meticulous dance among residents and support organizations as they accept or reject, keep or replace, certain values and norms that encourage a sense of community. The challenges of overcoming trauma, adjusting to new surroundings, negotiating new values, creating a new place attachment, building new social networks, collaborating with external organizations for support without becoming dependent, and rebuilding their livelihoods is a complex and time-consuming task. Above all, as seen in the cases discussed, it calls for a dialectical process between residents and sponsoring NGOs.

As an outcome, the success of creating community can be measured by how people treat one another, think about their neighbors, work collaboratively toward common goals, and experience a sense of ease in the place they call home. It is this social dimension that denotes the distinction between constructing a resettlement and fostering a community. These outcomes are often viewed as secondary to building infrastructure and economic development, which is an important foundation—following Maslow's (1943) hierarchy of needs, people need shelter and food first. But if the goal really is to "build back better," then governments and organizations must also invest in social development from the beginning; it's a crucial component of the long-term, sustainable success of the resettlements that they are trying to build.

The book thus far has focused on resettlement outcomes and the characteristics of the organization and residents that influenced the outcomes. This chapter will use the path dependency model to describe the *process* of the creation of a new culture within heterogeneous resettlements, specifically Suyapa and Pino Alto. The theory's four iterative stages—initial conditions, formation of community culture, conciliation, and increasing returns—uncover important and often overlooked characteristics of the resettlement social development process. These features cast into sharper relief the link between NGO strategies and successful or unsuccessful resettlement outcomes.

The four stages can be likened to the development of a person. Initial conditions are similar to the genetic makeup, inherent talents, and future potential of an individual. These conditions may shape but do not define outcomes. The formation of community culture is similar to the socialization process. Residents and the organization dialogue about the vision and social norms for the resettlement. As this occurs, the future potential of the resettlement narrows as distinct structures are constructed and reproduced. Conciliation is analogous to the way in which individuals accept, or rebel against, certain beliefs or behaviors encouraged by friends, family, or society. In the resettlements, residents deliberate among themselves and with the sponsoring organizations to discern what behaviors will be permitted and whose vision for the new community will be implemented. In some cases, organizations may have significantly greater influence over this process, mandating certain behavior. In others, the conciliation process may be more chaotic as more individual voices argue individual perspectives, in the absence of well-developed institutions that could mediate such conflict. Lastly, increasing returns are akin to the internalization of behaviors as normal. Just like people, resettlement culture over time becomes embedded as ordinary and natural and is passed along to future residents and subsequent generations.[1] Below, path dependence will be discussed in the context of Suyapa and Pino Alto.

INITIAL CONDITIONS

As discussed in chapters 1, 5, and 6, Suyapa and Pino Alto shared many initial conditions. Both resettlements had residents with similar demographics in terms of race, post-Mitch trauma, origin of pre-Mitch neighborhood, socioeconomic status, and so forth. Residents were also strangers, arriving from locations throughout the city with low bonding social capital to new heterogeneous resettlements. La Iglesia and La Internacional are also comparable in their goals of building a model community and in the infrastructure, house size, and geographic location of the resettlements they constructed. El Valle resettlement residents came from peripheral impoverished areas, such as unsanctioned periurban areas, which often suffered from higher crime and lower social capital compared to wealthier suburbs (Shaw and McKay 1942; Jargowsky and Park 2009). Post-disaster primary and secondary trauma and the process of relocation to a place without established bonding social capital combined to create a particularly vulnerable population, one likely to encounter significant challenges in creating a unifying culture. These similarities suggest that the resettlements could have had a parallel development trajectory if they had engaged in similar key practices (Goldstone 1998). At least theoretically, each could have created the community culture that would support the development of a socially healthy community.

Early differences in the populations and in the NGO's choices irrevocably shaped each resettlement's development. These differences in initial conditions—resident background and demographics, organizational strategies, NGO religious or secular background, resource input over time, commitment timeframe (short or long term), resettlement design, resident training before resettlement, and so forth—impacted the potential to create new visions and social norms within the resettlements and laid the groundwork for the formation of unique and distinct community cultures.

In Suyapa, La Iglesia's social worker, Belkis, connects the religious background of the organization to its success. She states, "The community has the Church, the spiritual part. The spiritual work that has been done here by the Church has helped. It has allowed this community to be what it wants, a peaceful community." It is not that Catholicism is a better religion on its merits. To residents, Catholicism is the dominant faith in Honduras and is deeply embedded in political, social, and cultural life. Thus, La Iglesia benefited from the legitimacy of the Catholic Church, the salience of its strategies and values, and the recognition of its structure (the NGO-resident relationship was hierarchically similar to the Church's relationship with parishioners). Therefore, the vision and norms espoused by La Iglesia, seen as an arm of the Church, were more easily embraced by Suyapa residents regardless of their religious preferences. La Internacional, despite being very well respected, could not tie its vision to larger religious or cultural paradigms—and its partnership approach, not a traditional or familiar type of relationship, may not have sufficiently resonated with residents.

The material resource input and NGO timeframe reinforced the early, divergent paths taken by each resettlement. It would seem plausible that the more money spent on infrastructure, social development, staff, and community programs, the more successful the future community would be. This did not prove to be the case in these sites. By 2002, La Iglesia had spent a total of about 100 million lempiras ($6,060,600; 16.5 L = $1) on Suyapa, while La Internacional had spent about 387.5 million lempiras ($23,484,850) on Pino Alto. The cost per household is $10,360 in Suyapa and $18,787 in Pino Alto. Part of this difference is attributed to the excellent infrastructure, especially water piping and filtration, that Pino Alto maintains. Still, more resources do not necessarily equal better social health outcomes.

From 2002 to 2011, the amount of material input into each resettlement shifted. According to La Iglesia, through mortgage payments Suyapa residents collectively repaid upward of 80 million lempiras, or $4,210,526 (~$7,200 per household adjusted for inflation; 19 L = $1), which La Iglesia redirected toward social projects. The mortgages enabled the organization to maintain a surplus of funds. This was a strategic choice, since La Iglesia knew that it would have to withdraw from the project for financial reasons once the houses were built. In order to instill values such as work ethic and commitment in the community, they directed residents to pay small mortgages that were then reinvested into the resettlement and allowed La Iglesia to continue serving as an active guiding presence. According to Doña Rosa, the collective value of the homes has increased to 180 million lempiras, an 80 percent return over ten years. She argues that this is due to the reputation of Suyapa as a safe and peaceful place to live.

After an exhaustive search of La Internacional's records and requests for information, I have been unable to obtain the amount spent by the organization on the resettlement after 2002. It is probable that La Internacional spent much more per capita than La Iglesia initially, but that La Iglesia spent more over time (through the reinvestment of mortgage payments), since La Internacional had difficulty procuring funding for social programming and officially left the resettlement in 2007. La Internacional had multiple obligations throughout the country, and its resources were spread thin as various emergencies appeared each year. Without enough revenue to sustain the long-term development of Pino Alto, La Internacional could not justify using its limited funds to support a fully developed resettlement when hundreds of thousands of Hondurans were suffering due to prolonged droughts, floods, and storms (GFDRR 2010).

Even without knowing La Internacional's figures, the evidence still indicates that La Iglesia likely provided less initial material input into the resettlement and still produced better social health outcomes. The fact that La Internacional had only a limited timeframe in Pino Alto may have encouraged the organization to focus its resources on creating excellent, lasting infrastructure at the expense of neglecting the resettlement's social development. By contrast, La Iglesia had a long-term commitment to the resettlement and could balance its spending between infrastructure and social programs.

Social science scholars (Newman 1973; Scudder and Colson 1982; Olshansky and Chang 2009; Iuchi 2010; Aldrich 2012a) have singled out the importance of resettlement design in fostering a socially healthy community, especially after a disaster. Pino Alto is a well-planned and designed resettlement. La Internacional expended significant time and resources in designing the infrastructure to encourage social development. La Iglesia, though it had a smaller resettlement and less land, also did the best that it could to design a resettlement that was sensitive to the residents' needs and prepared for future hazards.

Both resettlements include a central space for community interaction, with houses built extending outward from the central space, in a typical Spanish design. These designs differed in two ways. The first was the usability of the central space. In Pino Alto, the central space was not conducive to social interaction. In my time in Pino Alto, I saw people sit with umbrellas for short periods, and children used the space for small soccer games, but it was not a common gathering area due to the heat, lack of shade, and constant wind blowing dust. In Suyapa, although the central space was much smaller, it was paved, ornamental plants dotted the park, a few trees provided shade, and a water fountain would run on occasion. The space was more user-friendly and situated in the middle of town next to the market.

The location of the central market was also vitally important. In Suyapa, the market was located next to the park, near the bus station, and near the church. It was a seven-minute walk from the farthest house, with little elevation change. The entire market was covered, allowing it be a refuge for residents during a rainstorm or from the heat of the sun. In Pino Alto, the market was far for most residents, and only a handful of shops remained open after the murder of the two security guards. Reyna and her son David lived in Suyapa and moved to Pino Alto. In reference to the markets, David mentioned, "Suyapa has a market environment because it is in the central section and here [Pino Alto] it is outside [the community]." Instead, Pino Alto had thriving informal *pulperías* found throughout the resettlement. This phenomenon is likely a direct effect of the lack of a centralized market.

It is predictable that Suyapa would have higher social capital and collective efficacy due to urban planning; its design was much more conducive to social interaction, and the population was much smaller. Pino Alto residents tended to stay within their neighborhood blocks, meeting in the shade of their homes or along the narrow corridors between houses and buying from the nearby *pulpería*. Suyapa residents flocked to the park and market often just to be near the liveliest part of town. The lack of useful communal space, the size of the resettlement, and fewer community-wide activities led to factionalism in Pino Alto, in which residents' social networks became parochial; each network comprised immediate neighbors and those on the same block and possibly in the same barrio. Without a sense of community throughout the entire resettlement, the barrios balkanized and some began to create their own identity.

The literature substantiates the thesis that initial conditions matter. Putnam (1993) found that the regions of Italy with the most successful democratic institutions were those with relatively healthy and well-developed civil society in the nineteenth century. In a similar vein, Fukuyama (1995) argues that cultures of "low trust" are at an economic disadvantage in the global economy due to the challenges of developing large and complex social institutions. Jeannotte (2003, 47; see also Buchan 2003; Aldrich 2013) notes the importance of buy-in to these norms:

> Cultural participation helps to connect individuals to the social spaces occupied by others and encourages "buy-in" to institutional rules and shared norms of behavior. Without this "buy-in," individuals are unlikely to enter into willing collaboration with others and without that cooperation, civic engagement and social capital—key components of social cohesion—may be weakened.

Putnam (1993), Fukuyama (1995), and Jeannotte (2003) identify initial characteristics as the best predictors of future success for social institutions. Likewise, the initial conditions discussed above also direct each community's trajectory in this study.

FORMATION OF COMMUNITY CULTURE

Pierson's (2000, 251) claim that "large consequences may result from relatively small or contingent events" restates a crucial point: initial conditions matter as much as, if not more than, later interventions. So do early efforts to build a collective vision and social norms, which can provide the fertile soil from which bonding and bridging social capital, collective efficacy, social cohesion, and civic participation can develop. The unique characteristics of a heterogeneous resettlement—a lack of long-term social networks and a *new* resettlement—ensured that each resettlement's culture ultimately could take different forms. Organizations and early residents were afforded the opportunity and the challenge of defining a collective vision and norms to support it.[2]

As discussed, each NGO chose a different development strategy. La Iglesia utilized a SAGE approach, focusing on the creation of social structures and institutions through sustainment, accompaniment, guidance, and resident empowerment. La Internacional employed a partnership approach that encouraged agency among resettlement leaders and self-help development. What proved difficult to know beforehand, without the benefit of theory, exemplars, or hindsight, were other key characteristics and processes—scope of work, selection process, community development before resettlement, social development, buy-in, social control, time commitment, and the type of leadership support—that would give each resettlement a particular trajectory. Each organization, undoubtedly, struggled with these issues as best as it could, given the resources available. When I asked La Iglesia's and La Internacional's directors about which community development theories they had drawn upon, neither named specific theories; both mentioned that they did their best with the resources and knowledge they had available, often improvising as each new decision arose. Neither knew much about or followed a particular community development theory.

Additionally, in both Suyapa and Pino Alto, the collective vision and social norms were initially defined by the organization in concert with residents, though implementation was significantly different. The following paragraphs will discuss the influence of each NGO in the development of a collective vision and the enforcement of the social norms that would bring it into being.

Imagine a group of thousands of strangers brought to a new place to live together. Each individual would have his or her own opinion about what that new place should look like, how it should run, what the rules should be, and what was best for the whole. Each has a set of norms and values they have lived by that they have internalized but that may or may not resonate with others. How does this group define a common set of social rules, especially if these rules differ from what they previously had been familiar with? How is power distributed? Who leads? How is bonding social capital created? Who deals with conflict among residents? And how does a collective vision develop? The issues that arise in the community development process are numerous. As Suyapa and Pino Alto illustrate, in the liminal space of initial resettlement, in which everyone is arriving during the absence of an embedded normative culture, a collective vision and social norms must be created ex nihilo.

La Internacional and La Iglesia had high expectations for their respective resettlements. Suyapa and Pino Alto were claimed to be model communities with the ambition of developing an exemplar for future resettlements worldwide. To do so, in conjunction with residents, both organizations attempted to envision, as clearly as possible, what the resettlement and residents were supposed to become.

Even before the relocation of future residents, each organization had begun socializing prospective residents toward a collective vision and set of behaviors that would foster that vision. La Internacional focused most of its efforts on individual development (development *in* community) in the *macro-albergues*. They created capacity-building courses covering such issues as self-esteem, tourism, customer service, human relations, and various employment skills. When they were actually building homes, La Internacional promoted the idea that "the construction of the home is not an end, but rather a medium to arrive at community development" (CESAL 2008, 74). The organization put forth six social goals during the construction stage: ensuring equal participation by families in construction projects, maintaining security at the resettlement site, providing appropriate housing for each family, managing conflicts, fortifying and generating constructive abilities and skills to encourage income generation as well as continued maintenance of the home, and completing community development by sensitizing residents to respect the work that they put into in the community (CESAL 2008, 75–76). Following the La Internacional philosophy, these capacity-building opportunities and goals lean toward personal or household development rather than the building of a cohesive community.

It would seem likely that Pino Alto residents, most of whom had arrived from the same *macro-albergues* (where many of them lived together for years) and who also worked together for forty weeks before moving into the resettlement, would bond. The social cohesion that often comes from proximity could encourage the development of bonding social capital and buy-in to a collective vision, especially in comparison to Suyapa residents.

Yet, in Pino Alto, the formation of a collective vision was not this simple. A large number of people moved into the resettlement at the same time who were not necessarily from the same *albergues*. In some cases, residents had jobs in the capital and hired workers to take their place over the forty-week work commitment period. Furthermore, the geographic layout of the resettlement fails to facilitate social interaction. The greater number of households also diluted relationships; the quantity and heterogeneity of people made it challenging to reach broad consensus on a unifying vision. Lastly, the social networks and cohesion built in the *albergues* were disrupted once the relocation happened. Many *albergue* neighbors were separated in Pino Alto, disrupting previous social capital. In short, the experience of resettlement for many Pino Alto residents was chaotic, inhibiting the creation of a common vision.

In contrast, La Iglesia, after selecting the first two hundred families, required that a representative of each family attend weekly capacity-building workshops for six months before the families arrived in the resettlement.[3] These workshops covered themes regarding resettlement expectations, leadership training, the logistics of how the resettlement would work, and seminars on "what it means to live in community" (CESAL 2008, 78–79). By the end of 1999, La Iglesia had imprinted upon future residents a clear vision, viable political structures, and social norms that would support residents' move forward in community building immediately upon relocation. The first two hundred families also moved in together within a short time span. The clear expectations, weekly meetings, and act of arriving together inculcated into the residents' minds the collective vision of a healthy model community.

La Internacional's partnership approach and short time frame made it much harder to achieve its ends. La Internacional, although stating a clear vision, limited its involvement in the creation of social structures and community culture that would turn the vision into a reality, instead handing the process over to residents. Without formal leadership by La Internacional, the novice and mostly untrained *patronato* was unable to promote a unifying vision. Residents, lacking guidance, regressed from the ideal vision of a model resettlement to the problematic cultures they had previously known in Tegucigalpa. Beliefs and values found in these neighborhoods tended to isolate individuals, discourage civic participation and social capital, and ultimately, discourage active participation in transforming the resettlement into a community.

In Suyapa, La Iglesia distributed a document on norms of conduct and living in community (*Manual de normas de conducta y convivencia comunitaria*). This document, written in conjunction with the arrival of the first two hundred families, defined resettlement norms, which differed from and were stricter than those found in Tegucigalpa. The manual became the blueprint for the resettlement, and each resident had to sign a contract saying that they and their family agreed to live by the code of conduct. Although it was contested over time and through formal sanctions, Suyapa maintained the initial collective vision developed by La Iglesia and the first two hundred families. The imposition of sanctions, coupled with its long-term commitment and investment (financial and otherwise), buttressed the vision set forth by La Iglesia in the initial stages of resettlement, further encouraging future success.

La Iglesia clearly promoted the vision and enforced social norms. Belkis, the La Iglesia social worker, spells out the values Suyapa had laid out from the beginning:

> There are regulations from the point of view as in the *Manual of Conduct Standards and Community Cooperation* . . . to establish minimum standards of living, with respect to neighbors, trying to build solidarity among neighbors, and within the community. Another condition is the whole process of training to be brought into the community. This process has been important since its inception, a constant process of training. Another thing is good communication and openness in the issues in which La Iglesia has had to be firm and truthful in order not to impair the vision created from the beginning. For example, we have been approached by residents who wanted a gaming center or a bar since they do not exist here [in Suyapa]. But you know that opening the doors to this type of business is opening the door to all kinds of problems.

Belkis describes the instruments used by La Iglesia, including the formal code of conduct, continued training, and its ability to limit resident agency. As mentioned in chapter 5, guiding the resettlement through social intervention was an indispensable part of La Iglesia praxis. The use of clear and legitimate cultural norms, cultivated by La Iglesia with input from residents, provided the structural framework for the growth of a stronger, healthier resettlement culture. The organization could (and did) sanction residents for their behavior, encouraged training and social interaction in many areas (creating a foundation for strong leadership to emerge), and did not permit certain types of businesses, such as bars or gambling casinos, within the boundaries of the resettlement.

In Pino Alto, norms and rules were in place as well, but there was no way to enforce them; the *patronato* was weak and La Internacional, with its hands-off partnership approach and lack of power, had little ability to ensure compliance. Unlike La Iglesia, La Internacional could not stop residents from turning their houses into *cantinas* or gang hangouts. As Pastor Eduardo shared with me, "There is a hidden bar on almost every block." The increased disorder, whether higher levels of physical disorder, social disorder as evidenced by crime rates, or political disorder illustrated in the corruption and ineffective *patronato*, likely led to further disorder. As Keizer, Lindenberg, and Steg (2008, 1685) point out, "Early disorder diagnosis and intervention are of vital importance when fighting the spread of disorder." This did not happen in Pino Alto. The importance of social norm development and enforcement cannot be overstated in building community.

CONCILIATION OF COMMUNITY CULTURE

Perhaps the most complex and long-lived process of moving a resettlement toward community is the conciliation of culture. Again, residents from dozens of different neighborhoods were relocated together. Defining a collective vision and a set of social norms is relatively straightforward; obtaining buy-in and commitment is much more complex. How then does an organization or resettlement leadership maintain the common vision and social norms in the midst of such diversity? Comparing the outcomes of Suyapa and Pino Alto, one finds that evidence suggests that the role of the NGO either strengthened or degraded the initially created community culture.

NGOs taking on the role of community developers in much of the global south face enormous challenges to create spaces protected from a culture of violence, gang issues, police or judicial corruption, and crime. Working without a strong state presence and with diverse cultural frameworks between residents, the organizations felt it necessary to implement stricter guidelines than those that had existed in Tegucigalpa to maintain order in the resettlement communities. In the cases of Suyapa and Pino Alto, many of the rules were the same, but enforcement differed dramatically.

Suyapa had much stricter practices of social control due, in large part, to the influence of La Iglesia. Tied to its philosophy, La Iglesia's actions underscored the importance of social order. Residents followed the rules to avoid informal and formal sanctions imposed by resettlement leaders and the NGO. Residents were socialized to follow and later maintain the rules, which then became the cultural expectation and value (collective efficacy) of the resettlement. Due to the high integration of La Iglesia, the organization was able to intervene through formal sanctions, such as removing or threatening to remove problematic residents, while also empowering many residents to impose informal and formal sanctions upon each other. Positive sanctions could be as simple as general acceptance in the resettlement or as significant as public recognition by the CCS or La Iglesia. Negative sanctions would often begin as resident gossip but could, at the extreme end, lead to La Iglesia's removing a family from their home and the resettlement. Residents found it more worthwhile to work toward the collective vision both because they believed in the idea and because they did not want to be sanctioned for not subscribing. Their actions consequently strengthened common vision and norm formation.

Social order reinforced particular norms in Suyapa, and these norms, in turn, reproduced a concomitant level of social order. As outlined below, the same can go for neighborly trust, community participation, and collective efficacy. The philosophy and practice of La Iglesia, which included input from residents from the very beginning and over time, were the critical elements in the creation of the social norms that would influence the residents' behavior. Similarly, it has been found that if no new vision or norms are put into place, then residents will relapse to previous norms (Inglehart and Baker 2000). If this is the case, what one would expect to see in those resettlements with weaker social norm formation is a return to norms common in residents' former neighborhoods in Tegucigalpa (often including high distrust and violence [Call 2000; Coleman and Argueta 2008] and a breakdown of norms or norm cascading [Finnemore and Sikkink 1998]). This would be due in part to conflict among stakeholders preventing the creation of a common set of social norms.

Within Suyapa, strong social control mechanisms, due to La Iglesia's control over the mortgages and the daily presence of the NGO in the lives of the community, were in place. David, a previous Suyapa resident who now lives in Pino Alto, articulated his understanding of the differences in social order between the two resettlements:

> [Delinquency] is a big problem here in Pino Alto. There are a lot of drugs, and the police do not interfere much even though it is their job. In Suyapa the police are the same but the influence of La Iglesia is very important, because La Iglesia provides order. There [in Suyapa] gangs started to form and they [La Iglesia] told the people, well, you must control your children or leave.

Santiago, a La Iglesia employee, provided a further explanation. He pointed out that it was not specifically the delinquents who would lose their home, but more often their mother or another relative, since homeowners were responsible for the actions of all those living under their roof. This mechanism of social control made an enormous difference. As explained earlier, Suyapa residents were more concerned about La Iglesia taking their home, in stark contrast with Pino Alto residents, who were less apprehensive.

For the first nine years of Suyapa's existence, La Iglesia staff were present in the resettlement for a minimum of five (but as many as seven) days a week, collecting payments, working on infrastructure, starting new projects, resolving problems and conflicts, or engaging in other activities related to the well-being of the resettlement. Employees would check each home monthly to ensure that it was resident-occupied (not used as a second home or rented to outsiders). Oscar, a full-time social worker for La Iglesia, describes the NGO's role:

I think it's very important that you also have the presence of La Iglesia within the housing project through its staff. I think it helps because they [the staff] are there to address problems encountered in daily life and they are in the community as servants of the community. [The staff] can mediate in situations because when things are off track and the community is losing the vision with which the housing project was created, then La Iglesia staff can intervene so that the community can take the right path.

From his perspective, the organization kept the community focused (sustained), supported the vision over time (accompanied), and intervened when necessary (guided), impacting the reproduction of the new set of social norms. La Iglesia also focused on resident empowerment through capacity building before and after relocation, increasing responsibility of the CCS and collaborations wherein residents decided on and built projects with materials provided by the organization paid for by their mortgages.

Unlike La Iglesia, La Internacional left residents to their own devices when it came to creating community. The partnership approach meant residents had to take care of their own trauma, vulnerabilities, and social problems. Without the support of the NGO, Pino Alto residents were unable to develop the new social norms that would provide the foundation for better resettlement social health. Although La Internacional did tremendous work with residents in the *macro-albergues* from 1998 to their arrival in Pino Alto in 2004, resident vulnerability inhibited their ability to maintain a common vision without oversight and assistance. The NGO stayed for only three years to provide support once residents moved into Pino Alto, where a larger, more heterogeneous population made social cohesion more difficult and made a longer presence perhaps even more necessary.

La Internacional lacked the social control mechanisms employed by La Iglesia. It did not have the ability or desire to take houses away from residents, nor did it have the resources to maintain staff working in the resettlement or checking on home occupation. The organization's focus is disaster relief, not long-term development. As described in chapter 6, the NGO had no plans to be tied to the growth or outcomes of Pino Alto, nor did it believe its job was to shape the resettlement's political decisions or protect it against corruption and delinquency.

Crime often breeds more crime (Wilson and Kelling 1982; Keizer, Lindenberg, and Steg 2008). In Pino Alto, when residents sold alcohol or sold their houses to nonresidents, or when police officers were assaulted and the assailants remained unpunished, others were implicitly permitted to do the same. Some of the behavior and social norms of their former neighborhoods in Tegucigalpa reemerged. Murders became common, and people were increasingly afraid to leave their homes. Crime thus limited social cohesion, social capital, and participation. When corruption and nepotism became problems in Pino Alto, many residents gave up on the political system, believing that voting was pointless. Decreasing collective efficacy and participation, in turn, lessened trust and increased crime. Social health spiraled downward as a particular resettlement culture became entrenched.

The evolving vision and norms, for better or worse, were subsequently shared with the next cohort of residents. A new resettlement culture had begun to take on a life of its own and set the parameters for what was acceptable and normal in Suyapa and Pino Alto.

INCREASING RETURNS

As McMillan and Chavis (1986, 13) point out, "Influence of a member on the community and influence of the community on a member operate concurrently, and one might expect to see the force of both operating simultaneously in a tightly knit community." In the case of Suyapa and Pino Alto, visions and social norms solidified and stabilized over time.[4] The following examples illustrate the changing nature of resettlement to community by comparing resident experiences from arrival (2002–2004) and after several years (2009–2010). Residents were asked about life situation, community participation, trust in neighbors, delinquency, leadership, and livelihood. In short, did a self-reinforcing feedback loop, like a snowball moving downhill, build over time?

To evaluate the different levels of community participation found in 2009–2010, I asked whether the resident's participation had changed since arriving in the resettlement. While no statistically significant difference appears between Pino Alto (23 percent) and the other resettlements (21 percent), 47 percent of Suyapa residents responded affirmatively. This finding supports the claim that community participation is a process, not an initial demographic difference, and that a stronger mechanism encouraging participation existed in Suyapa, which reinforced a common community culture.

Turning to neighborly trust, the same conclusions hold true to a lesser extent. When asked, "Your trust in your neighbors has: decreased, stayed the same, or increased during your time in the community?" more than half of Suyapa residents (55 percent) report that their trust had increased, higher than Pino Alto (33 percent) and the average resettlement (45 percent). The opposite is also meaningful. In Pino Alto, 16 percent of residents claim their trust in neighbors decreased over time, while only 7 percent of Suyapa and the average resettlement had a similar response. As one characteristic of social capital, these statistics illustrate that Suyapa's overall process has been much more positive and successful than that of Pino Alto or the other resettlements.

Following the pattern, delinquency also identifies Pino Alto as an outlier. When asked to compare delinquency when they arrived in the resettlement (approximately 2004) to their life in 2009–2010, Pino Alto residents were almost equally split between delinquency decreasing, staying the same, or increasing—and all three are statistically significant in comparison to Suyapa and the average. What is striking is the fact that in Pino Alto, almost three times more residents (36 percent) believe that delinquency is increasing than in Suyapa (13 percent) and the control resettlements (10 percent). The opposite is also true. Two-thirds of Suyapa and the control resettlement residents believe that delinquency is actually decreasing, while only one-third of Pino Alto residents have the same belief. This perception illustrates how residents feel not only about their past but also about the fate of their respective resettlements. Despite being complex and poorly understood, the perception of crime has been found to have a "chilling effect" on social capital and community participation (Saegert and Winkel 2004), which may help explain the interaction of these different social health characteristics. Scholars discuss how social integration and individual perceptions of collective efficacy have an inverse relationship to concern about crime, leading one to speculate as to the self-reinforcing cycle of increasing fear of crime lowering social capital and participation, which in turn would increase the fear of crime (Gibson, Zhaoa, Lovrich, and Gaffney 2002)

Like community participation, Suyapa stands out as the anomaly in how residents feel about resettlement leadership over time. Many more residents in the control resettlements (52 percent) and Pino Alto (62 percent) express that their leadership is actually worse now than when their resettlement was founded compared to Suyapa residents (15 percent). Furthermore, nearly a third of Suyapa residents believe their leadership is doing better, while only 11 percent of Pino Alto and 13 percent of the control group have the same opinion. Two conclusions can be drawn from this. First, as discussed earlier, the strong presence of La Iglesia may have been a powerful factor in supporting the CCS's ability to take root in the resettlement, whereas in Pino Alto the *patronato* did not have the same support and for that reason, had the opposite results. Second, since corruption is endemic on all levels of Honduran society (Human Rights Watch 2016; Transparency International 2016), it is no surprise that without external influences Pino Alto's *patronato* would also take advantage of the system. The SAGE approach, with deliberate intervention in governance and slow transference of power over multiple years, enabled the CCS to develop a transparent and democratic foundation.

In sum, like the adage "one can know a tree by its fruit," culture formation can often be seen in a community's social health (most commonly discussed in reference to crime—Etzioni 2000; Cooter 2000). The divergent outcomes in social health of Pino Alto and Suyapa can be linked to the different community development approaches implemented by each respective supporting organization. Additionally, the creation and reinforcement of a collective vision and social norms throughout the process are critical for developing a foundation on which the resettlement can thrive. The absence of support in the process can lead to resettlements fracturing along religious, political, social, geographic (barrio), or other lines, undermining broader bonding social capital, cohesion, and collective efficacy. In the end, divided resettlements will have greater difficulty surmounting social problems and building future resilience.

LONG-TERM RESETTLEMENT AND COMMUNITY DEVELOPMENT

Successful resettlements required a clear strategy to address vulnerability through individual and collective capacity building, the development of resettlement culture that builds social health, the creation of a sense of community, and structures to guide and maintain these characteristics. In a heterogeneous resettlement, this process takes a long time and requires long-term organizational support (eight to ten years).[5]

Different NGO time commitments to the resettlement promoted or demoted the increasing returns of the conciliated resettlement culture. The initial decision by La Iglesia to remain involved with the resettlement for fifteen years contrasted with the uncertain commitment of La Internacional. Suyapa residents expressed a feeling of reassurance and comfort in the knowledge that the organization would not leave abruptly. This knowledge provided stability and much-valued support, given the context of traumatized relocated disaster survivors. La Internacional, however, adjusted its timeline multiple times, though it never intended to remain involved in the development of the community. The changing time frame created a sense of insecurity and the concern among Pino Alto residents that they would be left alone.

Pledges of extended accompaniment by organizations also provided consistency to residents. The relocation process and initial years within a resettlement can be chaotic as economic, political, and social relationships are negotiated. The progression of resettlement residents (who are initially strangers) to becoming neighbors is lengthy and tenuous, as the development of social capital, collective efficacy, social cohesion, and collective vision do not appear within a few months or even a few years. Doña Rosa highlights the importance of sustained accompaniment: "In Suyapa it took six years for the resettlement to become a community. . . . It was after six years that people finally started working together as a community; working together on community projects." Resettlements that did not have the benefit of consistent organizational accompaniment had greater difficulty in bringing residents together to address common social problems. Most resettlements without support were much more vulnerable to problematic elements such as drugs, gangs, and corruption.

Additionally, the NGO time commitment impacts the social reproduction of the collective vision and social norms. A vision and norms were going to develop in some form; as discussed in chapter 3, without a replacement, residents naturally returned to the culture of their previous Tegucigalpa neighborhood. Since organizations wanted the resettlement to be a healthier place to live than residents' original neighborhoods, they put forth expectations and norms, including goals like lower alcoholism, less crime and violence, more civic participation, and greater social capital than in the capital city. New goals, though, were not enough. Long-term, continual reinforcement of the expectations and norms was required, through informal and formal sanction, to embed the new culture. For example, in Suyapa, La Iglesia's consistently strong presence reinforced the desired "model community" culture. Since La Internacional did not possess the resources for a long-term commitment, it could only share its collective vision but could not reinforce it.

An extended timeline also facilitated the establishment of new institutions over time. The data suggests that certain resident and resettlement characteristics make the residents vulnerable to negative influences and fracturing. La Iglesia, implementing a SAGE strategy over nearly a decade, fortified new community institutions, which enhanced the development of political bodies, cooperatives, the formal market, and community cohesion around social problems. Suyapa's institutions, accompanied by La Iglesia, were able to avoid major corruption, nepotism, high crime, conflict, and the massive theft of resettlement materials. As the institutions strengthened over time, La Iglesia handed over further control and power. The citizens were proud of their resettlement, and they valued preserving institutions that made possible the realization of such a lofty vision. Internal and external affirmation encouraged Suyapa residents. Over time their optimism and feelings of empowered agency grew as they witnessed the dividends of their hard work: a socially healthy resettlement with solid institutions and independence from La Iglesia. As Don Hernán said, "Estamos en el paraíso" (we are in paradise). Pino Alto residents were not so fortunate. Although they worked equally hard to develop their resettlement into a model community, violence and corruption undermined the initial spirit of efficacy and empowerment, leaving many feeling resigned to living in a resettlement of strangers.

In the words of Arnold Toynbee (1889–1975), the English economic historian and social reformer, "Apathy can be overcome by enthusiasm, and enthusiasm can only be aroused by two things: first, an ideal, which takes the imagination by storm, and second, a definite intelligible plan for carrying that ideal into practice" (quoted in Forbes.com 2014). Although both Suyapa and Pino Alto had the ideals (in the form of a vision and new social norms), it was La Iglesia that provided the intelligible plan (SAGE strategy) that made the continuation of Suyapa's ideal possible.

PRACTICAL APPLICATION

António Guterres, UN High Commissioner for Refugees from 2005 to 2015, expressed that "we are witnessing a paradigm change, an unchecked slide into an era in which the scale of global forced displacement as well as the response required is now clearly dwarfing anything seen before" (UNHCR 2015a). There is little doubt that climate change will result in the climate refugee crisis continuing to grow, necessitating mass relocation and resettlement on an unprecedented scale. Taking just one example, scholars believe that there could be a mass immigration of up to fifty million people from Bangladesh by 2050 (Harris 2014). Forced displacement due to war, development projects, pollution, and so forth, is scaling up the need for coherent and holistic strategies to help people "build back better" wherever they rebuild. Although many of these crises are beyond our control, those of us involved in displacement issues, whether as scholars, practitioners, or policymakers, can influence *how* relocation and resettlement happen.[6]

The experiences of Suyapa and Pino Alto exemplify that a resettlement is not a community initially, but it can become one with support. Theorists and development agencies have broadly focused on economic development, individual and family well-being, and infrastructure as ways to define successful resettlement, although they are arguably inadequate. For example, the creation of strong economic mechanisms does not alone provide social health. A strong marketplace and high levels of resident wealth clearly have benefits, both financially and socially, but they cannot buy low crime, civic participation, or a collective vision. Similarly, the built infrastructure, NGO expenditures, or resident demographics do not presuppose a particular development trajectory. Leadership training, economic opportunities, and capacity building, among other strategic support measures, benefited the resettlements and should not be undervalued. At the same time, these alone did not provide the social structures necessary to develop a sense of community.

In-community development has become commonplace. The broader neoliberal political economic paradigm is interested in financial growth, especially by household (see McMichael 2016). Additionally, houses built and wells dug, of course, are the easiest to count and prove to donors that the NGO has accomplished its goals (Damberger 2011). By focusing on the trees, agencies have missed the forest. These features do not fully capture the social characteristics, especially culture, that transform a resettlement into a socially healthy community.

In this book I argue that the development "of community," specifically the formation and reinforcement of social norms and vision over time, is equally important to the economic growth and infrastructure of a resettlement. A community is more than the sum of its parts. La Iglesia took extraordinary steps to define and reinforce a unique and healthy culture in Suyapa. It *sustained* the resettlement through provision of resources and assets, *accompanied* residents for twelve years, *guided* the creation of new institutions and a healthy community culture while supporting the resettlement against external and internal threats, and *empowered* residents to shoulder increasing responsibility over time. The SAGE approach led to some conflict, but it also resulted in much higher social health measures than those in Pino Alto and the other five resettlements studies.

La Internacional also took important steps toward the development of a sustainable, self-governing model community, but its commitment was short-term, its focus was a model community based solely on the values of individual empowerment and self-definition, and it followed a partnership strategy. Many Pino Alto residents wished La Internacional had assumed a stronger presence and intervention role within the resettlement to keep conflict to a minimum, but those are not the characteristics of partnership-style leadership. Thus, La Iglesia, more successfully than La Internacional, formed and maintained a collective vision and social norms that would be internalized and reproduced by subsequent residents.

Although the technical assistance and self-help community development paradigms are often seen as binary, La Iglesia's development strategy and La Internacional's practices utilized a little of both. In resettlement and community building, decisions are made by the sponsoring organization without the knowledge or consent of future residents. Various time and resource restraints made full resident participation difficult, but each organization worked diligently to include initial residents in the resettlement decision-making, design, and development processes. Thus, this discussion is not as much about a technocratic versus resident-led approach as it is about how *both* can be implemented, depending on the circumstances (see Alesch, Arendt, and Holly 2009).

It seems, therefore, that under specific post-disaster resettlement or refugee conditions there may be a much greater need for sustainment, accompaniment, guidance, and empowerment *of community* to promote and maintain a particular collective vision and social norms over time. A SAGE approach, depending on context, may best provide the structure and increasing returns necessary for long-term social health development.

QUESTIONS AND FUTURE RESEARCH

The evidence in this comparative case study suggests that a SAGE approach to new heterogeneous resettlement development will lead to socially healthier communities over time. Still, numerous complications remain. For example, what is to be done with the families who do not meet a selection standard or who are pushed out of their homes because of their children's behavior? Is this not reproducing a system of stratification? The answer—of course it is. In an ideal world, all people would have access to the same resources, no matter their background, circumstances, or decisions. In the real world, NGOs have limited resources, skills, time, and human power to help as many people as they can. In Honduras, permitting even one gang-affiliated family to keep a home risks the health of the entire resettlement. Decisions must be made with the hope that those who are not chosen will find other resources. This is not acceptable to some theorists and activists, yet it remains the reality of scarce resources and must be acknowledged; subsequent alternative strategies must be proposed.

It has also been documented that disaster recovery has all too often made survivors' lives worse rather than better (Jha et al. 2010). Further comparative investigations into recovery and resettlement are called for to ensure that the billions of dollars poured into the building and rebuilding of infrastructure are buttressed by social structures that emphasize *the social well-being of survivors and community over time*. This long-term focus, coupled with the creation and maintenance of a community culture, ensures that future resettlements are indeed providing opportunities for residents to develop to their fullest potential, individually and collectively. With the guidance and support of NGO or government programs, transformative resettlement can take place, turning strangers into neighbors living in a community characterized by social health.

Further research is also needed to elaborate on how various actors shape the community development process. Governments, in both the global north and global south, often take an ad hoc approach to disaster recovery issues. They frequently do not have the financial or technical capacity to develop in-depth plans to deal with the human impact of natural hazards in a holistic and long-term way. In the global north, organizations work collaboratively with government to support the resettlement of individuals or entire communities. How this collaboration happens, and which level of government takes responsibility for implementing strategies that benefit social health, often remain unclear—sometimes leading to significant failure, as exemplified in the St. Louis, Missouri, Pruitt-Igoe public housing experiment (Friedrichs 2011). Defining clear roles about funding, infrastructure, social support, and timelines can and must be developed in a dialectical relationship with future residents. In the global south, nation-states often lack adequate resources to address the resettlement of thousands of citizens or migrants and depend on NGOs to provide services and development. However, as witnessed in Suyapa and Campo Cielo, organizations can mitigate or exacerbate the social problems in resettlements. If an organization decides to take on a project such as the resettlement of disaster survivors, it must ensure that it can follow the Hippocratic Oath and do no harm, not only during the relief and recovery phase but in the development phase as well.

Finally, a large theoretical gap remains in understanding all factors contributing to how strangers come together under different circumstances and build a new culture and sense of community. The world will benefit from future investigations that can discern how people with diverse assets and vulnerabilities do this cohesively and what may be the ways in which external groups and organizations can best facilitate the process. One can imagine future new peri-urban areas, refugee camps, post-disaster resettlements, dormitories, and even prisons as being fundamentally different if early intervention and long-term accompaniment and guidance can support the creation of a healthy initial culture and social relationships that will be passed on to forthcoming cohorts.

When resettlement or relocation is conceptualized as a long-term development process rather than a short-term recovery effort, and when it is understood as the inception, implementation, and maturation of infrastructure *and* social structures, the process of slowly building social capital, collective efficacy, vision, and civic participation, and maintaining low crime rates, are likely to begin down a sustainable path. This, in turn, will lead to the results we all hope for—a better life for survivors and their children.

Table A.1 Resettlement Surveys

Resettlement	Number of household surveys conducted	Approximate number of occupied homes [+]	Percentage of homes surveyed
Suyapa	449	583	77
Pino Alto (Random Sample)	506	1285	39
La Tierra	321	498	64
Campo Cielo	261	353	74
Valle Verde	224	317	71
Cerro Viejo	43	70	61
Santa Fe	114	150	76
Total	1918	3359	—

[+] On average, about 10% of homes are vacant or only have limited use (e.g., vacation homes).

Table A.2 Suyapa and Pino Alto Infrastructure and Housing

	Suyapa	Pino Alto
Geographic location	El Valle	El Valle
Subsections	9	10
Community buildings		
Community center	1	0
Library	1 (multi-use room)	1 (not in use)
Internet café	1 (private)	1 (private)
Educational/vocational workshops	4 buildings	~10 multi-use buildings
	Intermittent closures of buildings	Intermittent closures of buildings
Police station	1 (2 full-time police officers)	1 (2 full-time police officers)
Offices	1 La Iglesia	1 La Internacional office (closed)
	1 Comité Cívico Social	1 Junta de Agua
		1 Patronato
Schools	0 preschools, 1 elementary, 1 middle/high school	2 preschools, 1 elementary, 1 middle/high school
Small parks	7	2
Clinics	1	1
Full-time doctors/nurses	1; 1–2	1; 2
Churches		
Catholic	1 (permanent building)	1 (land and temporary building)
Evangelical	3 (either just outside of the resettlement or in residents' homes)	10
Protestant	0	1 (Methodist)
Economic spaces		
Large market	1 (55 total store stalls; 44 occupied, 11 empty)	1 (88 total store stalls, 10 occupied, 78 empty)
Percentage of streets with *pulperías*	60	89

Table A.3 Housing Information (2010 Lempiras and US Dollars)

HOUSES	Suyapa	Pino Alto
Total cost of community	~100,000,000 lempiras (~$6,060,600)	~387,500,000 lempiras (~$23,484,850)[1]
Cost per home (with infrastructure)	196,000 lempiras ($10,360)	349,500 lempiras ($18,492)
# of houses	583, two houses were combined as an office for La Iglesia	1,285 total homes
Cost to buy	271,000 or 300,000 lempiras	0
Cost in work hours	0 weeks, 0 hours	40 weeks, 500 hours
Monthly payment first year (2002)	750 lempiras, $35 (in 2002 lempiras/dollars)	No payments on mortgage
Interest on home per year	8% (average inflation costs)	None
Mortgage timeline	15 years	0
Homes paid off	4% of families have had their debt forgiven due to economic circumstances	N/A
Homes in debt	0–3 months—72%	N/A
Avg. number of houses empty	~25 (4% of total)	Few (~2–3% of total)
Design	1 bathroom, 1 living room, 1 kitchen area, 1 or 2 bedrooms	1 bathroom, 1 living room, 1 kitchen area, 1 or 2 bedrooms
Material	Cement block or brick	Cement block or brick
Type of home	Duplex or single family	Duplex or single family

1. (Ortega Dolz 2002)

Table A.4 Community Utilities, Transportation, and Surrounding Communities

	Suyapa	Pino Alto
Water	2–3 days a week for about six hours—the water is semipotable (ideally not for drinking, although most residents drink the water)	All the time—the water is potable
Electricity	About 95% of the time	About 95% of the time
Garbage	2 days a week	2 days a week
Sewage	Biofiltration, treatment tanks, then gravity-fed to local river	Treatment tanks
Farmland	About 4 acres	None
Streets	Good condition	Good condition
Street types	Paved (about 30%), dirt (about 70%), in the community about 20% paved	To the community 90% paved, in the community 5% paved
Bus	Every ½ hour 5 a.m. to 7 p.m., less frequent on weekends	Every ½ hour 5 a.m. to 4 p.m., less frequent on weekends
Bus to Teguc.	1.25 to 2 hours	1.25 to 2 hours

Table A.5 Resettlement Survey Schedule (Spanish)

1. Demográficos de los miembros

1.1   ¿Qué es su nombre completo?

1.2   Sexo (*Varón [1], Mujer [2]*)

1.3   ¿Cuántos años tiene usted?

1.4   ¿Cuál es su más alto nivel de la educación? *No educación [0], básica hasta 9 grado [1], secundaria [2], universidad [3], graduado [4]*

1.5   ¿Dirección completa de su vivienda? Sector____ Peatonal____ # de casa____

1.6   ¿Dónde (qué colonia/barrio) vivió usted antes del Huracán Mitch?

1.7   ¿Cuál era su ocupación antes del huracán?

1.8   ¿Ahora, cuál es su ocupación?

1.9   ¿Y dónde (qué colonia o barrio) trabaja usted ahora?

1.10   ¿Piensa usted que su trabajo es: *peor [1], igual [2], o mejor [3]* que antes del huracán?

1.11   ¿A qué iglesia pertenece usted? *Católica [1], Protestante [2], Evangélica [3], ninguno [4], u otra [5]. ¿Cuál?*

1.12   ¿Cada cuanto asiste usted a su iglesia: *no asisto [1], fechas especiales [2], una vez por semana [3], dos días o más por semana [4]*?

1.13   ¿Cómo encontró usted la oportunidad de vivir en la comunidad? *Por una organización [1], una iglesia [2], familiares [3], otro [4]? ¿Cuál?*

1.14   ¿Por qué usted escogió vivir en la comunidad en vez de una otra comunidad?

1.15   ¿Cuántos años tiene de vivir en la comunidad? *De 0-3 años [1], 4-6 años [2], 7+ [3], o desde el inicio [4]*

1.16   ¿Está casado usted? *No [0], sí [1]*

1.17   ¿Cuántos adultos viven en la casa en total?_____ [ ] varones [ ] mujeres

1.18   ¿Cuántos niños (menos de 18 años) viven en su casa ahora?

1.19   Generalmente, ¿ahora, su salud es *mal [1], normal [2], o bien [3]*?

1.20   ¿Cuál es el ingreso promedio mensual familiar? *0-600 lempiras [1], 600-1.200 [2], 1.200-4.500 [3], 4.500-5.500 [4], 5.500-8.000 [5], 8.000-11.000 [6], 11.000 adelante [7]*

1.21   ¿Qué porcentaje de su ingreso recibe usted de remesas? *0 [1], 1-10 [2], 11-20 [3], 21-30 [4], 31-40 [5], o 40 o más [6]*

2. Calidad de vida: comparación antes y ahora

2.1   En comparación con _____ *[repita el nombre de la comunidad donde vivió antes del Mitch en 1.6]*, ¿La delincuencia en la comunidad" es menor [1], igual [2], o más [3]?

2.2   En comparación con _____ *[repita el nombre de la comunidad donde vivió antes del Mitch en 1.6]*, ¿Su confianza con sus vecinos aquí es: menor [1], igual [2], o mayor [3]?

2.3   En comparación con _____ *[repita el nombre de la comunidad donde vivió antes del Mitch en 1.6]*, ¿Su participación en la comunidad es: menor [1], igual [2], o mayor [3]?

Table A.5 Continued

2.4 En comparación con _____ *[repita el nombre de la comunidad donde vivió antes del Mitch en 1.6]*, ¿Su situación de vida es: *peor [1], casi igual [2], o mejor [3]* ahora?

4. La política, poder político, liderazgo

4.1 ¿Cree usted que puede influir en las decisiones políticas de la comunidad? *No [0], sí [1]*

4.2 Cuánto confía usted en la política de la comunidad: *¿nada [1], poco [2], o mucho [3]?*

5. Participación cívica, capital social, unidad, y religión

5.1a ¿Usted participa en las votaciones? *No [0], sí [1]*

5.1b ¿Participa usted en alguna organización de la comunidad? *No [0], sí [1]*

5.1c ¿Participa usted en la iglesia? *No [0], sí [1]*

5.1d ¿Está involucrado usted en formaciones, proyectos o actividades de la comunidad? *No [0], sí [1]*

5.1e *Sí a las últimas preguntas:* ¿Cuántas horas cada semana participa usted en una organización o iglesia de la comunidad? *No participó [0], Cuando es necesario [1], 1-2 horas [2], 3-4 horas [3], o 5+ horas [4]*

5.1f ¿Participó usted en los cursos de formación que ofreció la ONG u otra organización en su comunidad? *(como salud, liderazgo, familia) No [0], sí [1] ¿En qué año(s)? ¿Qué tema(s)?*

5.1g ¿Si haya un proyecto de servicio en la comunidad, usted participaría en una manera? *No [0], sí [1]*

5.2a Hay una liga de fútbol en la comunidad. ¿Usted o una persona de su casa participa en el campeonato? *No [0], sí [1] Si participó: ¿Cuántas personas participaron?* _____

5.2b *Si participó:* ¿Piensa usted que el campeonato llevó: *ningún [1], algunos [2], o muchos beneficios sociales [3]?* ¿Cuáles? _____

5.3a ¿Cuánto confía usted en sus vecinos? *nada [1], poco [2], o mucho [3]*

5.3b ¿ Si usted tiene una necesidad, piensa que su vecino le ayudaría? *No [0], sí [1]*

5.3c ¿Si un ladrón intenta ingresar a su casa, considera que sus vecinos lo interrumpirían? *No [0], sí [1]*

5.3d ¿Si alguien intenta vender drogas a sus hijos u otros niños en la comunidad, piensa que sus vecinos lo denunciarían o agarrarían? *No [0], sí [1]*

5.4a ¿Usted cree que los vecinos comparten los mismos valores que usted *(familia, fe, educación)*? *No [0], sí [1]*

5.4b ¿Hay un sentido de vivir en "comunidad" aquí? *No [0], sí [1]*

5.4c En su opinión, ¿la comunidad es: *desunida [1], semi-unida (más o menos unida) [2], o muy unida [3]?*

5.5a ¿La religión ha tenido un efecto en el desarrollo de la comunidad? *No [0], sí [1]*

5.5b *Sí a la última pregunta:* ¿Un efecto *negativo [1], neutral [2], o positivo [3]?*

Table A.5 Continued

6. Familiaridad con la colonia y los vecinos

6.1a ¿Usted sabe dónde están los límites (los bordes) de todos los sectores en la comunidad? *No [0], sí [1]*

6.1b ¿Cómo se llama el presidente del patronato? *No sabe [0], sí sabe [1]*

6.2a ¿Ud. reconoce por su rostro a las personas de la comunidad: es *muy difícil [1], difícil [2], fácil [3], o muy fácil [4]*?

6.2b ¿Ud. reconoce gente externa de la comunidad: es *muy difícil [1], difícil [2], fácil [3], o muy fácil [4]*?

6.3 ¿Usted cree que su comunidad es una comunidad modelo para el país? *No [0], sí [1]* ¿Por qué?

7. Control informal y delincuencia

7.1a Usted piensa que, en general, los vecinos controlan a sus niños: ¿*Mal [1], bien [2], o muy bien [3]*?

7.1b Usted piensa que, durante el año, los vecinos envían los niños a la escuela: ¿*casi nunca [1], a veces [2], o casi siempre [3]*?

7.1c ¿A usted le preocupa que la organización puede quitarle a su casa por su mala conducta en la comunidad? *No [0], sí [1]*

7.1d ¿Usted ha tenido problemas con La Organización? *No [0], sí [1]*

7.1e ¿En los últimos años, usted quisiera que La Organización: *se fuera lo más rápido posible [1], tuviera una influencia menor [2], tuviera la misma influencia [3], o tuviera una influencia mayor [4]* en la comunidad?

7.2a ¿Cómo se siente usted en la comunidad: *inseguro [1], más o menos seguro [2], o muy seguro [3]*?

7.2b ¿Usted o cualquier persona de su familia ha sido una víctima de delincuencia en su comunidad? *No [0], sí [1]* ¿Cuántas veces?

7.2c ¿En su comunidad, usted tiene miedo salir por las noches? *No [0], sí [1]*

7.3a ¿Aquí, grupos de jóvenes reunidos en las calles haciendo "osio" *(hacer nada)*: *no es problema [1], es un poco problema [2], o es un gran problema [3]*?

7.3b ¿En La Comunidad, la venta y uso de drogas y alcohol: *no es problema [1], es un medio problema [2], o es un gran problema [3]*?

7.3c ¿En su comunidad, el grafiti en las paredes: *no es problema [1], es un problema pequeño [2], o es un problema grande [3]*?

7.3d ¿Aquí, las casas y calles sucias y descuidadas: *no son problemas [1], son problemas pequeños [2], o son grandes problemas [3]*?

7.3e ¿Usted conoce una persona de la comunidad que es miembro de una mara? *No [0], sí [1]*

7.4 ¿Usted siente que puede denunciar las delincuencias que pasan en su comunidad? *No [0], sí [1]*

Table A.5 Continued

8. Desastre, trauma, y ayuda de la organización

8.1a   ¿Qué tipos de trauma ha sufrido usted del desastre de Huracán Mitch? *(Escriba todos los números que dice) Ninguno [0], psicológico/emocional [1], físico [2], material [3], u otro [4] ¿Cuál?*

8.1b   En su opinión, ¿su trauma de Huracán Mitch: fue *muy mal [1], mal [2], o normal [3]?*

8.1c   ¿Usted u otros miembros de la familia todavía tienen secuelas de trauma del desastre? *No [0], sí [1]*

8.2a   ¿La organización les ha ayudado a enfrentar el trauma del desastre? *No [0], sí [1] ¿Cómo? (clases, tratamiento, etc.)*

8.2b   ¿Dónde vivió usted después del huracán pero antes de llegar a la comunidad? *en un macro-albergue [1], con familiares [2], alquiló una casa o apartamento [3], en la misma casa reparada [4], u otra [5]. Si es 5, escriba.*

8.2c   Después del huracán, en su nuevo hogar *(por ejemplo, con familiares, en los macro-albergues, etc.)*, ¿Cómo fue su vida allá? *No sufrió [1], sufrió un poco [2], o sufrió mucho [3].*

9. Cambios individuales y en la comunidad en el largo plazo (Estas preguntas son similares)

9.1a   ¿Su participación en la comunidad *ha disminuido [1], se quedó igual [2], o ha aumentado [3]* durante su tiempo en la comunidad?

9.1b   ¿Su confianza en los vecinos *ha disminuido [1], se quedó igual [2], o ha aumentado [3]* durante su tiempo aquí?

9.2   Generalmente, ¿desde el principio hasta la fecha su vida aquí en la comunidad es: *peor [1], igual [2], o mejor [3]?*

9.3   ¿Desde el principio hasta la fecha la delincuencia en la comunidad es: *menor [1], se quedó igual [2], o más [3]?*

9.4   ¿Desde el principio hasta la fecha el funcionamiento del Comité Cívico es: *peor [1], igual [2], o mejor [3]?*

9.5a   ¿Qué son tres cosas que a usted no le gustan de La Comunidad? *[Escriba atrás]*

9.5b   ¿Qué son tres cosas que a usted le gustan de La Comunidad? *[Escriba atrás]*

9.6   ¿Hoy la comunidad se ve en un camino: *malo [1], bueno [2], o muy bueno [3]?* ¿Por qué? *[Escriba atrás]*

Table A.6 Resettlement Survey Schedule (English)

1. Demographics

1.1   What is your name?

1.2   Sex (Male [1], Female [2])

1.3   How old are you?

1.4   What is your highest level of education? (No education [0], basic to 8th grade [1], secondary [2], university [3], graduate degree [4])

1.5   What is your address?

1.6   Where (in which *colonia* or barrio) did you live before Hurricane Mitch?

1.7   What was your occupation before the hurricane?

1.8   What is your occupation now?

1.9   Where (in which *colonia* or barrio) do you work now?

1.10   Do you have a worse [1], equal [2], or better [3] job now compared to before the hurricane?

1.11   What is your faith? (Catholic [1], Protestant [2], Evangelical [3], or other [4]). If other, what?

1.12   How often do you attend services: do not attend [1], holy days [2], one time a week [3], or two times or more a week [4]?

1.13   How did you find out about the opportunity to live in X resettlement? Through an organization [1], a church [2], family [3], or other [4]? If other, how?

1.14   Why did you choose X resettlement over other resettlements?

1.15   How many years have you lived in X resettlement? (0–3 years [1], 4–6 years [2], since the beginning [3])

1.16   Are you married? (No [1], Yes [2])

1.17   How many adults live in your house right now? ___ Men?___ Women?___

1.18   How many children (under 18 years old) live in your house right now?___

1.19   Generally, is your health: poor [1], normal [2], or good [3]?

1.20   What is your monthly household income? (0–600 lempiras [1], 600–1.200 [2], 1.200–4.500 [3], 4.500–5.500 [4], 5.500–8.000 [5], 8.000–11.000[6], or 11.000 or more [7])

1.21   What percent of your household income do you receive from remittances? (0 percent [1], 1–10[2], 11–20, [3] 21–30[4], 31–40[5], 41+ [6])

2. Quality of Life: Before Mitch vs. Now

2.1   Compared to the community you lived in prior to Mitch, is there less [1], equal [2], or more [3] crime in X resettlement?

2.2   Compared to the community you lived in prior to Mitch, do you trust your neighbors less [1], equal [2], or more [3]in X resettlement?

2.3   Compared to the community you lived in prior to Mitch, do you participate in community activities less [1], equal [2], or more [3] in X resettlement?

2.4   Compared to the community you lived in prior to Mitch, is your life situation worse [1], equal [2], or better [3] in X resettlement?

Table A.6 Continued

4. Politics, Political Power, and Leadership

4.1   Do you think you can influence political decision-making in the resettlement? (No [0], Yes [1])

4.2   How much do you trust your leaders? (None [1], some [2], a lot [3])

5. Civic Participation, Trust, Unity, and Religion

5.1a   Do you vote? (No [0], yes [1])

5.1b   Do you participate in a community organization? (No [0], Yes [1])

5.1c   Do you participate in the church? (No [0], Yes [1])

5.1d   Are you involved in workshops, projects, or activities in the community? (No [0], Yes [1])

5.1e   *If yes to the last question:* How many hours a week do you participate in the community? (0 [0], 1–2 hours [1], 3–4 hours [2], 5+ hours [3])

5.1f   Do you take classes given by an external NGO? (No [0], Yes [1])

5.1g   If there was a service project in the community, would you participate? (No [0], Yes [1])

5.2a   X resettlement has a soccer league. Have you or someone in your household participated or do you currently participate? (No [0], Yes [1])

5.2b   If the interviewee participated, do you think the league offers: none [1], some [2] or many [3] social benefits? Which ones?

5.3a   Generally, how much do you trust your neighbors: none [1], some [2], a lot [3]?

5.3b   Do you think your neighbors would help you if you needed help? (No [0], Yes [1])

5.3c   If a thief was robbing your house, would a neighbor intervene? (No [0], Yes [1])

5.3d   If someone was selling drugs to your children, would a neighbor intervene? (No [0], Yes [1])

5.4a   Do you believe other community members share the same values as you? (No [0], Yes [1])

5.4b   Is there a feeling of community here? (No [0], Yes [1])

5.4c   In your opinion, is the community not united [1], semi-united [2], or very united [3]?

5.5a   Do you believe religion has played a role in the community development process? (No [0], Yes [1])

5.5b   If yes to the last question: a negative [1], neutral [2], or positive [3] role?

6. Familiarity with the Neighborhood and Neighbors

6.1a   Do you know the names of all of the barrios (or the geographic boundaries) in X resettlement? (No [0], Yes [1])

6.1b   What is the name of the president of the *patronato*? (The person does not know [0], the person knows [1])

6.2a   Do you recognize few [1], some [2], or many [3] people by face in the community?

6.2b   To recognize an outsider of the community, is it very difficult [1], difficult [2], easy [3], or very easy [4]?

6.3   Do you believe X resettlement is a model community for Honduras? (No [0], Yes [1]) Why or why not?

Table A.6 Continued

7. Informal Social Control and Delinquency

7.1a   In general, do your neighbors control their children: poorly [1], fine [2], very well [3]?

7.1b   In general, do your neighbors send their children to school: almost never [1], sometimes [2], almost all of the time [3]?

7.1c   Do you worry the organization may take your home for bad conduct? (No [0], Yes [1])

7.1d   Have you had any problems with the organization? (No [0], Yes [1])

7.1e   Do you wish the organization had in the last few years: left earlier [1], played a lesser role [2], stayed the same [3], played a more important role [4] in the community?

7.2a   Do you feel unsafe [1], fairly safe [2], very safe [3] in your community?

7.2b   Have you been a victim of crime in X resettlement? (No [0], Yes [1]) How many times?

7.2c   Are you afraid to be out at night in your community? (No [0], Yes [1])

7.3a   In your resettlement, groups of young people hanging out in the street doing nothing: is not a problem [1], is a small problem [2], is a big problem [3]?

7.3b   In your resettlement, the selling and use of drugs and alcohol: is not a problem [1], is a small problem [2], is a big problem [3]?

7.3c   In your resettlement, graffiti on the walls: is not a problem [1], is a small problem [2], is a big problem [3]?

7.3d   In your resettlement, houses and streets that are dirty and not taken care of: are not a problem [1], are a small problem [2], are a big problem [3]?

7.3e   Do you know someone in the community who is a member of a gang? (No [0], Yes [1])

7.4   Do you feel you can report a crime that happens in the resettlement? (No [0], Yes [1])

8. Disaster, Trauma, and Organizational Support

8.1a   What types of trauma (psychological [1], emotional [2], physical [3], material [4], all [15]), did you suffer? Mark all that apply.

8.1b   In your opinion, your trauma from Hurricane Mitch was: not bad [1], bad [2], or very bad [3]?

8.1c   Are you or a family member still dealing with the trauma of the disaster? (No [0], Yes [1])

8.2a   Did the supporting organization help you deal with this trauma? (No [0], Yes [1]) In what ways?

8.2b   After the hurricane but before the resettlement, where did you live? Temporary shelters [1], with family or friends [2], rented an apartment [3], lived in same home [4], or other [5].

8.2c   Did you suffer: not at all [1], a little [2], or a lot [3] in that situation?

Table A.6 Continued

9. Individual and Community Changes over Time

9.1a   Has your civic participation decreased [1], stayed the same [2], or increased [3] during your time in the resettlement? Why?

9.1b   Has your trust in your neighbors decreased [1], stayed the same [2], or increased [3] during your time in the community?

9.2   Generally speaking, is your life in the community today worse [1], the same [2], or better [3] than when you first arrived?

9.3   Has the crime decreased [1], stayed the same [2], or increased [3] during your time in the community?

9.4   Today the *patronato* functions worse [1], the same [2], or better [3] than they did in the beginning?

9.5a   What are three things you do not like about the resettlement?

9.5b   What are three things you like about the resettlement?

9.6   Today is the community on a bad [1], good [2], or very good [3] trajectory? Why?

CHAPTER 1

1. Pseudonyms are used for all resettlements, residents, and respondents.

2. *Heterogeneous* refers to the relocation of people from different neighborhoods or communities into the same resettlement. This is a different type of resettlement than one in which an entire neighborhood is relocated together.

3. Institutional review board approval was received in 2008 and renewed through 2013 (study number 0809P46722).

4. Honduras is considered one of the most violent countries in the world and often has the highest homicide rate in the world depending on year (UNODC 2015).

CHAPTER 2

1. To put it in perspective for the United States, it was more powerful than Katrina (905 to 902 millibars), maintained Category 5 status for twice as long, stayed in the country longer, displaced millions more (Mitch displaced more than 2,000,000, Katrina 250,000), and killed ten times as many people.

2. A Honduran friend was shot at while driving home from working in one resettlement. I was convinced the seven resettlements would be sufficient.

3. The Tegucigalpa neighborhood where resettlement residents lived before Hurricane Mitch will be used as a proxy for socioeconomic status and social vulnerability (see Cutter et al. 2003).

4. When I refer to Tegucigalpa throughout the rest of the book, I am referring to all neighborhoods within the Tegucigalpa metro area, including Comayaguela.

5. The sponsoring NGO returned to working in La Tierra in 2014 after a six-year hiatus.

6. There were, of course, also differences in the resettlements. These differences include religion, religiosity, household size, resettlement size, post-Mitch living situation, and number of communities from which the residents were drawn. These characteristics and their consequences will be discussed at length in chapters 4 and 5.

7. See also the International Development Bank report by Buvinic, Morrison, and Shifter (1999) and Caldera and Jiménez's 2006 book, *Prevención de maras y pandillas: realidad y desafíos*.

8. In Honduras, most adults have dealt with corruption by paying bribes. In my experience, many police checkpoints are erected for the primary purpose of shaking down drivers. Even orphanages are not immune; the orphanage van was stopped like other cars and a bribe paid to avoid a lengthy confrontation.

CHAPTER 3

1. See Seidman 2013 and Browne 2015 for excellent work on reconstruction over time in New Orleans after Katrina.

2. Although only peripherally tied to a disaster, Kirk's 2015 investigation on the out-

comes of formerly incarcerated individuals after Hurricane Katrina is one of the few longitudinal studies of relocated indivduals.

3. Resettlement is often done by moving entire neighborhoods or communities together. The population is homogeneous by geographic location and likely shares, to some extent, previous community culture and history.

4. See also Woolcock and Narayan 2000.

5. Residents who arrived earlier had greater opportunity to define and design space.

6. Two other important approaches exist: conflict and interactional. However, within the seven resettlements discussed here, the sponsoring NGOs utilized technical assistance and self-help models.

7. See the examples of the Suyapa Comité Cívico Social in chapter 5 and the Pino Alto CODELES in chapter 6.

8. This new theory is meant to supplement previous explanations, especially in post-disaster heterogeneous resettlements. Although the data suggests that the premises are sound and likely can inform other types of relocation and resettlement, each project must be examined in context.

9. This is one of the great failures of previous resettlements. If an organization or state is willing to take on the responsibility of building infrastructure for disaster survivors, it must also be willing to expend the resources to build social structures, or the situation could become much worse. By not participating, organizations still guide the development process, likely in a negative way.

10. See also Friedmann 1992; Craig and Mayo 1995; and Mohan and Stokke 2000.

11. USAID (1997) developed its own policy entitled New Partnership Initiative.

12. Residents also mentioned the critical role of the NGOs. In almost every interview I conducted with community residents and leaders, I asked, "Why did Suyapa and Pino Alto turn out so much differently?" The answer almost always included the phrase, "La Iglesia."

13. Path dependence is, in many ways, similar to the interactional approach (Wilkinson 1991) in examining community development.

14. As sections of the resettlement are completed, residents are invited to move. This process may take months or years.

15. Even in a natural experiment, social conditions are not identical. Suyapa and Pino Alto did not have identical initial conditions. However, the conditions were similar enough to provide each the opportunity to choose a similar path. In other words, each resettlement's fate was not predetermined.

16. Pierson 2000 refers to this stage as subsequent processes.

CHAPTER 4

1. C. Rubin, one of the foremost scholars on disaster recovery, currently affiliated with George Washington University. Personal communication, June 10, 2011.

2. Logistical challenges—safety, cost, and the time it would take to survey residents in over one hundred *colonias*—made obtaining data on the other four indicators difficult.

3. There is little data to compare homicide rates cross-nationally before 1996.

4. As one Honduran police officer mentioned, homicides are the most accurate crime statistics because there is always a body. This is especially true in the global south, wherein data is unreliable and crime underreported.

5. Many Hondurans and foreigners, including me, have found themselves being fol-

lowed in a threatening way and have had to duck into a store until the person(s) have left, leave the store through a side entrance, or call for friends to pick them up.

6. This may be due to a low number of events, making statistical significance difficult to ensure.

7. Pino Alto has been heralded as a major success story by La Internacional.

8. A 2011 LAPOP survey of one thousand Hondurans found that 65 percent of respondents think crime increased a lot in the last twelve months (Latinobarometro 2011c).

9. The differences in stranger and neighbor recognition cannot be attributed only to size, as all of the control resettlements (which have a smaller population than Suyapa and Pino Alto) had even lower recognition levels.

10. Some argue that this is a result of time rather than place. I take resident opinions more literally. Since the past is continually being constructed, opinions ebb and flow. In late 2009 and early 2010, when the survey was taken, residents believed their lives were better (see Johnson and Sherman 1990 for more on past reconstruction).

11. This question is left undefined intentionally.

CHAPTER 5

1. This governing political body will be further described in chapter 6.

2. The actual question was asked in reference to the last few years before the organization left. See appendix, table A.5, question 7.1e.

3. Crime continues to be the number-one concern of Hondurans (OSAC 2015; UNODC 2011). Honduras has high crime and very low conviction rates. If someone was actually convicted of a crime, it is likely no resettlement would allow them in.

4. Interestingly, this observation was affirmed by Maori community leaders after the Christchurch, New Zealand, earthquake in 2011. The Maori went directly to the Marae (spiritual and community meeting place) for support.

5. Gang affiliation is not hidden in Honduras. Living in certain areas, tattoos, clothing, and other characteristics may evidence gang participation.

6. Mortgage payments also provided La Iglesia a revolving balance to be used at the discretion of the CCS and the organization to address communal needs, such as repairing roads, improving the waterworks system, or constructing a new building.

7. People were strongly encouraged to stay in the community. One formal way of doing so was by legally defining the mortgage as rent until year ten. After year ten, people could sell their house only to La Iglesia and would receive a percentage of their mortgage back.

8. Even though La Iglesia promised to stay for fifteen years, after twelve years there was a clear desire on behalf of Suyapa and the organization to separate. La Iglesia continues to support the resettlement as of this writing, but only on a very minimal basis.

9. La Iglesia's social workers were highly involved in community affairs. They worked closely with families in many areas, including employment, and therefore knew more or less who could pay the mortgage and who could not.

10. Objectively, they were removed for both reasons.

CHAPTER 6

1. The two security guards were murdered on the market site. This will be discussed in greater depth later in the chapter.

2. W. Siembieda. Personal communication, June 17, 2009.

3. According to La Internacional staff, this avoided earlier problems of residents' stealing materials from other homes to strengthen their own.

4. The lempira-to-US-dollar exchange was 19.5 to 1 in 2010.

5. The largest post-Mitch donations came from the United States, Spain, and Switzerland.

6. However, this was not the case. Dozens of houses were sold, and La Internacional had little recourse to stop it from happening. This brought in new residents who had not been vetted, leading to a lack of social cohesion and feelings of insecurity by long-term residents.

CHAPTER 7

1. The construction of culture is similar to social construction theory generally (Berger and Luckmann 1966).

2. Francis 1999 found that during forced relocation by the World Bank in Madagascar, poor outcomes partially stemmed from a lack of initial clarity concerning the goals of resettlement. Also, as seen in other resettlements, such as Campo Cielo or Santa Fe, if those initial conditions are not there, if survivors are forced to build a sense of community without resources or support, they will have a much more difficult time creating the relationships and vision necessary for future social health.

3. If a family representative did not attend, the family risked losing their chance at having a home in Suyapa.

4. This is similar to Mahoney's self-reinforcing sequence, in which the "the contingent period corresponds with the initial adoption of a particular institutional arrangement, while the deterministic pattern corresponds with the stable reproduction of this institution over time" (2000: 535). See also Goldstone 1998 and David 2000.

5. These numbers are based on the experiences of El Valle resettlements. Of course, each resettlement is different, and the time frame must be adjusted to fit the particular context.

6. The contexts and needs of displaced persons are diverse. Although this book targets only a minority of resettlement contexts, resettlements with heterogeneous populations in a weak state, there are potential lessons for other relocation or resettlement settings.

REFERENCES

Adams, Helen, Ryan Alaniz, Robin Bronen, and Karen McNamara. 2015. "Maintaining and Building 'Place' through Managed and Forced Community Relocations: Lessons for a Climate Changed World." *UNU-EHS Working Paper Series* No. 8. Bonn: United Nations University Institute of Environment and Human Security.

Addams, Jane. 1910. *Twenty Years at Hull House: With Autobiographical Notes.* New York: Macmillan.

Adger, W. Neil, Terry P. Hughes, Carl Folke, Stephen R. Carpenter, and Johan Rockström. 2005. "Social-Ecological Resilience to Coastal Disasters." *Science* 309 (5737): 1036–1039.

Alaniz, Ryan. 2012. "Unsupervised Recovery: Post-disaster NGO Recovery and Adaptation Strategies in Honduras." *SOURCE: Studies of the University: Research, Council, Education Publication Series of United Nations University Institute for Environment and Human Security* 16: 110–124.

Aldrich, Daniel P. 2010. "Fixing Recovery: Social Capital in Post-Crisis Resilience." *Journal of Homeland Security* 6: 1–10.

———. 2011. "The Power of People: Social Capital's Role in Recovery from the 1995 Kobe Earthquake." *Natural Hazards* 56 (3): 595–611.

———. 2012a. *Building Resilience: Social Capital in Post-disaster Recovery.* Chicago: University of Chicago Press.

———. 2012b. "Social, Not Physical, Infrastructure: The Critical Role of Civil Society After the 1923 Tokyo Earthquake." *Disasters* 36 (3): 398–419.

———. 2013. "Rethinking Civil Society–State Relations in Japan after the Fukushima Accident." *Polity* 45 (2): 249–264.

Aldrich, Daniel P., and Yasuyuki Sawada. 2015. "The Physical and Social Determinants of Mortality in the 3.11 Tsunami." *Social Science & Medicine* 124: 66–75.

Alesch, Daniel J., Lucy A. Arendt, and James N. Holly. 2009. *Managing for Long-Term Community Recovery in the Aftermath of Disaster.* Denver: Public Entity Risk Institute.

Ali Badri, S., Ali Asgary, A. R. Eftekhari, and Jason Levy. 2006. "Post-disaster Resettlement, Development and Change: A Case Study of the 1990 Manjil Earthquake in Iran." *Disasters* 30 (4): 451–468.

Alinsky, Saul. 1971. *Rules for Radicals; A Practical Primer for Realistic Radicals.* New York: Random House.

Aminzade, Ronald. 1992. "Historical Sociology and Time." *Sociological Methods and Research* 20 (4): 456–480.

———. 2013. *Race, Nation, and Citizenship in Post-Colonial Africa: The Case of Tanzania.* Cambridge: University of Cambridge Press.

Amos, Valerie. 2011. "ECOSOC Humanitarian Affairs Segment 2011 Closing Remarks [July 21]." United Nations. http://www.un.org/en/ecosoc/julyhls/pdf11/has_erc_ecosoc _2011_closing_remarks 21_july_2011.pdf.

Arnson, Cynthia J. 2009. "The Crisis in Honduras." Woodrow Wilson International Center. Retrieved September 6, 2016. https://www.wilsoncenter.org/article/weak-institutions -and-the-honduran-crisis.

Barnes, Diane. 2001. "Resettled Refugees' Attachment to Their Original and Subsequent

Homelands: Long-Term Vietnamese Refugees in Australia." *Journal of Refugee Studies* 14 (4): 394–411.

Barr, Abigail. 2004. "Forging Effective New Communities: The Evolution of Civil Society in Zimbabwean Resettlement Villages." *World Development* 32 (10), 1753–1766.

Barrios, Roberto E., Marco T. Medina, James P. Stansbury, and Rosa Palencia. 2000. "Nutritional Status of Children Under Five Years of Age in Three Hurricane-Affected Areas of Honduras." *Pan American Journal of Public Health.* 8 (6): 380–384.

BBC (British Broadcasting Corporation). 2011. "Honduras Arrests 176 Police in Corruption Purge." November 3. http://www.bbc.co.uk/.

Beck, Frank D. 2001. "Struggles in Building Community." *Sociological Inquiry* 71 (4): 455–457.

Belli, Charlotte. 2008. "Impacto social de los ecomateriales, Proyecto Betania, Honduras." http://www.ecosur.org.

Berger, Peter, and Thomas Luckmann. (1991 [1966]). *The Social Construction of Reality: A Treatise in the Sociology of Knowledge.* United Kingdom: Penguin.

Berke, Philip, and Timothy Beatley. 1997. *After the Hurricane: Linking Recovery to Sustainable Development in the Caribbean.* Baltimore: Johns Hopkins University Press.

Bhutan. 2016. Gross National Happiness Commission. Retrieved on November 24, 2016. http://www.gnhc.gov.bt/.

Black, Richard, Nigel W. Arnell, W. Neil Adger, David Thomas, and Andrew Geddes. 2013. "Migration, Immobility and Displacement Outcomes Following Extreme Events." *Environmental Science & Policy* 27: S32–S43.

Boeni, Teddy, and Rohit Jigyasuii. 2005. "Cultural Considerations for Post Disaster Reconstruction Post-Tsunami Challenges." UNDP Conference. Retrieved November 24, 2011. http://www.adpc.net/.

Boettke, Peter, Emily Chamlee-Wright, Peter Gordon, Sanford Ikeda, Peter T. Leeson, and Russell Sobel. 2007. "The Political, Economic, and Social Aspects of Katrina." *Southern Economic Journal* 74 (2): 363–376.

Bolin, Robert, and Lois Stanford. 1998. "The Northridge Earthquake: Community-Based Approaches to Unmet Recovery Needs." *Disasters* 22 (1): 21–38.

Bornstein, Erica. 2005. *The Spirit of Development: Protestant NGOs, Morality, and Economics in Zimbabwe.* New York: Routledge.

Bourdieu, Pierre. 1986. "The Forms of Capital." In Handbook of Theory and Research for the Sociology of Education, edited by J. G. Richardson, 241–258. New York: Greenwood.

Bridger, Jeffrey C., and A. E. Luloff. 2001. "Building the Sustainable Community: Is Social Capital the Answer?" *Sociological Inquiry* 71 (4): 458–472.

Browne, Katherine E. 2015. *Standing in the Need: Culture, Comfort, and Coming Home after Katrina.* Austin: University of Texas Press.

Buchan, Dianne. 2003. "Buy-In and Social Capital: By-Products of Social Impact Assessment." *Impact Assessment and Project Appraisal* 21 (3): 168.

Bursik, Robert. J. Jr., and Jim Webb. 1982. "Community Change and Patterns of Delinquency." *American Journal of Sociology* 88 (1): 24–42.

Buvinic, Mayra, Andrew Morrison, and Michael Shifter. 1999. "Violence in Latin America and the Caribbean: A Framework for Action (Technical Study)." Inter-American Development Bank Sustainable Development Department. http://www.bvsde.paho.org/.

Caldera, Hilda, and Guillermo Jiménez. 2006. *Prevención de maras y pandillas: realidad y desafíos.* Tegucigalpa: IHNFA.

Call, Charles T. 2000. "Sustainable Development in Central America: The Challenges of Violence, Injustice, and Insecurity." Hamburg: Institut für Iberoamerika-Kunde. http://www.giga-hamburg.de/content/ilas/ze2020/call.pdf.

Candland, Christopher. 2001. "Faith as Social Capital: Religion and Community Development in Southern Asia." In *Social Capital as a Policy Resource*, edited by John Montgomery and Alex Inkeles, 129–148. New York: Springer.

Cardona, Omar D. 2004. "The Need for Rethinking the Concepts of Vulnerability and Risk from a Holistic Perspective: A Necessary Review and Criticism for Effective Risk Management." In *Mapping Vulnerability: Disasters, Development and People*, edited by G. Bankoff, G. Frerks, and D. Hillhorst. London: Earth Scan Publishers.

Cary, Lee J. 1970. *Community Development as a Process*. Columbia: University of Missouri Press.

Castellanos, Plutarco. 2011. "Transformación del sector salud." A presentation by the former minister of health. Tegucigalpa, Honduras. March.

CEC (Community Empowerment Collective). 2014. "Empowerment." http://cec.vcn.bc.ca/cmp/modules/emp-go.htm.

Cernea, Michael M. 1997. "The Risks and Reconstruction Model for Resettling Displaced Populations." *World Development* 25, 1569–1587.

———. 2000. "Risks, Safeguards, and Reconstruction: A Model for Population Displacement and Resettlement." In *Risks and Reconstruction: Experiences of Resettlers and Refugees*, edited by Michael M. Cernea and Chris McDowell, 11–55. Washington, DC: World Bank Publications.

———. 2003. "For a New Economics of Resettlement: A Sociological Critique of the Compensation Principle." *International Social Science Journal* 55 (175): 37–45.

Cernea, Michael M., and Chris McDowell, eds. 2000. *Risks and Reconstruction: Experiences of Resettlers and Refugees*. Washington, DC: World Bank Publications.

CESAL (Centro de Estudios y Solidaridad con América Latina). 2008. *Diez años después del Mitch: reconstrucción y desarrollo; la intervención de CESAL en El Valle*. Madrid: CESAL.

Chambers, Robert. 1997. *Whose Reality Counts? Putting the Last First*. London: Intermediate Technology Publications.

Chamlee-Wright, Emily. 2010. *The Cultural and Political Economy of Recovery: Social Learning in a Post-disaster Environment*, vol. 12. New York: Routledge.

Chamlee-Wright, Emily, and Virgil Henry Storr. 2011. "Social Capital as Collective Narratives and Post-disaster Community Recovery." *The Sociological Review* 59 (2): 266–282.

Christenson, James A., and Jerry W. Robinson. 1989. *Community Development in Perspective*. Ames: Iowa State University Press.

CIA World Factbook. 2015. *Median Age: Honduras*. Retrieved on June 29, 2015. https://www.cia.gov/library/publications/the-world-factbook/fields/2177.html.

———. 2016. *Honduras*. https://www.cia.gov/library/publications/the-world-factbook/geos/ho.html.

CIES (Council for International Exchange of Scholars). 2016. "Fulbright Specialist Opportunities—Refugee-Resettlement." Retrieved January 22, 2016. http://www.cies.org/refugee-resettlement.

CMCD (Chief Minister and Cabinet of Australia). 2011. http://www.cmd.act.gov.au/.

CODELES. 2005. Seguimiento de CODELES, Pino Alto. Pino Alto internal document.

Coleman, James S. 1988. "Social Capital in the Creation of Human Capital." *American Journal of Sociology* 94: S95–S120.

Coleman, Kenneth, and José René Argueta. 2008. "Delincuencia y criminalidad en las estadísticas de Honduras, 2008: el impacto de la governalidad." LAPOP, Vanderbilt University, and USAID. http://www.vanderbilt.edu.

Consultoría. 2011. "La policía bajo la lupa." Centro Nacional De Consultoría. http://www.centronacionaldeconsultoria.com.

Cooter, Robert D. 2000. "Do Good Laws Make Good Citizens? An Economic Analysis of Internalized Norms." *Virginia Law Review* 86 (8): 1577–1601.

Craig, Gary, 2002. "Towards the Measurement of Empowerment: The Evaluation of Community Development." *Community Development* 33 (1): 124–146.

Craig, Gary, and Marjorie Mayo. 1995. *Community Empowerment: A Reader in Participation and Development.* London: Zed Books.

Crenshaw, Kimberle. 1991. "Mapping the Margins: Intersectionality, Identity Politics, and Violence Against Women of Color." *Stanford Law Review*: 43(6): 1241–1299.

Cutter, Susan L., Bryan J. Boruff, and W. Lynn Shirley. 2003. "Social Vulnerability to Environmental Hazards." *Social Science Quarterly* 84 (2): 242–261.

Damberger, David. 2011. "What Happens When an NGO Admits Failure." TED Talk. (https://www.ted.com/speakers/david_damberger).

David, Paul A. 1985. "Clio and the Economics of QWERTY." *American Economic Review* 75: 332–337.

———. 2000. "Path Dependence, Its Critics, and the Quest for 'Historical Economics.'" In *Evolution and Path Dependence in Economic Ideas: Past and Present*, edited by P. Garrouste and S. Ioannides, 15–40. Cheltenham, England: Edward Elgar Publishing.

De Wet, C. J. (2006). *Development-Induced Displacement: Problems, Policies, and People*, vol. 18. New York: Berghahn Books.

Dijkstra, Geske. 2011. "The PRSP Approach and the Illusion of Improved Aid Effectiveness: Lessons from Bolivia, Honduras and Nicaragua." *Development Policy Review* 29 (s1): s111–s133.

Dougherty, Michael L., and Rocio Peralta. 2010. "The Politics of Protected Areas: Environmental Capital and Community Conflict in Guatemala." In *Mobilizing Communities: Asset Building as a Community Development Strategy*, edited by Gary Paul Green and Ann Goetting, 247–63. Philadelphia: Temple University Press.

Du, Fachun. 2012. "Ecological Resettlement of Tibetan Herders in the Sanjiangyuan: A Case Study in Madoi County of Qinghai." *Nomadic Peoples*, 116–133.

Dudley, Steven. 2016. Honduras Elites and Organized Crime: Introduction. International Development Research Center. http://www.insightcrime.org/investigations/honduras-elites-and-organized-crime-introduction.

Durkheim, Emile. 1979 [1897]. *Suicide.* New York: The Free Press.

———. 1984 [1893]. *The Division of Labor in Society*, translated by W. D. Hall. New York: The Free Press.

———. 1995 [1912]. *The Elementary Forms of Religious Life*, translated by Karen E. Fields. New York: The Free Press.

Econstats. 2010. *Unemployment Rate IMF World Economic Outlook*. Retrieved November 24, 2011. http://www.econstats.com/weo/V021.htm.

Edwards, Michael. 1999. "International Development NGOs: Agents of Foreign Aid or Vehicles for International Cooperation?" *Nonprofit and Voluntary Sector Quarterly* 28 (1): 25–37.

Edwards, Michael, and David Hulme. 1996. "Too Close for Comfort? The Impact of Official Aid on Nongovernmental Organizations." *World Development* 24: 961–973.

El Heraldo. 2006. "Familias desalojadas se toman carretera." February 23. http://www
.elheraldo.hn/.

Ellerman, David. 2007. "Helping Self-Help: The Fundamental Conundrum of Development
Assistance." *Journal of Socio-Economics* 36 (4): 561–577.

Ellis, Sue, and Sultan Barakat. 1996. "From Relief to Development: The Long-Term Effects
of 'Temporary' Accommodation on Refugees and Displaced Persons in the Republic of
Croatia." *Disasters* 20 (2): 111–124.

Ensor, Marisa O., ed. 2010. *The Legacy of Hurricane Mitch: Lessons from Post-disaster Reconstruction in Honduras.* Tucson: The University of Arizona Press.

Erikson, Kai T. 1976. *Everything in Its Path: Destruction of Community in the Buffalo Creek
Flood.* New York: Simon and Schuster.

Escobar, Arturo. 1995. *Encountering Development: The Making and Unmaking of the Third
World.* Princeton, NJ: Princeton University Press.

Esnard, Ann-Margaret, and Alka Sapat. 2014. *Displaced by Disaster: Recovery and Resilience
in a Globalizing World.* New York: Routledge Press.

Etzioni, Amitai. 1995. "The Responsive Community: A Communitarian Perspective." *American Sociological Review* 61: 1–11.

———. 2000. "Social Norms: Internalization, Persuasion, and History." *Law and Society
Review* 34 (1): 157–78.

Euraque, Dario A. 1996. *Reinterpreting the Banana Republic: Region and State in Honduras,
1870-1972.* Chapel Hill: University of North Carolina Press.

Europa World Online. 2016. *Honduras.* London: Routledge. Retrieved September 6, 2016.
http://www.europaworld.com/entry/hn.

FBI (Federal Bureau of Investigation). 2011. "Crime in the United States: Arrests 2010."
http://www.fbi.gov/.

FEMA (Federal Emergency Management Agency). 2011. "National Disaster Recovery
Framework: Strengthening Disaster Recovery for the Nation." http://www.fema.gov
/pdf/recoveryframework/ndrf.pdf.

Finnemore, Martha, and Kathryn Sikkink. 1998. "International Norm Dynamics and Political Change." *International Organization* 52 (4): 887–917.

Flora, Cornelia Butler, and Jan L. Flora. 2003. *Rural Communities: Legacy and Change.* Boulder, CO: Westview Press.

Flyvbjerg, Bent. 2011. "Case Study." In *The Sage Handbook of Qualitative Research,* 4th ed.,
edited by Norman K. Denzin and Yvonna S. Lincoln, 301–316. Thousand Oaks, CA:
Sage Publications.

Forbes.com. 2014. "Thoughts on the Business of Life." http://thoughts.forbes.com/thoughts
/enthusiasm-arnold-toynbee-apathy-can-only.

Fothergill, Alice, and Lori A. Peek. 2004. "Poverty and Disasters in the United States: A Review of Recent Sociological Findings." *Natural Hazards* 32 (1): 89–110.

Francis, Paul. "Involuntary Resettlement in Urban Development: Plan, Performance and
Outcome in the World Bank-funded Antananarivo Plain Project, Madagascar." *Journal
of Refugee Studies* 12, no. 2 (1999): 180–202.

Friedmann, John. 1992. *Empowerment: The Politics of Alternative Development.* Oxford:
Blackwell.

Friedrichs, Chad. 2011. *Pruitt-Igoe Myth: An Urban History.* Unicorn Stencil Documentary
Films.

Fromm, Erich, and Michael Maccoby. 1970. *Social Character in a Mexican Village.* Upper
Saddle River, NJ: Prentice Hall.

Fukuyama, Francis. 1995. "Social Capital and the Global Economy." *Foreign Affairs* 74 (5): 89–103.

Fussell, Elizabeth. 2015. "The Long-Term Recovery of New Orleans' Population after Hurricane Katrina." *American Behavioral Scientist* 59 (10): 1231–1245.

Galea, Sandro, Chris R. Brewin, Michael Gruber, Russell T. Jones, Daniel W. King, Lynda A. King, Richard J. McNally, Robert J. Ursano, Maria Petukhova, and Ronald C. Kessler. 2007. "Exposure to Hurricane-Related Stressors and Mental Illness After Hurricane Katrina." *Archives of General Psychiatry* 64 (12): 1427–1434.

GFDRR (Global Facility for Disaster Reducation and Recovery). 2010. "Disaster Risk Management in Central America: Honduras." Washington DC: The World Bank. www.gfdrr .org/sites/gfdrr.org/files/Honduras_DRM.pdf.

Gibson, Chris L., Jihong Zhaoa, Nicholas P. Lovrich, and Michael J. Gaffney. 2002. "Social Integration, Individual Perceptions of Collective Efficacy, and Fear of Crime in Three Cities." *Justice Quarterly* 19 (3): 537–564.

Gifford, Paul. 1994. "Some Recent Developments in African Christianity." *African Affairs* 93 (373): 513–534.

Gill, Duane. 2007. "Secondary Trauma or Secondary Disaster? Insights from Hurricane Katrina." *Sociological Spectrum* 27: 613–632.

Gillespie, Nicole A., and Leon Mann. 2004. "Transformational Leadership and Shared Values: The Building Blocks of Trust." *Journal of Managerial Psychology* 19 (6): 588–607.

Gladwell, Malcolm. 2015. "Starting Over: Many Katrina Victims Left New Orleans for Good. What Can We Learn From Them?" *The New Yorker*. August 24. www.newyorker.com.

Goe, W. Richard, and Sean Noonan. "The Sociology of Community." In *21st Century Sociology: A Reference Handbook*, vol. 21, edited by Clifton D. Bryant and Dennis L. Peck, 455–464. Thousand Oaks, CA: Sage Publications.

Goenjian, Armen K., Alan M. Steinberg, Louis M. Najarian, Lynn A. Fairbanks, Madeline Tashjian, and Robert S. Pynoos. 2000. "Prospective Study of Posttraumatic Stress, Anxiety, and Depressive Reactions After Earthquake and Political Violence." *American Journal of Psychiatry* 157: 911–895.

Goldstone, Jack A. 1998. "Initial Conditions, General Laws, Path Dependence, and Explanation in Historical Sociology." *The American Journal of Sociology* 104 (3): 829–845.

Gorjestani, Nicolas. 2001. "Indigenous Knowledge for Development: Opportunities and Challenges." World Bank. Retrieved October 7, 2011. http://www.worldbank.org/.

Gould, Roger V. 1991. "Multiple Networks and Mobilization in the Paris Commune, 1871." *American Sociological Review* 56 (6): 716–729.

Gray, Rob, Jan Bebbington, and David Collison. 2006. "NGOs, Civil Society and Accountability: Making the People Accountable to Capital." *Accounting, Auditing & Accountability Journal* 19 (3): 319–348.

Green, Bonnie L., Jacob D. Lindy, Mary C. Grace, Goldine C. Glesser, Anthony C. Leonard, Mindy Korol, and Carolyn Winget. 1990. "Buffalo Creek Survivors in the Second Decade: Stability of Stress Symptoms." *American Journal of Orthopsychiatry* 60: 43–54.

Green, Gary Paul. 2011. "The Self-Help Approach to Community Development." In *Introduction to Community Development: Theory, Practice, and Service Learning*, edited by Jerry W. Robinson and Gary Paul Green, 71–84. Thousand Oaks, CA: Sage Publications.

Green, Gary Paul, and Anna Haines. 2015. *Asset Building & Community Development*. Thousand Oaks, CA: Sage Publications.

Guardian. 2015. "The Migrants Who Fled Violence for the US Only to be Sent Back to Their

Deaths." October 12. http://www.theguardian.com/world/2015/oct/12/deportation -migrants-flee-honduras-guatemala-salvador.

Gusfield, Joseph R. 1975. *Community: A Critical Response.* New York: Harper & Row.

Gutmann, Matthew C. 1996. *The Meanings of Macho: Being a Man in Mexico City.* Berkeley: University of California Press.

Hailey, John. 2000. "NGO Partners: The Characteristics of Effective Development Partnerships." In *Public-Private Partnerships: Theory and Practice in International Perspective*, edited by Stephen P. Osborne, 313–323. New York: Routledge.

Hall, Anthony. 1994. "Grassroots Action for Resettlement Planning: Brazil and Beyond." *World Development* 22 (12): 1793–1809.

Harris, Gardiner. 2014. "Borrowed Time on Disappearing Land: Facing Rising Seas, Bangladesh Confronts the Consequences of Climate Change." *New York Times.* March 28. http://www.nytimes.com.

Hart, Timothy C., and Callie Rennison. 2003. "Reporting Crime to the Police, 1992–2000." Bureau of Justice Statistics. http://www.icasa.org/.

Harvey, Mark H. 2013. "Consensus-Based Community Development, Concentrated Rural Poverty, and Local Institutional Structures: The Obstacle of Race in the Lower Mississippi Delta." *Community Development* 44 (2): 257–273.

Hillery, George A. 1955. "Definitions of Community: Areas of Agreement." *Rural Sociology* 20: 111–123.

Hoffman, Susanna M., and Anthony Oliver-Smith. 1999. "Anthropology and the Angry Earth: An Overview." In *The Angry Earth: Disaster in Anthropological Perspective*, edited by A. Oliver-Smith and S. M. Hoffman, 1–16. London: Routledge.

Holt, Julius. 1981. "Camps as Communities." *Disasters* 5 (3): 176–179.

Honduras Weekly. 2011. "Honduran Homicide Rate Doubles in 10 Years." January 11. http:// www.hondurasweekly.com/.

Human Rights Watch. 2016. "Honduras: Events of 2015." Retrieved September 26, 2016. https://www.hrw.org/world-report/2016/country-chapters/honduras.

IADB (Inter-American Development Bank). 1999. "Vulnerabilidad ecologia y social." Consultative Group for the Reconstruction and Transformation of Central America. http:// www.iadb.org/.

———. 2000. "Central America after Hurricane Mitch: The Challenge of Turning a Disaster into an Opportunity." Retrieved July 28, 2011. http://www.iadb.org/regions/.

IFRC (International Federation of the Red Cross and Red Crescent). 2006. *Review of The International Federation of the Red Cross and Red Crescent Recovery Operations: Summary Report.* http://www.ifrc.org.

IISP (Institute for Innovation in Social Policy). 2011. "Social Indicator Projects: American and International." http://iisp.vassar.edu/socialindicator.html.

Inglehart, Ronald, and Wayne E. Baker. 2000. "Modernization, Cultural Change, and the Persistence of Traditional Values." *American Sociological Review* 65 (1): 19–51.

Ingram, Jane C., Guillermo Franco, Cristina Rumbaitis-del Rio, and Bjian Khazai. 2006. "Post-disaster Recovery Dilemmas: Challenges in Balancing Short-Term and Long-Term Needs for Vulnerability Reduction." *Environmental Science & Policy* 9 (7): 607–613.

Insight Crime. 2015. "Gangs in Honduras." http://www.insightcrime.org/images/PDFs /2015/HondurasGangs.pdf.

Institute of Medicine. 2015. *Healthy, Resilient, and Sustainable Communities After Disasters: Strategies, Opportunities, and Planning for Recovery.* Washington, DC: The National Academies Press, 2015. http://www.nap.edu/18996.

IPCC (Intergovernmental Panel on Climate Change). 2013. *Fifth Assessment Report*. http://www.ipcc.ch/.

Iuchi, Kanako. 2010. "Redefining A Place to Live: Decisions, Planning Processes and Outcomes After Disasters." PhD diss. Urbana-Champaign: University of Illinois.

Jackson, Jeffrey T. 2005. *The Globalizers: Development Workers in Action*. Baltimore: Johns Hopkins University Press.

Jackson, Laura E. 2003. "The Relationship of Urban Design to Human Health and Condition." *Landscape and Urban Planning* 64: 191–200.

Jargowsky, Paul A., and Yoonhwan Park. 2009. "Cause or Consequence? Suburbanization and Crime in US Metropolitan Areas." *Crime & Delinquency* 55 (1): 28–50.

Jeannotte, M Sharon. 2003. "Singing Alone? The Contribution of Cultural Capital to Social Cohesion and Sustainable Communities." *The International Journal of Cultural Policy* 9 (1): 35–49.

Jeffrey, Paul. 1999. "Rhetoric and Reconstruction in Post-Mitch Honduras." *NACLA Report on the Americas* 33(2): 28–37.

Jha, Abhas K., Jennifer Duyne Barenstein, Priscilla M. Phelps, Daniel Pittet, and Stephen Sena. 2010. *Safer Homes, Stronger Communities: A Handbook for Reconstructing after Natural Disasters*, chapter 12. Washington, DC: World Bank.

Johnson, Marcia K., and Steven J. Sherman. 1990. "Constructing and Reconstructing the Past and the Future in the Present." In Handbook of Motivation and Cognition: Foundations of Social Behavior, vol. 2, edited by Tory E. Higgins and Richard M. Sorrentinos, 482–526. New York: Guilford Press.

Kahn, Carrie. 2013. "In Honduran Crimes, Police Are Seen as Part of the Problem." July 15. http://www.npr.org/blogs/parallels/2013/07/15/196262813/The-Police-Are-A-Major-Part-Of-The-Crime-Problem-In-Honduras.

Kawachi, Ichiro, Bruce P. Kennedy, and Richard G. Wilkinson. 1999. "Crime: Social Disorganization and Relative Deprivation." *Social Science & Medicine* 48 (6): 719–731.

Keizer, Kees, Siegwart Lindenberg, and Linda Steg. 2008. "The Spreading of Disorder." *Science* 322: 1681–1685.

Kipling, Rudyard. 1998 [1899]. "White Man's Burden." *Peace Review* 10(3): 311–312.

Kirk, David S. 2015. "A Natural Experiment of the Consequences of Concentrating Former Prisoners in the Same Neighborhoods." *Proceedings of the National Academy of Sciences* 112 (22): 6943–6948. June 2. doi:10.1073/pnas.1501987112.

Klein, Naomi. 2007. *The Shock Doctrine: The Rise of Disaster Capitalism*. New York: Metropolitan Books.

Koss, Mary P. 1992. "The Under-Detection of Rape: Methodological Choices Influence Incidence Estimates." *The Society for the Psychological Study of Social Issues* 48 (1): 61–75.

Koss, Mary P., and Christine A. Gidycz. 1985. "Sexual Experiences Survey: Reliability and Validity." *Journal of Consulting and Clinical Psychology* 53 (3): 422–423.

Krasner, Stephen D. 1988. "Sovereignty: An Institutional Perspective." *Comparative Political Studies* 21 (1): 66–94.

Kretzmann, John P., and John McKnight. 1993. *Building Communities From the Inside Out*. Evanston, IL: Center for Urban Affairs and Policy Research, Neighborhood Innovations Network.

La Iglesia. 2009. "President Remarks." Benefit dinner for La Iglesia, October 3. Tegucigalpa, Honduras.

———. 2010. "Informe." Internal document.

La Iglesia and CESAL. 2004. "Estudio de línea de base: diagnóstico situacional del proyecto habitacional Suyapa." Internal document.

La Internacional. 2002. *La intervención de La Internacional en El Valle: el plan Pino Alto.* Original internal document.

———. 2004. "Pino Alto." Compact Disc.

———. 2007. *Monografía de Pino Alto.* Internal document.

———. 2011. "Bienvenidos; Historia." Retrieved July 7, 2011, from website of pseudonymous organization.

La Internacional, Spain. 2002. "Mitch: De la emergencia al desarrollo—Honduras." Internal document.

La Internacional and Pino Alto. 2007. "Informe." Internal document.

Latinobarometro. 2011a. "Confidence in Police." http://www.latinobarometro.org.

———. 2011b. "Honduras: Perception of Progress in the Country." http://www.latinobarometro.org.

———. 2011c. "Honduras: Has Crime Increased or Decreased?" http://www.latinobarometro.org.

La Tribuna. 2010. "Honduras con menor transparencia presupuestaria de Centroamérica." November 9. http://www.latribuna.hn.

———. 2014. "Les quitan la vida a dos jóvenes." October 25. http://www.latribuna.hn/2014/10/25/les-quitan-la-vida-a-dos-jovenes/.

Leon, Patricio, and Allan Lavell. 1996. "Comunidades urbanas en Centro América: vulnerabilidad a desastres." *Desastres y Sociedad* 7 (4): 57–78. http://www.desenredando.org.

Levi, Margaret. 1997. "A Model, a Method, and a Map: Rational Choice in Comparative and Historical Analysis." In *Comparative Politics: Rationality, Culture, and Structure*, edited by Mark I. Lichbach and Alan S. Zuckerman, 19–41. Cambridge: Cambridge University Press.

Leyva, Hector M. 2001. "Delincuencia y criminalidad en las estadísticas de Honduras, 1996–2000." Tegucigalpa: Gobierno de la República de Honduras y Programa de las Naciones Unidas para el Desarrollo.

Lister, Sarah. 2000. "Power in Partnership? An Analysis of an NGO's Relationships with Its Partners." *Journal of International Development* 12: 227–239.

Lizarralde, Gonzalo, Cassidy Johnson, and Colin Davidson, eds. 2009. *Rebuilding After Disasters: From Emergency to Sustainability.* New York: Routledge.

Lloyd, Marion. 2005. "Honduras Recovery Offers Lessons: Massive Rebuilding Followed '98 Storm." *The Boston Globe.* September 23. http://www.boston.com/.

Logan, John. 2003. "Life and Death in the City: Neighborhoods in Context." *Contexts* 2 (2): 33–40.

Lummis, C. D. 1991. "Development Against Democracy." *Alternatives* 161: 31–66.

MacDonald, John S., and Leatrice D. MacDonald. 1964. "Chain Migration, Ethnic Neighborhood Formation and Social Networks." *The Milbank Memorial Fund Quarterly* 42 (1): 82–97.

Mahoney, James. 2000. "Path Dependence in Historical Sociology." *Theory and Society* 29 (4): 507–548.

Masci, David. 2014. "Why has Pentecostalism Grown so Dramatically in Latin America?" Pew Research, FactTank. November 14. http://www.pewresearch.org/fact-tank/2014/11/14/why-has-pentecostalism-grown-so-dramatically-in-latin-america/.

Maslow, Abraham Harold. 1943. "A Theory of Human Motivation." *Psychological Review* 50 (4): 370–396.

McMichael, Philip. 2016. *Development and Social Change: A Global Perspective.* Thousand Oaks, CA: Pine Forge Press.

McMillan, David W. 1996. "Sense of Community." *Journal of Community Psychology* 24 (4): (1996): 315–325.

McMillan, David W., and David M. Chavis. 1986. "Sense of Community: A Definition and Theory." *Journal of Community Psychology* 14 (1): 6–23.

McPherson, Miller, Lynn Smith-Lovin, and James M. Cook. 2001. "Birds of a Feather: Homophily in Social Networks." *Annual Review of Sociology* 27: 415–444.

Merrill, Tim. 1995. "Honduras: A Country Study." Washington, DC: Federal Research Division, Library of Congress. http://countrystudies.us/honduras/.

Met (Meteorological) Office. 2011. "Hurricane Mitch Fact Sheet." Devon, UK: Public Weather Service. http://www.metoffice.gov.uk/.

Meyer, David S. 2007. *The Politics of Protest: Social Movements in America.* New York: Oxford University Press.

Mohan, Giles, and Kristian Stokke. 2000. "Participatory Development and Empowerment: The Dangers of Localism." *Third World Quarterly* 21 (2): 247–268.

Morello-Frosch, Rachel, Phil Brown, Mercedes Lyson, Alison Cohen, and Kimberly Krupa. 2011. "Community Voice, Vision, and Resilience in Post-Hurricane Katrina Recovery." *Environmental Justice* 4 (1): 71–80.

Morrow, Betty Hearn. 1999. "Identifying and Mapping Community Vulnerability." *Disasters* 23 (1): 1–18.

MPNPE (Ministerio de Planificación Nacional y Política Económica). 2007. *Índice de desarrollo social 2007.* San José, Costa Rica: MIDEPLAN.

Najarian, Louis M., Armen K. Goenjian, David Pelcovitz, Francine Mandel, and Berj Najarian. 2001. "The Effect of Relocation after a Natural Disaster." *Journal of Traumatic Stress* 14 (3): 511–526.

Nakagawa, Yuko, and Rajib Shaw. 2004. "Social Capital: A Missing Link to Disaster Recovery." *International Journal of Mass Emergencies and Disasters* 22 (1): 5–34.

National Geographic Society. 2016. "Climate Refugee." http://www.nationalgeographic.org/encyclopedia/climate-refugee.

Nawyn, Stephanie. 2006. "Faith, Ethnicity, and Culture in Refugee Resettlement." *American Behavioral Scientist* 49 (11): 1509–1527.

NCPC (National Crime Prevention Council). 2016. "Neighborhood Watch." http://www.ncpc.org/topics/home-and-neighborhood-safety/neighborhood-watch.

Neria, Y., A. Nandi, and S. Galea. 2008. "Post-traumatic Stress Disorder Following Disasters: A Systematic Review." *Psychological Medicine* 38: 467–480.

Newman, Oscar. 1973. *Defensible Space: Crime Prevention Through Urban Design.* New York: Collier Books.

NOAA (National Oceanic and Atmospheric Administration). 1998. "Hurricane Mitch Special Coverage." NOAA. http://www.osei.noaa.gov/mitch.html.

———. 2009. "Mitch: The Deadliest Atlantic Hurricane Since 1780." http://www.ncdc.noaa.gov/oa/reports/mitch/mitch.html.

Nolen-Hoeksema, Susan, and Jannay Morrow. 1991. "A Prospective Study of Depression and Posttraumatic Stress Symptoms after a Natural Disaster: The 1989 Loma Prieta Earthquake." *Journal of Personality and Social Psychology* 61 (1): 115–121.

North, Carol S., Aya Kawasaki, Edward L. Spitznagel, and Barry A. Hong. 2004. "The Course of PTSD, Major Depression, Substance Abuse, and Somatization after a Natural Disaster." *Journal of Nervous & Mental Disease* 192 (12): 823–829.

NSNI (National Social Norms Institute). 2014. Social Norms Definition. University of Virginia. http://www.socialnorm.org/.

OECD-DAC (Organization for Economic Cooperation and Development-Development Assistance Committee). 1991. "Guidelines for Aid Agencies on Involuntary Displacement and Resettlement in Development Projects." Retrieved April 28, 2012. http://www.oecd .org/.

Oliver-Smith, Anthony. 1991. "Successes and Failures in Post-disaster Resettlement." *Disasters* 15 (1): 12–23.

———. 1992 (1986). *The Martyred City: Death and Rebirth in the Andes*. Albuquerque: University of New Mexico Press.

———. 2005. "Communities after Catastrophe: Reconstructing the Material, Reconstituting the Social." *Community Building in the 21st Century*. Santa Fe, NM: School of American Research Press.

———, ed. 2009. *Development and Dispossession: The Crisis of Forced Displacement and Resettlement*. Santa Fe, NM: School for Advanced Research Advanced Seminar.

———. 2010. *Defying Displacement: Grassroots Resistance and the Critique of Development*. Austin: University of Texas Press.

Olshansky, Robert B., Laurie A. Johnson, and Ken C. Topping. 2006. "Rebuilding Communities Following Disaster: Lessons from Kobe and Los Angeles." *Built Environment* 32 (4): 354–374.

Olshansky, Robert B., Lewis D. Hopkins, and Laurie A. Johnson. 2012. "Disaster and Recovery: Processes Compressed in Time." *Natural Hazards Review* 13 (3): 173–178.

Olshansky, Robert. B., and Stephanie Chang. 2009. "Planning for Disaster Recovery: Emerging Research Needs and Challenges." *Progress in Planning* 72 (4): 200–209.

Ortega Dolz, Patricia. 2002. "Un milagro en El Valle: Honduras hace realidad el proyecto Pino Alto y mira hacia el desarrollo." *El País*. August 12. www.elpais.com.

OSAC (US Department of State-Overseas Security Advisory Council). 2015. "Honduras 2015 Crime and Safety Report." https://www.osac.gov.

Page, Scott E. 2006. "Path Dependence." *Quarterly Journal of Political Science* 1: 87–115.

Palencia, Gustavo. 2014. "Honduras Murder Rate Falls in 2013, but Remains World's Highest." *Chicago Tribune*. February 17. http://articles.chicagotribune.com/2014-02-17/news /sns-rt-honduras-homicides-20140217_1_gustavo-palencia-tegucigalpa-murder-rate -honduras.

Pierson, Paul. 1993. "When Effect Becomes Cause: Policy Feedback and Political Change." *World Politics* 45 (04): 595–628.

———. 2000. "Path Dependence, Increasing Returns, and the Study of Politics." *American Political Science Review* 94 (2): 251–67.

Pine, Adrienne. 2008. *Working Hard, Drinking Hard: On Violence and Survival in Honduras*. Berkeley: University of California Press.

Pino Alto. 2005. Borrador final de estatuas de patronato de Pino Alto. Pino Alto internal document.

Portes, Alejandro. 1998. "Social Capital: Its Origins and Applications in Modern Sociology." *Annual Review of Sociology* 24 (1): 1–24.

Plunkett, Hazel. 1995. "The Nicaraguan Community Movement: In Defence of Life." In

Community Empowerment: A Reader in Participation and Development, edited by Gary Craig and Majorie Mayo, 194–205. London: Zed Books.

Putnam, Robert. 1993. *Making Democracy Work: Civic Traditions in Modern Italy*. Princeton, NJ: Princeton University Press.

———. 2000. *Bowling Alone: The Collapse and Revival of American Community*. New York: Simon and Schuster.

Quarantelli, Enrico L. 2005. "A Social Science Research Agenda for the Disasters of the 21st Century: Theoretical, Methodological, and Empirical Issues and Their Professional Implementation." In *What Is a Disaster? New Answers to Old Questions*, edited by Ronald W. Perry and Enrico L. Quarantelli, 325–396. Philadelphia: Xlibris.

Ragin, Charles C. 1987. *The Comparative Method: Moving Beyond Qualitative and Quantitative Methods*. Berkeley: University of California.

Reduniversitaria. 2009. "El Valle: De la reconstrucción al desarrollo 2.000–2.009." *II Congreso Internacional de Desarrollo Humano Madrid*. http://www.reduniversitaria.es/.

República de Panamá, Ministerio de Economia y Finanzas. 2006. *Percepciones de la comunidad: encuesta de niveles de vida 2003*. Panama City: Government of Panama.

Ritchie, Liesel A. 2012. "Individual Stress, Collective Trauma, and Social Capital in the Wake of the *Exxon Valdez* oil spill." *Sociological Inquiry* 82 (2): 187–211.

Ritchie, Liesel Ashley, and Duane A. Gill. 2007. "Social Capital Theory as an Integrating Theoretical Framework in Technological Disaster Research." *Sociological Spectrum* 27: 103–129.

Robinson, Jerry W., and Frank Fear. 2011. *The Technical Assistance Approach* in *Introduction to Community Development: Theory, Practice, and Service Learning*. Thousand Oaks, CA: Sage Publications.

Robinson, William I. 2004. *Transnational Conflicts: Central America, Social Change and Globalization*. New York: Verso Press.

Ruhl, J. Mark. 2010. "Honduras Unravels." *Journal of Democracy* 21 (2): 93–107.

Saegert, Susan, and Gary Winkel. 2004. "Crime, Social Capital, and Community Participation." *American Journal of Community Psychology* 34 (3–4): 219–233.

Sampson, Robert J., and W. Byron Groves. 1989. "Community Structure and Crime: Testing Social-Disorganization Theory." *American Journal of Sociology* 94 (4): 774–802.

Sampson, Robert J., and Stephen W. Raudenbush. 1999. "Systematic Social Observation of Public Spaces: A New Look at Disorder in Urban Neighborhoods." *The American Journal of Sociology* 105 (3): 603–651.

Sampson, Robert J., Stephen W. Raudenbush, and Felton Earls. 1997. "Neighborhoods and Violent Crime: A Multilevel Study of Collective Efficacy." *Science* 277: 918–924.

Sampson, Robert, and William Julius Wilson. 1995. "Toward a Theory of Race, Crime and Urban Inequality." In *Crime and Inequality*, edited by John Hagan and Ruth D. Peterson. Palo Alto, CA: Stanford University Press.

Schwartz, Norman B. 1981. "Anthropology Views of Community and Community Development." *Human Organization* 40 (4): 313–322.

Scott, Katherine. 2010. "Community Vitality: A Report of The Canadian Index of Wellbeing." Waterloo, Canada: Canadian Council on Social Development. http://www.ciw.ca/.

Scudder, Thayer, and Elizabeth Colson. 1982. "From Welfare to Development: A Conceptual Framework for the Analysis of Dislocated People." In *Involuntary Migration and Resettlement*, edited by Art Hansen and Anthony Oliver-Smith. 267–287. Boulder, CO: Westview Press.

Seidman, Karl F. 2013. *Coming Home to New Orleans: Neighborhood Rebuilding After Katrina.* New York: Oxford University Press.

Sengupta, Somini. 1998. "Bishops Appeal for Aid to Hurricane Victims." *New York Times.* November 30, 1998.

Shaffer, Ron E., and Gene. F. Summers. 1989. "Community Economic Development." In *Community Development in Perspective*, edited by James A. Christenson and Jerry W. Robinson, 173–195. Ames: Iowa State University Press.

Shaw, Clifford R., and Henry D. McKay. 1942. *Juvenile Delinquency in Urban Areas.* Chicago: University of Chicago Press.

Sherwell, Phillip. 2015. "Welcome to Honduras, the Most Dangerous Country on the Planet." *The Telegraph.* http://www.telegraph.co.uk/news/worldnews/centralamericaandthe caribbean/honduras/10454018/Welcome-to-Honduras-the-most-dangerous-country-on -the-planet.html.

Sieder, Rachel. 1995. "Honduras: The Politics of Exception and Military Reformism (1972–1978)." *Journal of Latin American Studies* 27 (1): 106–127.

Silverman, Robert Mark. 2004. *Community-Based Organizations: The Intersection of Social Capital and Local Context in Contemporary Urban Society.* Farmington Hills, MI: Wayne State University Press.

SJP (Seguridad, Justicia y Paz). 2014. "The 50 Most Violent Cities in the World." http://www .seguridadjusticiaypaz.org.mx/biblioteca/prensa/summary/5-prensa/199-the-50-most -violent-cities-in-the-world-2014.

Smelser, Neil J. 1998. "The Rational and the Ambivalent in the Social Sciences: 1997 Presidential Address." *American Sociological Review* 63 (1): 1–15.

Smith, Gavin, and Dennis Wenger. 2007. "Sustainable Disaster Recovery: Operationalizing an Existing Agenda." In *Handbook of Disaster Research*, edited by Havidan Rodriquez, Enrico L. Quarantelli, and Russell R. Dynes, 234–257. New York: Springer.

Snarr, Neil, and Leonard Brown. 1978. "Post-disaster Housing in Honduras after Hurricane Fifi: An Assessment." *Mass Emergencies* 2: 239–250. http://www.massemergencies.org.

Snow, David A., Louis A. Zurcher Jr., and Sheldon Ekland-Olson. 1980. "Social Networks and Social Movements: A Microstructural Approach to Differential Recruitment." *American Sociological Review* 787–801.

Stefanovics, Tomás. 1999. *A propósito del "Mitch."* Tegucigalpa, Honduras: Editorial Universitaria, Universidad Nacional Autónoma de Honduras.

Steinberg, Florian. 2007. "Housing Reconstruction and Rehabilitation in Aceh and Nias, Indonesia—Rebuilding Lives." *Habitat International* 31: 150–166.

Summers, Gene F. 1986. "Rural Community Development." *Annual Review of Sociology* 12: 347–371.

Sutherland, Ben. 2004. "'Sustainable Relief' is Needed." *British Broadcasting News.* September 14. http://news.bbc.co.uk/1/hi/sci/tech/3655416.stm.

Swidler, Ann. 1986. "Culture in Action: Symbols and Strategies." *American Sociological Review* 51 (2): 273–286.

Sylves, Richard. 2011. "Theory of Disaster Recovery." Federal Emergency Management Higher Education Conference. http://training.fema.gov/hiedu/11conf/presentations /alaniz%20-%20peri-theory%20of%20disaster%20recovery.docx.

Tellman, Beth, Ryan Alaniz, Andrea Rivera, and Diana Contreras. 2014. "Violence as an Obstacle to Livelihood Resilience in the Context of Climate Change." *United Nations University Institute for Environment and Human Security* 3. www.collections.unu.edu/eserv /UNU:2859/resilience_academy_wp3.pdf.

Thelen, Kathleen. 1999. "Historical Institutionalism in Comparative Politics." *Annual Review of Political Science* 2 (1): 369–404.

Thomas, Shaun A. 2007. "Lies, Damn Lies, and Rumors: An Analysis of Collective Efficacy, Rumors, and Fear in the Wake of Katrina." *Sociological Spectrum* 27 (6): 679–703.

Tierney, Kathleen. 2007. "From the Margins to the Mainstream? Disaster Research at the Crossroads." *Annual Review of Sociology* 33: 503–525.

Tönnies, Ferdinand. 2001 [1887]. *Community and Civil Society*. Cambridge: Cambridge University Press.

Transparency International. 2016. "Corruption Perception Index." www.transparency.org.

Turner, Ralph H., and Lewis M. Killian. 1972. *Collective Behavior*. Englewood Cliffs, NJ: Prentice Hall.

UNDP (United Nations Development Programme). 2007. "Delincuencia y criminalidad en las estadísticas de Honduras, 1996–2000." Programa de las Naciones Unidas para el Desarrollo.

———. 2008. "UNDP Policy on Early Recovery." Retrieved October 2, 2016. http://www.pacificdisaster.net/pdnadmin/data/original/UNDP_2008_Policy_early_recovery.pdf.

———. 2015. "2014 Human Development Report." Retrieved August 29, 2015. http://www.undp.org.

UNHCR (United Nations High Commission on Refugees). 2015a. "Global Trends: Forced Displacement in 2014." http://www.unhcr.org.

———. 2015b. "Worldwide Displacement Hits All-Time High as War and Persecution Increase." http://www.unhcr.org/558193896.html.

UNICEF (United Nations Children's Fund). 2010. "Ten Years after Hurricane Mitch, Honduras is Once Again Hit by Natural Disaster." http://www.unicef.org/infobycountry/honduras_45850.html. [This version is slightly different from the original video shown by UNICEF, which has been deleted.]

UNISDR (United Nations International Strategy for Disaster Reduction). 2012. "Terminology: Recovery." http://www.unisdr.org.

UNODC (United Nations Office on Drugs and Crime). 2007. "Crime and Development in Central America: Caught in the Crossfire." United Nations Publication. http://www.unodc.org.

———. 2011. "Transnational Organized Crime in Central America and the Caribbean: A Threat Assessment." *United Nations Publication*. http://www.unodc.org.

———. 2015. *Global Study on Homicide*. http://www.unodc.org/gsh/.

———. 2016. *Homicide Data*. http://www.data.unodc.org/.

USAID (United States Agency for International Development). 1997. "New Partnership Initiative (NPI) Resource Guide: A Strategic Guide to Development Partnering." http://www.usaid.gov.

USGS (United States Geological Survey). 2002. "Hurricane Mitch: Peak Discharge for Selected Rivers in Honduras." http://mitchnts1.cr.usgs.gov.

Washington Post. 2011. "Honduras: The World's Homicide Capital." November 13. http://www.washingtonpost.com/.

Weber, Max. 1968. "The Types of Legitimate Domination." In *Economy and Society*, vol. 3, edited by Guenther Roth and Claus Wittich212–301. New York: Bedminster Press.

———. [1947] 2009. *The Theory of Social and Economic Organization*. New York: Simon and Schuster.

Whyte, William Foote. 1943. *Street Corner Society*. Chicago: University of Chicago Press.

Wilkinson, Kenneth P. 1991. *The Community in Rural America* no. 95. Westport: Greenwood Publishing Group.

Wilson, James Q., and George L. Kelling. 1982. "Broken Windows: The Police and Neighborhood Safety." *Atlantic Monthly*. http://www.manhattan-institute.org/pdf/_atlantic _monthly-broken_windows.pdf.

Wolseth, Jon. 2008. "Safety and Sanctuary: Pentecostalism and Youth Gang Violence in Honduras." *Latin American Perspectives* 35 (4): 96–111.

Woolcock, Michael. 1998. "Social Capital and Economic Development: Toward a Theoretical Synthesis and Policy Framework." *Theory and Society* 27 (2): 151–208.

Woolcock, Michael, and Deepa Narayan. 2000. "Social Capital: Implications for Development Theory, Research, and Policy." *World Bank Research Observer* 15 (2): 225–249.

World Bank. 2013. World Bank Country Survey: Honduras. http://microdata.worldbank .org/index.php/catalog/1895.

———. 2014. "Involuntary Resettlement Portfolio Review Phase II: Resettlement Implementation." http://pubdocs.worldbank.org/pubdocs/publicdoc/2015/3/96781425483120443 /involuntary-resettlement-portfolio-review-phase2.pdf.

———. 2015a. "Poverty and Equity Data." http://povertydata.worldbank.org/poverty/region /LAC.

———. 2015b. "World Bank Acknowledges Shortcomings in Resettlement Projects, Announces Action Plan to Fix Problems." http://www.worldbank.org/en/news/press-release /2015/03/04/world-bank-shortcomings-resettlement-projects-plan-fix-problems.

———. 2016a. "Intentional Homicides (per 100,000)." http://data.worldbank.org/.

———. 2016b. "Honduras Data." http://data.worldbank.org/.

World Health Organization. 2003. Alliance for Healthy Cities. http://www.who.int/life -course/partners/alliance-healthy-cities/en/.

Wuthnow, Robert. 1999. "Mobilizing Civic Engagement: The Changing Impact of Religious Involvement." In *Civic Engagement in American Democracy*, edited by Theda Skocpol and Morris P. Fiorina, 331–363. Washington, DC: Brookings Institution Press.

Yandong, Zhao. 2007. "Social Capital and Post-disaster Recovery: A Sociological Study of Natural Disaster." *Sociological Studies* (5): 164–187.

Zablocki, Benjamin David. 1971. *The Joyful Community: An Account of the Bruderhof, a Communal Movement Now in Its Third Generation*. Chicago: University of Chicago Press.

Zahran, Sammy, Tara O'Connor Shelley, Lori Peek, and Samuel D. Brody. 2009. "Natural Disasters and Social Order: Modeling Crime Outcomes in Florida." *International Journal of Mass Emergencies and Disasters* 27 (1): 26–52.

Zizek, Slavoj. 2010. "First as Tragedy, Then as Farce." *Royal Society for the Encouragement of the Arts*. https://www.thersa.org/discover/videos/rsa-animate/2010/08/rsa-animate -first-as-tragedy-then-as-farce-.

neighbors, 69–70; and religion, 115; and religiosity, 85; and remittances, 114; and resident diversity, 29; and resident feelings of security, 65; resident feelings toward La Iglesia, 100–102, 101f; resident satisfaction with, 84; and social capital, 68–69; and social control, 141; and social health, 149; versus Tegucigalpa, 59; and Tegucigalpa neighborhoods of origin, 56; and Tegucigalpa residents, 14; and violence, 1; vision for, 49

technical assistance: "of" versus "in" community, 39; and community development, 149; and dependency, 104, 130; explanation of, 35–37; and NGOs, 166n6; and partnership approach, 42–43; and SAGE approach, 40, 90, 99–100, 102; and self-help approach, 3, 22–23, 38

Tegucigalpa: compared to Pino Alto, 115; cultural influences of, 80; culture of, 139; and government corruption, 19–20; high crime rate of, 57; and Hurricane Mitch, 10, 32; and local government, 86–87; and low trust, 60–61; norms in, 94–95; and Pino Alto's heterogeneity, 119; and Pino Alto's leadership, 119; and Pino Alto's vision problem, 50; police perception of, 78; and post-Mitch homelessness, 124–125; and resettlement after Mitch, 11–12, 13; and resettlement residents, 1; versus resettlements, 59, 64, 73; and resident diversity, 29; and social health issues, 49; social health of, 56–59; as source of resettlement residents, 14; and Suyapa's economy, 81; unhealthiness of, 33

Tohoku earthquake and tsunami, 31

trauma: and community development, 131; and disaster survivors, 26–28, 91, 133; as factor to overcome, 31; isolated study of, 5; long-term effects of, 24; and NGO support, 143; and resettlement residents, 2, 14, 31, 34, 40, 48, 54; and resettlement survey, 7; and self-help approach, 38; and Suyapa residents, 94; and vulnerability, 26–28

trust: and collective efficacy, 69; and inconsistent NGO timeline, 91; and path dependence, 49; in resettlements versus Tegucigalpa, 60; as SAGE element, 40; and social capital, 30, 144–145; as social health metric, 54; and social order, 142

underemployment, 18
unemployment, 61, 66, 103
United Nations, 12
United Nations Development Programme, 52
United Nations High Commission on Refugees, 6
United Nations International Strategy for Disaster Reduction, 52
United States: and Central American gangs, 18; and Honduras, 17; and Hurricane Mitch, 11, 168n5; and Hurricane Katrina, 165n1; and Pino Alto, 121; and security, 57; and women, 82
UN Millennium Goals, 12
urban planning, 25, 136. See also community development
USAID (United States Agency for International Development), 11, 19–20, 166n11

Valle Verde, 15, 17
values: and community-building process, 131–132; as elements of community, 35; and formation of community culture, 137; and heterogeneous resettlements, 29; negotiation of, 33; and path dependence, 47; and resettlement resident selection, 91, 92; and social health, 54; and Suyapa selection process, 140. See also SAGE
violence: and gang wars, 18–19; Honduran levels of, 55, 57; in Honduras, 17, 20–21; in Pino Alto, 16, 127; in resettlements, 1; and Tegucigalpa, 12. See also crime
vision: and CCS, 94; "in" versus "of" community, 149; and community building,